# WORKING WITH ASPECTS OF LANGUAGE

*MANSOOR ALYESHMERNI*
*University of Minnesota*

*PAUL TAUBR*
*University of Minnesota*

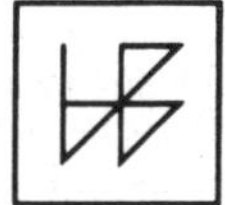



*Harcourt, Brace & World, Inc.*

*New York Chicago San Francisco Atlanta*

ISBN: 0-15-503866-4

Library of Congress Catalog Card Number: 76-113703

Printed in the United States of America

# Preface

This workbook is designed to be useful in introductory courses in general language study or English. Although it can accompany other texts of similar scope, it is primarily a companion piece of readings and exercises for Dwight Bolinger's *Aspects of Language* (Harcourt, Brace & World, 1968). The workbook contains exercises in: the biological basis of language; phonology (including distinctive features); morphology; the concept of grammar; traditional, structural, and transformational grammar; sociolinguistics and doctrines of usage; principles of language change and history of English; graphology; and the application of the semantic differential.

The principal goal of this manual is to encourage the student to make generalizations about language through his increased awareness of facts about his own language. The few examples in foreign languages are intended only to emphasize the universality of the processes involved. No exercise (except the one on Webster's *Third*) demands reference sources other than a desk dictionary and the student's native linguistic competence.

The instructor's manual for this workbook provides suggestions for varying the order of the fourteen chapters, depending on emphasis in instruction, and grouping the exercises according to topic. It also provides a bibliography of useful sources for each chapter, suggestions for effective use of each exercise, and answers to the exercises.

Material for the exercises has been drawn from many standard sources as well as from individual works acknowledged. We have been especially influenced in format and content by two workbooks: John Algeo and Thomas Pyles, *Problems in the Origin and Development of the English Language* (Harcourt, Brace & World, 1966) and Harold King, *Guide and Workbook in the Structure of English* (Prentice-Hall, 1967). In this workbook each author is responsible for the content as follows: Mansoor Alyeshmerni, Chapters 3, 4, 5, 6, 7, 8, 11 (except Exercises 4 and 5), and Exercise 2 of Chapter 2; Paul Taubr, Chapters 2, 9, 10, 11 (Exercises 4 and 5), 12, 13, and 14. We share the responsibility for Chapter 1.

We are indebted to Professor Bolinger and to Professor John Algeo for the benefit of their comments on all chapters of the manuscript. We are grateful also to Professors Harold Allen, Walter Lehn, and Larry Hutchinson for their suggestions and assistance. We wish to thank Professor Daniel Bryan, director of the Communication Program of the University of Minnesota, as well as the staff and students in the program for their comments and suggestions. We also wish to thank Margaret Lessinger for her research, and Marcia Taubr for her encouragement; we appreciate their assistance in the preparation of the manuscript at all stages.

Mansoor Alyeshmerni
Paul Taubr

# Contents

| | |
|---|---|
| Socrates: | What do you say of him [the young boy who has just been guided to solve a problem in geometry], Meno? Were not all these answers given out of his own head? |
| Meno: | Yes, they were all his own. |
| Socrates: | And yet, as we were just now saying, he did not know [how to solve geometry problems]? |
| Meno: | True. |
| Socrates: | Then he who does not know still has true notions of that which he does not know? |
| Meno: | He has. |
| Socrates: | Without any one teaching him he will recover his knowledge for himself, *if he is only asked questions?* |

(emphasis added)

From "The Meno," *The Dialogues of Plato,* translated by Benjamin Jowett, Vol. I, 4th ed. (Oxford, Eng.: Clarendon Press, 1953). Reprinted by permission of the Clarendon Press, Oxford.

# 1

# Born to Speak

Are children born to speak? Is speaking instinctive behavior, or is it a cultural achievement, like the ability to ride a bicycle? One way of answering the question is through the study of how children learn to speak. If children learn language largely through imitation, then it is not instinctive but, in a sense, nearly memorized behavior. The traditional view holds for imitation. In the first reading in this chapter, Philip B. Gough explores this possibility.

By what criteria can one judge whether an activity is instinctive or not? Is speech similar to such an indubitably instinctive activity as walking? Exercise 1 begins with a reading giving four criteria for distinguishing instinctive from acquired activity. Following the reading you are given some evidence that is commonly used to support the instinct hypothesis of language development. Exercise 2 presents a brief statement by Edward Sapir attacking such an hypothesis, which you are to defend, attack, or qualify.

Among the evidence for the instinctiveness of language is the regularity in the stages in which children learn to speak. The third exercise gives you some experience with Dwight Bolinger's scheme for classifying these stages.

## *READING:*

## *THE LIMITATIONS OF IMITATION: THE PROBLEM OF LANGUAGE ACQUISITION*[1]

**PHILIP B. GOUGH**

The child must be taught many things in school, but before he gets there he has learned something without which he could scarcely be taught anything at all; he has learned his native language. This fact is so commonplace that it has failed to excite our wonder, in part because we have thought we understood if not in detail, at least in outline, the way

[1]From Alexander Frazier, ed., *New Directions in Elementary English* (Champaign, Ill.: National Council of Teachers of English, 1967), pp. 92–97. Reprinted with the permission of the National Council of Teachers of English and Philip B. Gough. The author's research is supported by a grant from the U.S. Public Health Service (MH11869-01).

in which language is acquired. But recent work in psycholinguistics suggests that language is not learned in the way we have supposed, that the child's feat is far more wonderful than we have imagined.

In this paper, I hope to illustrate this work by showing how it casts doubt on what I take to be the traditional and prevailing view of language acquisition, that language is learned largely through imitation. In this view, the child tries to mimic his parents' speech. If he is successful, he is reinforced; if he errs, he is corrected. Once he has mastered certain forms, he will generalize what he has learned to create novel utterances, he will extend what he knows by analogy.

If one means by *imitation* simply that the child learns the language of his parents, then we cannot doubt that the child learns through imitation, for that is a fact. If they speak English, then so will he. But *imitation* is typically not used simply to describe this fact; it is used to explain it, to describe a process by which the child comes to speak like his parents. In this usage, the meaning of imitation is vague, but it clearly suggests a humble, mechanical process, one devoid of complex mental or intellectual activity, so that, in the extreme, the child is seen to resemble a parrot, or a kind of biological tape recorder, storing parental utterances for use at an appropriate moment.

It is this latter view of imitation I wish to challenge, for I hope to show that whatever the process of language acquisition, its accomplishment demands a high order of cognitive activity on the part of the child.

There are two ways to evaluate an hypothesis about the way something is learned. One is to observe how the learning develops, to see if it proceeds as it should; the other is to examine the final achievement, the product of learning, to see if it could have been learned in that way. Both of these tests can be applied to imitation as an hypothesis about language learning. Let us begin by examining the course of language learning.

## THE COURSE OF LANGUAGE LEARNING

Sometime around his second birthday, a child begins to sound like a man. Prior to this, he has mastered, to a reasonable degree of approximation, the phonology of his language, and he has acquired a workable vocabulary. But he has been limited to single-word utterances. Now he takes an important step toward linguistic adulthood; he begins to utter sentences.

The child's earliest sentences are not adult sentences. When we hear "Ride horsie" or "Want apple" or "White sweater on," we know that we are not listening to an adult. We should also recognize that we are not listening to an accurate imitation of adult speech, for these sentences are not good English. If the small child is a tape recorder, he is a faulty one, for he seldom produces a faithful reproduction of an adult sentence.

The metaphor of a faulty tape recorder holds, however. The child's productions do not appear to be random combinations of words; they look like recordings of adult sentences in which some words and word endings have been skipped, for we add a word or affix here and there to the child's utterances and get good sentences like "I want to ride a horsie" and "I want an apple." We have little trouble in understanding the child's sentences, and we might conceive of the child as producing economical imitations of adult sentences, leaving out redundant and uninformative elements. In fact, Brown and Fraser (1964) have observed that childish sentences are similar to those produced by an adult when words cost him money; they are telegraphic. Thus we might maintain that the child's telegraphic productions are simply imitations with omission.

If this is the case, then it behooves us to explain his omissions. One possibility is that they are simply failures of memory. When we use the term *imitation,* we use it loosely, for the child seldom echoes adult speech. His imitations, if they are such, are usually not immediate; they are delayed. It seems reasonable to suppose that he simply forgets parts of the utterance he is reproducing, and the result is "telegraphese."

If the child's telegraphic sentences are poorly remembered imitations, we would expect his direct and immediate imitations to be accurate. The child occasionally does produce immediate imitations, and, in fact, we can ask him to. Brown and Fraser (1964) have asked two- and three-year-old children to repeat sentences like "I showed you the book" and "I will not do that again." The children reply with sentences like "I show book" and "Do again." Their accuracy increases with age, but at any age, these solicited and direct imitations do not significantly differ, in length or complexity, from the child's spontaneous utterances.

Evidently the child's reductions of adult sentences cannot be blamed on failures of memory, for the child similarly reduces sentences he has just heard. If they are imitations, they are limited imitations. Those limitations decrease with age. But the decrease is not achieved through imitation, for the child's imitations do not seem to differ from his spontaneous productions (Ervin, 1964). We must look for another explanation of the increasing length and complexity of childish utterances, and this is a first reason for doubting the adequacy of imitation.

No one supposes that the child is purely imitative, for we are certain that he creates novel utterances. If many of the child's utterances seem to be telegraphic versions of adult sentences, many do not. When the child says "All gone outside" or "more page" or "there high," it is hard to imagine adult models for his utterances. Moreover, when the offspring of college graduates uses word forms like "comed" and "breaked" and "foots" and "sheeps" (those familiar errors commonly attributed to "regularization" of irregular nouns and verbs), it is not likely that he is repeating forms he has heard.

The usual explanation of such productions is that they are generalizations, extensions by analogy. This is a vague and unsatisfactory explanation, for there are any number of analogies which might be extended but are not, any number of generalizations the child might make but does not; and it would seem that an adequate explanation would predict which analogies or generalizations would occur, and why. But we might ignore this problem and assume that novel utterances are produced by generalization, to see where this assumption leads us.

The notion that novel utterances of this sort are generalizations implies that the child has a basis for generalizations; the idea of extension by analogy requires that the child know something to extend. In the case of the regularization of word endings for example, as in the plural of nouns or the past tense of verbs, we should expect to find the child forming regular plurals (boy-boys) and past tenses (walk-walked) before he extends these endings to the irregular nouns and verbs.

Ervin (1964) has found that the development of the plural noun proceeds in just this way. The appearance of regular plurals in the child's speech precedes by some weeks the first appearance of a regularized irregular; the child says "blocks" and "toys" and "dogs" considerably before he says "foots" or "sheeps" or "mans."

But Ervin has also found that the development of the past tense does not proceed in this way. Instead, the first past tenses used are the correct forms of the irregular verbs, forms like "came" and "went" and "broke." This is probably not surprising, for these are among the most frequently used forms in adult speech, and we might well expect the child to imitate them correctly. But the interesting and important fact is that when the child first learns to use the past tense of a very few regular forms, like "walked" and "watched," the correct irregulars disappear, to be replaced by incorrect over-generalizations. That is, despite the fact that the child has correctly imitated and practiced the correct past tense of these forms, and has presumably been reinforced for his usage, the forms disappear with the appearance of the regular tense system.

### GENERALIZATION AND EXTENSION OF BASIC PROCESSES

This fact is intriguing, for it suggests that when the child produces novel utterances, novel forms, he is not generalizing or extending some pattern which has been gradually accumulating in mechanically imitated forms. It suggests that extension by analogy and generalization are not secondary processes, operating on a basis of practiced and reinforced imitations. It suggests instead that generalization and extension are themselves basic, that the child does not record particular adult utterances but registers their pattern.

In fact, we should have reached this conclusion earlier. The assumption that the child produces some utterances through imitation and others through generalization leaves us in an uncomfortable position, for ultimately we must be forced to distinguish between them. We must assume that some of his utterances like "comed" and "foots" are generalizations, and not imitations, for we are confident that he has not heard these forms. But this should surely make us wonder whether many of his correct productions, like "walked" and "boys," are not generalization, too. And if any of the child's utterances might be generalizations, we might even wonder if they all are. Instead of assuming that the child says familiar things in imitation, and novel things through imitation and generalization, we might speculate that the child creates all that he says through a kind of "generalization"; that he internalizes the pattern, the rules, of his language, and uses that pattern or those rules to create each of his utterances.

Thus a second reason for doubting the adequacy of the imitation hypothesis is that it does not correctly predict the appearance of novel utterances in the course of development; moreover, it forces us to impose what seems to be an arbitrary classification on the productions of a child.

So far we have been looking at what the child says. We have tacitly assumed that the acquisition of language is the acquisition of language production. But there is a familiar observation which shows that this is a false assumption. The child not only learns to speak; he also learns to listen. And most observers . . . claim that the child learns to listen before he learns to speak, that comprehension precedes production.

We all know many more words than we use, and we hear more sentences than we utter. (We must, for we hear all those we utter, but not vice versa.) The same is true of children; moreover, most of us believe that they comprehend before they produce. A recent experiment by Fraser, Bellugi, and Brown (1963) has confirmed our beliefs.

These investigators compared three-and-a-half-year-old children's comprehension and production of ten grammatical contrasts, like the difference between the singular and plural forms of *be* (*is* vs. *are*), the singular and plural in the third person possessive pronoun (*his* or *her* vs. *their*), and the present progressive and past tenses of the verb (*is spilling* vs. *spilled*). They wrote a pair of sentences exemplifying each contrast (e.g., "The sheep are jumping" and "The sheep is jumping"), and drew a picture corresponding to each sentence (e.g., a picture of two sheep jumping over a stile and a picture of one sheep jumping while another watches).

Each child heard both sentences and saw both pictures. Then his comprehension of the contrast was measured by reading him one of the sentences and asking him to point to the correct picture; his production of the contrast was measured by pointing to one of the pictures and asking him to name it. With each contrast, comprehension exceeded production; more children pointed to the correct picture, given a sentence, than produced the contrast, given the picture.

(Of course, it might be objected that pointing at a picture is easier than uttering a sentence; this is surely true, but it does not explain the relative difficulty of the production task, for the children were able to utter the sentences, in an imitation task, more accurately than they could comprehend them.)

This result is not novel, but it does provide experimental confirmation of our casual observation that comprehension precedes production. Some children comprehended contrasts they could not produce, but no child was able to produce a contrast which he could not comprehend. Whatever the child needs to comprehend a sentence is necessary for his production of it; the child must learn how to comprehend a sentence before he can produce it. But this fact is crucial in evaluating the imitation hypothesis, for, while the child may imitate sentences, he could not possibly imitate the comprehension of them. There are many things a parent might do to indicate that he understood a sentence, and the child could observe these things. But he cannot see or hear or feel the comprehension itself, and surely one cannot imitate something one cannot even sense. Hence a third and seemingly insurmountable difficulty for the imitation hypothesis is that it demands that the child imitate something he cannot observe.

From studies of language development we can draw, then, at least three cogent arguments against the hypothesis that language is learned through imitation.

BIBLIOGRAPHY

Brown, R., and C. Fraser, "The Acquisition of Syntax," in U. Bellugi and R. Brown, eds., *The Acquisition of Language. Child Development Monographs,* 29, 1964, pp. 43–78.

Ervin, S. M., "Imitation and Structural Change in Children's Language," in E. Lenneberg, ed., *New Directions in the Study of Language.* Cambridge, Mass.: Massachusetts Institute of Technology Press, 1964, pp. 163–90.

Fraser, C., U. Bellugi, and R. Brown, "Control of Grammar in Imitation, Comprehension, and Production," *Journal of Verbal Learning and Verbal Behavior,* 2, 1963, pp. 121–35.

## EXERCISE 1: Language, Instinctive or Acquired?

By what criteria does one judge whether an activity is instinctive or the result of a cultural achievement? Eric Lenneberg gives four criteria for distinguishing an obviously instinctive activity (walking) from an obviously cultural achievement (writing):

A. Is the activity essentially invariant within the species?
B. Is there a history of the development of the activity within the species?
C. Is there evidence for an inherited predisposition for the activity?
D. Does the activity have its own specific physical center in the brain and any other part of the body?

Lenneberg compares walking (bipedal gait) and writing in the selection below. As you read this, consider where language belongs. Is it more like walking or writing?

## *READING:* The Four Criteria[2]

| *Bipedal Gait* | *Writing* |
|---|---|
| | Criterion A |
| *No intraspecies variations:* The species has only one type of locomotion; it is universal to all men. (This is a special case of the more general point that inherited traits have poor correlations—if any—with social groupings: cf. black hair or protruding zygoma.)[3] | *Intraspecies variations correlated with social organizations:* A number of very different successful writing systems have co-existed. The geographical distribution of writing systems follows cultural and social lines of demarcation. |

[2]"The Capacity for Language Acquisition," in Jerry A. Fodor and Jerrold J. Katz, eds., *The Structure of Language* (Englewood Cliffs, N. J.: Prentice-Hall, 1964), pp. 583–84. This essay is a revised version of "Language, Evolution, and Purposive Behavior," in S. Diamond, ed., *Culture in History: Essays in Honor of Paul Radin* (New York: Columbia University Press, 1960), pp. 869–93. All citations are from the 1964 version of the essay. Reprinted by permission of Columbia University Press.

[3]Note, however, that although there are no significant intraspecies variations in gait, there are many distinctive but minor cultural differences. For example, Weston La Barre has observed differences between the Bengali, Punjabi, and South Chinese walk. See his "Paralinguistics, Kinesics, and Cultural Anthropology," in Thomas A. Sebeok et al., eds., *Approaches to Semiotics* (The Hague: Mouton & Co., 1964), p. 195.—Eds.

### Criterion B

*No history within species:* We cannot trace the development of bipedal gait from a primitive to a complex stage throughout the history of human *cultures.* There are no geographical foci from which cultural diffusion of the trait seems to have emanated at earlier times. All human races have the same basic skeletal foot pattern. For significant variations in gait, we have to go back to fossil forms that represent a predecessor of modern man.

*Only history within species:* There are cultures where even the most primitive writing system is completely absent. We can follow the development of writing historically just as we can study the distribution of writing geographically. We can make good guesses as to the area of invention and development and trace the cultural diffusion over the surface of the globe and throughout the last few millenia of history. The emergence of writing is a relatively recent event.

### Criterion C

*Evidence for inherited predisposition:* Permanent and customary gait cannot be taught or learned by practice if the animal is not biologically constituted for this type of locomotion.

*No evidence for inherited predisposition:* Illiteracy in nonWestern societies is not ordinarily a sign of mental deficiency but of deficiency in training. The condition can be quickly corrected by appropriate practice.

### Criterion D

*Presumption of specific organic correlates:* In the case of gait, we do not have to *presume* organic correlates; we *know* them. However, behavioral traits that are regarded as the product of evolution (instincts) are also thought to be based on organic predispositions, in this case, on the grounds of circumstantial evidence and often in the absence of anatomical and physiological knowledge.

*No assumption of specific organic correlates:* We do, of course, assume a biological capacity for writing, but there is no evidence for innate predisposition for this activity. A child's contact with written documents or with pencil and paper does not ordinarily result in automatic acquisition of the trait. Nor do we suppose that the people in a society that has evolved no writing system to be genetically different from those of a writing society. It is axiomatic in anthropology that any normal infant can acquire all cultural traits of any society given the specific cultural upbringing.

A series of statements about language and language acquisition are given below. Each may be used to support one of the criteria given above in deciding that speech is instinctive behavior, rather than a result of cultural achievement. In the space provided beside each statement, place the letter of the criterion for which the statement may be construed as evidence.

_A_ 1. "All languages have ways of turning sentences into interrogatives, negatives, and commands." (Bolinger, p. 18)

____ 2. "There are differences in detail, but in broad outline languages are put together in similar ways. . . . One is reminded of what is so often said about sexual behavior—that it can be modified by social restrictions but never seriously changed." (Bolinger, pp. 17–18)

____ 3. "All languages use nominal phrases and verbal phrases, corresponding to the two major classes of noun and verb, and in all of them the number of nouns far exceeds the number of verbs. One can be fairly sure that a noun in one language translates a noun in another." (Bolinger, p. 18)

____ 4. An eight-year-old deaf child, who had never had any training or any contact with other deaf children, was admitted to a school for the deaf. Immediately upon his arrival he began to "talk" sign language with his contemporaries. "The existence of an innate impulse for symbolic communication can hardly be questioned." (Lenneberg, p. 589)

____ 5. Instinctive behavior develops according to patterns of organic maturation. Bolinger distinguishes five stages of language development. (See Exercise 3.)

____ 6. "All languages show at least two forms of interaction between verbal and nominal, typically 'intransitive' (the verbal is involved with only one nominal, as in ***Boys play***) and 'transitive' (the verbal is involved with two nominals, as in ***Boys like girls***)." (Bolinger, p. 18)

____ 7. As far back as we can reconstruct the languages of the world, there is no evidence that those spoken, say, four thousand years ago were different in nature from those spoken today.

____ 8. "Language development, or its substitute, is relatively independent of the infant's babbling or his ability to hear. The congenitally deaf who will usually fail to develop an intelligible vocal communication system, who either do not babble or to whom babbling is of no avail . . . , will nevertheless learn the intricacies of language and learn to communicate efficiently through writing. Apparently, even under these reduced circumstances of stimulation the miracle of development of a feeling for grammar takes place." (Lenneberg, p. 589)

____ 9. There is no evidence, direct or indirect, that man was ever without a fully developed language.

____ 10. Every language has words assembled according to set rules.

____ 11. "If in the case of lower animals we assume without compunction that the communication trait is the result of an *innate predisposition elicited by environmental circumstances,* we have no reason to assume . . . that the language trait of man is purely acquired behavior . . . ." (Lenneberg, p. 600)

____ 12. Every language has a small group of distinct and discrete sound units which combine to form the words and sentences of the language.

____ 13. We have no evidence that we can use to trace the spread of language at any particular place or time from a tribe having it to a tribe or tribes not having it.

____ 14. Every human culture has a language.

____ 15. "One still hears the foolish claim that a child of German ancestry ought to be able to learn German more easily than some other language. Our experience discredits this. An infant of whatever race learns whatever language it hears, one about as easily as another." (Bolinger, p. 2)

____ 16. In comparing the language development of identical and fraternal twins, one finds the following: the onset of speech and the speech development history of each child in a pair of identical twins is about the same. On the other hand, the onset of speech and the speech development history of each child in a pair of fraternal twins is often different.[4]

____ 17. There is no such thing as an incompletely developed language.

____ 18. "The organs of speech in their present form were shaped as much for sound production as nourishment. The human tongue is far more agile than it needs to be for purposes of eating. On the receiving end, the sensitivity of the human ear has been sharpened to the point that we can detect a movement of the eardrum that does not exceed one tenth of the diameter of a hydrogen molecule." (Bolinger, p. 3)

## EXERCISE 2: The Nature of Language Acquisition

The following passage by Edward Sapir, an early twentieth-century linguist (see Bolinger, pp. 190–91), differs remarkably from the point of view held by Gough. Write a paragraph supporting, contradicting, or qualifying the information in this passage.

## READING: The Nature of Language Acquisition[5]

Speech is so familiar a feature of daily life that we rarely pause to define it. It seems as natural to man as walking, and only less so than breathing. Yet it needs but a moment's reflection to convince us that this naturalness of speech is but an illusory feeling. The process of acquiring speech is, in sober fact, an utterly different sort of thing from the process of learning to walk. In the case of the latter function, culture, in other words, the traditional body of social usage, is not seriously brought into play. The child is individually

[4]Eric Lenneberg, "Are Biological Theories Compatible with Genetics?" in *Biological Foundations of Language* (New York: John Wiley & Sons, 1967), pp. 252–53.

[5]From *Language* by Edward Sapir, copyright, 1921, by Harcourt, Brace & World, Inc.; renewed, 1949, by Jean V. Sapir. Reprinted by permission of Harcourt, Brace & World, Inc. The selection, which appears on pp. 3–4 of *Language*, has been retitled.

equipped, by the complex set of factors that we term biological heredity, to make all the needed muscular and nervous adjustments that result in walking. Indeed, the very conformation of these muscles and of the appropriate parts of the nervous system may be said to be primarily adapted to the movements made in walking and in similar activities. In a very real sense the normal human being is predestined to walk, not because his elders will assist him to learn the art, but because his organism is prepared from birth, or even from the moment of conception, to take on all those expenditures of nervous energy and all those muscular adaptations that result in walking. To put it concisely, walking is an inherent, biological function of man.

Not so language. It is of course true that in a certain sense the individual is predestined to talk, but that is due entirely to the circumstance that he is born not merely in nature, but in the lap of a society that is certain, reasonably certain, to lead him to its traditions. Eliminate society and there is every reason to believe that he will learn to walk, if, indeed, he survives at all. But it is just as certain that he will never learn to talk, that is, to communicate ideas according to the traditional system of a particular society. Or, again, remove the new-born individual from the social environment into which he has come and transplant him to an utterly alien one. He will develop the art of walking in his new environment very much as he would have developed it in the old. But his speech will be completely at variance with the speech of his native environment. Walking, then, is a general human activity that varies only within circumscribed limits as we pass from individual to individual. Its variability is involuntary and purposeless. Speech is a human activity that varies without assignable limit as we pass from social group to social group, because it is a purely historical heritage of the group, the product of long-continued social usage. It varies as all creative effort varies—not as consciously, perhaps, but none the less as truly as do the religions, the beliefs, the customs, and the arts of different peoples. Walking is an organic, an instinctive, function (not, of course, itself an instinct); speech is a non-instinctive, acquired, "cultural" function.

## EXERCISE 3: Stages of Language Acquisition

Bolinger recognizes five stages in the child's acquisition of language. The first is the *holophrastic* stage, when each utterance is a word that has just one meaning. During the second stage, the *analytic* stage, the child discovers that what he considered a single word is in fact a combination of words. He notices in the third, or *syntactic,* stage that different classes of words occur in different places in a sentence, and that this variation affects meaning. The fourth stage is *structural,* when the child learns how to place utterances he had learned earlier within other utterances. The final stage is *stylistic,* when the child knows how to construct different sentences for the same meaning. Classify the sentences below as characteristic of one or another of these five stages. (These sentences are from *Aspects of Language.*)

1. *synt.* Mama eat cereal.
2. ______ Mapank.
3. ______ {I gave the dog the bone. / I gave the bone to the dog.} (The child knows that these are paraphrases.)
4. ______ Daddy sit chair.
5. ______ {Pank mama. / Mama pank.} (The child does not know that these are different in adult English.)
6. ______ House eat baby.
7. ______ Get daddy.
8. ______ {Spank mama. / Mama spank.} (The child knows that these are different.)
9. ______ Daddy sit baby chair.
10. ______ Kiss mama.
11. ______ Come-to mama.
12. ______ I'm going to the other side of the whole lake.
13. ______ What he did at work today?

# 2

# Some Traits of Language

## EXERCISE 1: Language Is Patterned Behavior

**A Pattern of English Word Order:**

The linguist approaches language as a set of patterns or rules. In the phrase ***several young Canadian girls,*** the order of the words is not random nor at the pleasure of the speaker, but is determined by the rules of English. Linguists have not ferreted out all the rules of such phrases, but any native speaker of English follows them automatically: he would know how to put ***violin, Italian, old,*** and ***the*** into the most common English order—***the old Italian violin.***

The object of this exercise is to call your attention to a rule of English which you already know but are probably not aware of using. This rule specifies the order of words in some simple phrases similar to the two above.

The procedure is this: first you are to apply the knowledge of English phrases that you have as a native speaker, and then you are to discover and write out explicitly the rule you applied so easily and automatically.

A. Rewrite each of the following lists of words into natural English order. The rule for this section is already written out below.

1. American/new/astronauts/the ___*the new American astronauts*___
2. latest/the/fashions/French ______________
3. lasses/Scottish/the/young ______________

The rule or pattern that you followed to change the order is this: you put ***the*** first, then the word giving the age of what is being talked about, and then the nationality of what is being talked about. To check this rule, give one new example of such a four-word phrase and see if the rule applies.

______________

B. Rewrite each list of words into natural English order.

1. five/the/freshmen/beginning ___*the five beginning freshmen*___
2. recent/the/accident/third ______________
3. peaches/fresh/the/three ______________

What system did you follow in reordering these lists?

______________________________________________

______________________________________________

To check the rule you have written above, write one new example of a similar four-word phrase below.

______________________________________________

C. We are now ready to combine these rules into one more useful rule. In the phrases we discussed in exercise A, we noted that the native speaker of English places age first, and then nationality. In exercise B, we noted that when age and number occur in one phrase, number comes first. In what order would age, number, and nationality come in a single phrase? To find out, insert ***three*** in its natural place in ***the old Spanish guitars.***

Between ____________________ and ____________________.

Where would you insert ***French*** in the phrase ***the third new girl?***

Between ____________________ and ____________________.

Give the order in which words giving age, nationality, and number come in many English noun phrases.

______________, ______________, ______________.

Check this rule by giving two new phrases of your own to which it applies.

______________________________________________

______________________________________________

This rule you have uncovered gives the most common word orders for such phrases. There are occasions when you would not order them this way. For example, if there were several young girls in a classroom and two were Scottish, you might have occasion to speak of ***the Scottish young girls*** rather than ***the young Scottish girls,*** according to the rule above. You would be speaking of the young ladies who were Scottish, not of the Scottish ladies who were young.

**Patterns of Negation and Interrogation:**

All languages have patterns that change one kind of sentence into another. This exercise is concerned with uncovering a little of what you know about changing English sentences from affirmative to negative and converting simple statements into questions.

A. *Negative Sentences.* Rewrite each of the following affirmative statements as a negation.

1. He could drive. *He could not drive.*
2. He could have driven. ____________________
3. He has gone. ____________________

The rule that you followed might be stated thus: positive statements are turned into negative statements by adding ***not*** after the first of the helping verbs (such as ***could, could have,*** or ***has***).

This rule works well enough when there is a helping verb in the sentence, but what happens when there is none? To find out, change the following sentences into negative sentences. (Be sure you have not added any new ideas to the sentence besides negation, such as 'ability' in ***could.***)

1. They drive to town. ______________________________

2. We drive to town. ______________________________

3. You walk to town. ______________________________

State the rule you used.

______________________________

______________________________

B. *Interrogative Sentences.* Rewrite each of the following statements as a question.

1. He could drive. ______ *Could he drive?* ______

2. He could have driven. ______________________________

3. He has been teaching. ______________________________

4. He is talking. ______________________________

State the rule.

______________________________

______________________________

This rule, like the first rule for negation, works well enough when the statements contain words such as ***could, have,*** and ***is.*** As a first step toward finding out the transformation you use in sentences without such words, change the following sentences into questions.

1. They drive. ______ *Do they drive?* ______

2. We drive. ______________________________

3. You walk. ______________________________

State the transformation.

______________________________

______________________________

C. *Negative-Interrogative Sentences.* Rewrite the following sentences according to the models.

1. He was going home at noon. ______ *Wasn't he going home at noon?* ______

2. He works on his car Saturdays. ______ *Doesn't he work on his car Saturdays?* ______

3. He walked to town. ______________________________

4. He always went home weekends. ______________________________

5. He has seen it already. ______________________________

State the pattern you followed.

______________________________

______________________________

Make up another pair of sentences, and check to see if the pattern works.

______________________________

______________________________

**Rules of Pronunciation in English:**

A. In the first two exercises you were made aware of the patterns of word order and of how English changes one kind of sentence into another. This exercise is devoted to uncovering some of the rules of English pronunciation that you know implicitly. The process will be the same as before: you will apply the rules, using your skill as a native speaker, and then you will write out explicitly what you have done. Read the following two sentences aloud.

1. Did you convict him of the crime?
2. Where was the convict taken?

Which syllable of ***convict*** was emphasized in the first sentence?

______________________________ In the second? ______________________________

The following pairs of words show the same pattern as ***convict.*** Underline the emphasized syllable of the words in bold face.

1. I ***combine*** them regularly.
   The ***combine*** is good for business.
2. He won't ***permit*** it.
   Do you need a ***permit?***
3. Did the ***contract*** give you trouble?
   Did you ***contract*** German measles?
4. How do you ***combat*** the common cold?
   The ***combat*** took place near Gettysburg.

State the pattern you followed in changing the stress in these words.

______________________________

______________________________

B. There are many patterns of pronunciation that tell the native speaker how to stress words as he changes their endings. For example, consider how you change the position of the main stress as you change the endings of the following words.

| | | |
|---|---|---|
| provoke | provocative | provocation |
| repeat | repetitive | repetition |
| derive | derivative | derivation |

Where is the stress placed in the words of the first column? ______________

Of the second column? ______________ Of the third column? ______________

## EXERCISE 2: Language Is Systematic

Examine these columns of corresponding words and phrases in four modern languages, and then follow the instructions given below. (In Persian the æ is pronounced somewhat like the ***a*** in ***bat,*** the ***č*** like ***ch*** in ***church,*** and the ***x*** like ***ch*** in German ***Bach.*** In Hebrew the ***š*** is pronounced like the ***sh*** in ***shin.***)

| | *English* | *German* | *Persian*° | *Hebrew* |
|---|---|---|---|---|
| 1. | man | Mann | mærd | iš |
| 2. | a man | ein Mann | mærdi | iš |
| 3. | the man | der Mann | an mærd | haiš |
| 4. | the woman | die Frau | an zæn | haiša |
| 5. | a good man | ein guter Mann | mærdi xub | iš tov |
| 6. | the good man | der gute Mann | an mærde xub | haiš hatov |
| 7. | a good woman | eine gute Frau | zæni xub | iša tova |
| 8. | the good woman | die gute Frau | an zæne xub | haiša hatova |
| 9. | a good house | ein gutes Haus | xane(y)i xub | bayit tov |
| 10. | the large house | das grosse Haus | an xane(y)e bozorg | habayit hagadol |
| 11. | a small house | ein kleines Haus | xane(y)i kuček | bayit katan |
| 12. | a large book | ein grosses Buch | ketabi bozorg | sefer gadol |
| 13. | a man's house | eines Mannes Haus | xane(y)e mærdi | beyt iš |
| 14. | the house of a man | das Haus eines Mannes | xane(y)e mærdi | beyt iš |
| 15. | the man's wife | des Mannes Frau | zæne an mærd | ešet haiš |
| 16. | the wife of the man | die Frau des Mannes | zæne an mærd | ešet haiš |
| 17. | The man is good. | Der Mann ist gut. | an mærd xubæst. | haiš tov. |
| 18. | The book is small. | Das Buch ist klein. | an ketab kučekæst. | hasefer katan. |
| 19. | The woman is good. | Die Frau ist gut. | an zæn xubæst. | haiša tova. |
| 20. | The house is small. | Das Haus ist klein. | an xane kučekæst. | habayit katan. |

A. Fill in the blanks in the vocabulary list for each language. Give the words, leaving off the endings. For example, when you find ***gute, guter, gutes,*** and ***gut*** all translated as 'good,' insert ***gut*** as the vocabulary item.

| *English* | *German* | *Persian* | *Hebrew* |
|---|---|---|---|
| 1. man | *Mann* | *mærd* | *iš* |
| 2. woman | ______ | ______ | ______ |
| 3. good | *gut* | ______ | ______ |
| 4. house | ______ | ______ | *báyit* |

°***An*** is translated as 'the' in this column. It is actually closer to ***that*** than to ***the,*** but it may be considered as ***the*** for the purposes of this exercise. The (*y*) may be ignored; it occurs between vowels when the second vowel is a suffix.

| | | | |
|---|---|---|---|
| 5. small | | | |
| 6. large | *gross* | | |
| 7. book | | | |
| 8. is | | | (none) |
| 9. a | | | (none) |
| 10. the | *der, die, das* | | |

B. By constructing the vocabularies, you have already learned much about the grammars of small portions of these languages. The following statements are true of one or more of these languages. Basing your conclusions on the limited data given, circle the languages for which each statement is true.

| | | | | |
|---|---|---|---|---|
| 1. There is an ending or word with the meaning of English ***a.*** | Eng | Ger | Per | Heb |
| 2. The adjective follows the noun. | Eng | Ger | Per | Heb |
| 3. The adjective changes according to the noun. | Eng | Ger | Per | Heb |
| 4. The adjective ending varies according to whether or not the definite article is present. | Eng | Ger | Per | Heb |
| 5. The word for the object possessed is altered to show possession, rather than the word for the possessor. | Eng | Ger | Per | Heb |
| 6. Possession is shown by endings. | Eng | Ger | Per | Heb |
| 7. Possession is shown by a preposition. | Eng | Ger | Per | Heb |
| 8. A separate word stands for ***is.*** | Eng | Ger | Per | Heb |
| 9. A suffix stands for ***is.*** | Eng | Ger | Per | Heb |
| 10. Nothing stands for ***is.*** | Eng | Ger | Per | Heb |

C. Translate each expression into the three other languages.

| | *English* | *German* | *Persian* | *Hebrew* |
|---|---|---|---|---|
| 1. | The small book | | | |
| 2. | | Das Buch ist gross | | |
| 3. | | | an xane(y)e kuček | |
| 4. | | | | haiš hagadol |

## EXERCISE 3: Language Is Largely Arbitrary

A. There is generally no necessary connection between the sound of a word and its meaning, beyond the agreement of those who use the word. Two classes of words, however, have a closer connection than this. One class is made up of words that are thought to imitate some natural noise, such as the sound an animal makes. Speakers of Urdu, a language of Pakistan and India, think the words in the first column below imitate various natural sounds. First, try to guess what the words imitate without looking at the second column. Fill in your guesses in the first blank column. Then match each imitative word with the words in the second column, writing the correct number in the second blank column. Check your answers with the key at the bottom of the page.

| | | | |
|---|---|---|---|
| ______________ | vow vow | ____ | 1. a cat |
| ______________ | myow | ____ | 2. a horse |
| ______________ | ba | ____ | 3. a slamming door |
| ______________ | sahee | ____ | 4. a bell |
| ______________ | cuck-roo-coo | ____ | 5. a cock |
| ______________ | bwack | ____ | 6. a dog |
| ______________ | guwru guwrun | ____ | 7. a sheep |
| ______________ | dhun | ____ | 8. a clock |
| ______________ | tik | ____ | 9. a pig |
| ______________ | ting-ting | ____ | 10. a duck |

B. The second class of words that have more than a simple arbitrary and conventional connection between sound and meaning consists of groups that are no more natural than the echoic words in Exercise A. Consider the words ***rump, bump, lump, thump,*** and ***chump.*** They have in common the ***-ump*** sound and the general meaning 'heaviness and bluntness.' In these words the sound itself suggests the meaning to an English speaker. Give other words that belong in this group.

______________________________________________________________

______________________________________________________________

Give the meaning held in common by the words in each group below, and add as many as you can to the list.

chew, chomp, munch, chaw ______________________________________

______________________________________________________________

screech, squeak, scream, squeal __________________________________

______________________________________________________________

flip, flop, flutter, flicker ______________________________________

______________________________________________________________

hiss, sizzle, swish, whish ______________________________________

______________________________________________________________

snuff, snore, snout, sneeze ______________________________________

______________________________________________________________

Key: 6, 1, 7, 2, 5, 10, 9, 3, 8, 4

# 3

# The Phonetic Elements

## EXERCISE 1: Articulation of Sounds

The chart below shows the organs of speech that regulate the flow of air from the lungs to create the sounds of speech. (Speech almost always takes place during exhalation only.) As the air leaves the lungs, it is modified by muscular actions of the *vocal cords*, the *uvula*, the *tongue*, the *jaw*, and the *lips*.

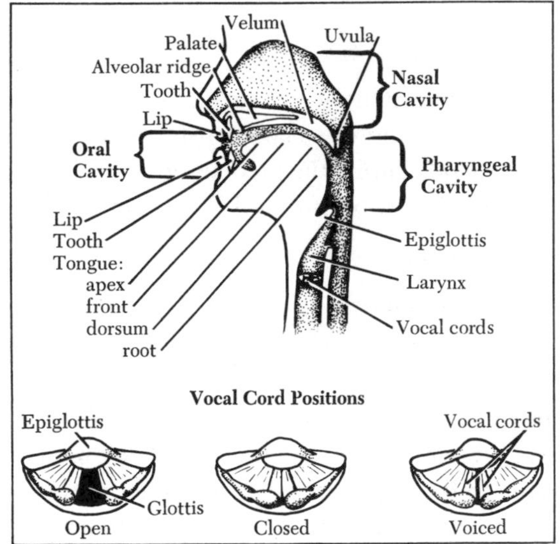


PRINCIPAL ORGANS OF SPEECH

**Articulation of Sounds I:**

The first modification of the air stream is the vibration of the muscles of the vocal cords. When these muscles are set in vibration, the sounds produced are called *voiced*. Compare the voiced sound ***z*** with the *voiceless* ***s***. If you place your hands on your ears and pronounce ***z*** and then ***s***, you will hear the vibrations which accompany the ***z*** but are missing in ***s***. Another test is to place your hand on your throat and repeat the sounds. All sounds in English may be distinguished as voiced or voiceless in this manner.

Place V beside a voiced sound and VL beside a voiceless sound.

| | | |
|---|---|---|
| __V__ b | ____ o (*oh*) | ____ r |
| ____ p | ____ t | ____ l |
| ____ f | ____ d | ____ m |
| ____ v | ____ th (***thin***) | ____ a (***ah***) |
| ____ y (***your***) | ____ th (***then***) | |

Try other vowels. They are all ________. The sounds ***m, n, l, r, y,*** and ***w*** are all ________.

**Articulation of Sounds II:**

The second possible modification takes place at the *velum.* If the velum is lowered, the sound produced by the other organs is characteristically nasal.

Which of these are nasal sounds? Place an N beside the nasal sounds.

| | |
|---|---|
| ____ b | ____ t |
| ____ m | ____ ng (***sing***) |
| ____ n | ____ f |

**Articulation of Sounds III:**

Before considering the modifications of sounds made by the lower jaw and the tongue, consider those of the lip muscles and the characteristic action of lip rounding.

Place an R beside those sounds during the production of which the lips are rounded. For example, the lips are rounded for ***w***, but for ***m*** they are not.

| | |
|---|---|
| ____ ow (***know***) | ____ s (***sing***) |
| ____ a (***Kate***) | ____ oo (***boots***) |
| ____ y (***yes***) | ____ l (***like***) |

**Articulation of Sounds IV:**

Most of the contrasts in the sounds of speech are made by modifying the relation of the *lower jaw* and the *tongue* to the *upper jaw.* The generally stationary organs of the upper jaw are called *points of articulation.* They are the *upper lip* and *teeth,* the *alveolar ridge,* the (hard) *palate,* the *velum* (or soft palate), and the *uvula.* The uvula and the upper lip are the only organs in the upper jaw that move. The organs along the lower jaw are called *articulators.* They are the *lower lip* and *teeth,* and the *apex, front,* and *dorsum* of the tongue. (See the diagram.) There are six major positions of articulation made by the relation of the articulator to the point of articulation. They are defined as follows:

| *Articulator* | *Point of Articulation* | *Position of Articulation* | *Examples* |
|---|---|---|---|
| 1. lower lip | upper lip | bilabial | m, b, ______ |
| 2. lower lip | upper teeth | labiodental | f, ______ |

| | | | |
|---|---|---|---|
| 3. apex of the tongue and lower teeth | upper teeth | interdental | th (***thin***) ______ (          ) |
| 4. apex of the tongue | alveolar ridge | apicoalveolar | n, t, s, l, r, ______ |
| 5. front of the tongue | palate | frontopalatal | sh, ______ |
| 6. dorsum of the tongue | velum | dorsovelar | k, ______ |

Add another example of a sound for each position in the spaces provided above. The answers may be checked on the phonetic chart on page 24.

The seventh position of articulation, the *glottal* position, is described as follows: when no organs other than the vocal folds are used in producing a sound, the sounds are called glottal. The ***h*** in ***he*** and the sound heard between the two parts of the colloquial negative ***hunh-uh*** are examples of this position of articulation.

**Articulation of Sounds V:**

Further modifications of sound are determined by the distance between the articulator and the point of articulation. (See the phonetic chart as you read the following.) The two may touch and stop the air stream for a moment; these sounds are called *stops* (***p, t, k, b, d, g***). Non-stop sounds are called *continuants*. The continuants may be divided into *fricatives*, in which the air is constricted at one of the positions of articulation (***f, th, s, sh,*** and ***h***), and other sounds collectively called *resonants*. [A group of sounds such as ***j*** (***judge***) and ***ch*** (***chin***) are made phonetically by a combination of a stop and a fricative. Such sounds are called *affricates* and are not considered continuants.] The resonants (***m, n, ng*** of ***sing, l, r, y,*** and ***w*** and all vowels) are either *nasal* (the first three) or *oral* (the remaining). In the articulation of the oral resonants, the air stream may leave from the side of the mouth as in ***l***, which is called a *lateral*, or it may leave through the more common *central* position. The central oral resonants are the *semivowels* (***r, y, w***) and the *vowels*. The jaw is lowest in the production of vowels. It is lower for some vowels than others. All this information is represented on the phonetic chart that follows.

Number the following three sets of consonants, vowels, and semivowels in the order of increasing jaw opening, starting with number (1) for the sound in which the jaw is the lowest compared to the other sounds in the set. The first set has been completed.

| I | II | III |
|---|---|---|
| _3_ t | ____ k | ____ a (***father***) |
| _2_ i (***bit***) | ____ a (***father***) | ____ i (***sit***) |
| _1_ a (***bat***) | ____ o (***note***) | ____ e (***set***) |
| | ____ oo (***good***) | |

## EXERCISE 2: A Classification of English Sounds

Since phonetics attempts to describe and classify all possible human language sounds, the phonetic chart below is only a subset of what would be included in a theoretically com-

# The Phonetic Chart

| Manner of Articulation \ Position of Articulation | | Bilabial | Labiodental | Interdental | Apicoalveolar | Frontopalatal | Dorsovelar | Glottal |
|---|---|---|---|---|---|---|---|---|
| Stop: Stop | VL<br>V | p (***pit***)<br>b (***bit***) | | | t (***tip***)<br>d (***dip***) | | k (***kit***)<br>g (***get***) | |
| Stop: Affricate | VL<br>V | | | | | č (***chip***)<br>ǰ (***jet***) | | |
| Continuant: Fricative | VL<br>V | | f (***fit***)<br>v (***vex***) | θ (***thin***)<br>ð (***then***) | s (***sit***)<br>z (***zip***) | š (***ship***)<br>ž (***azure***) | | h° (***hit***) |
| Continuant: Resonant: Nasal | (V) | m (***moon***) | | | n (***noon***) | | ŋ (***ring***) | |
| Continuant: Resonant: Oral: Lateral | (V) | | | | l (***loom***) | | | |
| Continuant: Resonant: Oral: Central: Semi-vowel | (V) | | | | r (***bar***)°° | y (***boy***) | w (***bow***) | |
| Continuant: Resonant: Oral: Central: Vowel | (V) | see vowel chart below | | | | | | |

Vowel chart (Degree of frontness ←→; Tongue height ↕):

| | Front | Central | Back |
|---|---|---|---|
| High | i (beat) | | u (boot) |
| Lower high | ɪ (bit) | ɨ† ɵ† | ʊ (put) |
| Mid | e (bait) | | o (boat) |
| Lower mid | ɛ (bet) | ə† | ɔ (bought) |
| Low | æ (bat) | ʌ (but) | a (pot) |

° This is similar in articulation to an aspirated voiceless vowel.

°° The ***r*** is not pronounced in New England and much of the South. In this chart semivowel = semiconsonant.

† The three reduced vowels ***ɨ*** (pity), ***ə***, often called *schwa* (sofa), and ***ɵ*** (willow) represent vowels usually. found in unstressed positions in words.

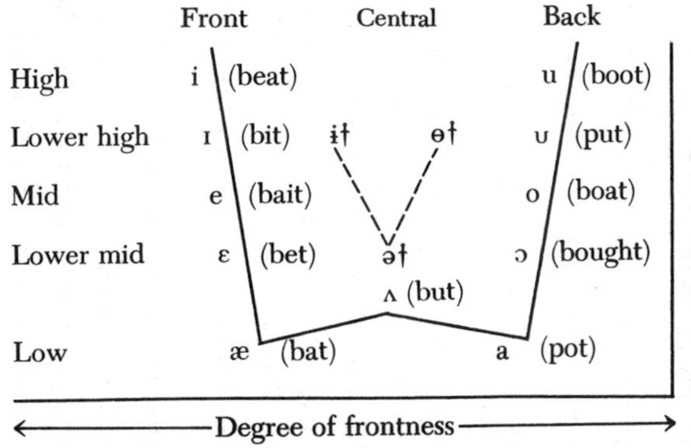

plete chart. Our concern is only with the phones, or sounds, that are found in most dialects of English. Further modification of the symbols used in this chart will be discussed under *allophones* in the next chapter.

**The Phonetic Chart:**

A. Why is the vowel chart placed where it is in relation to the consonants?

______________________________________________

______________________________________________

B. In which *position* are the consonantal sounds most numerous? ____________
Would you guess that these sounds are frequent in English? A recent statistical analysis of the English language provides the following figures for the relative frequency of each position of articulation:[1]

| | |
|---|---|
| Bilabial | 9.2% |
| Labiodental | 5.6% |
| Interdental | 4.2% |
| Apicoalveolar | 60.7% |
| Frontopalatal | 2.4% |
| Dorsovelar | 13.7% |
| Glottal | 4.1% |

C. The vowel chart is reproduced here so that you may represent the English diphthongs. A diphthong is a glide from one vowel to another, during the production of which the position of the tongue changes. One indicates this movement on a vowel chart by drawing an arrow with the base at the position where the tongue starts and the tip of the arrow where the tongue finishes. [y] symbolizes a movement to or from a high front position, and [w] to or from a high back position. Draw the diphthong arrows for these words: ***boy*** [ɔy], ***yore*** [yɔ], ***wan*** [wa], ***high*** [ay], ***Yamaha*** [ya], ***you*** [yu]. The diphthong of the word ***how*** [aw] is drawn for you. Label each arrow with the phonetic spelling of the diphthong. (There are several other diphthongs in some varieties of American English. If you use any of them, mark them on the chart on page 26.)

D. The phonetic chart can be expanded and modified to include all possible human sounds. Even within the limits of the incomplete phonetic chart given, there are empty spaces that represent possible sounds. Some of these are used in other languages; some in fact occur in English as variants of sounds found on the chart. Place the first five symbols defined below in the proper location on the phonetic chart:

1. [c] as in ***k*** of Persian ***yæk*** 'one': a voiceless frontopalatal stop.
2. [ß] as in ***b*** of Spanish ***La Habana, Cuba:*** a voiced bilabial fricative.
3. [x] as in ***ch*** of German ***lachen*** 'to laugh': a voiceless dorsovelar fricative.

[1]These figures were arrived at by adding the frequencies of the individual sounds as found in A. Hood Roberts, *A Statistical Linguistic Analysis of American English* (=*Janua Linguarum, Series Practica* 8) (The Hague: Mouton & Co., 1965), Fig. 5, p. 41.

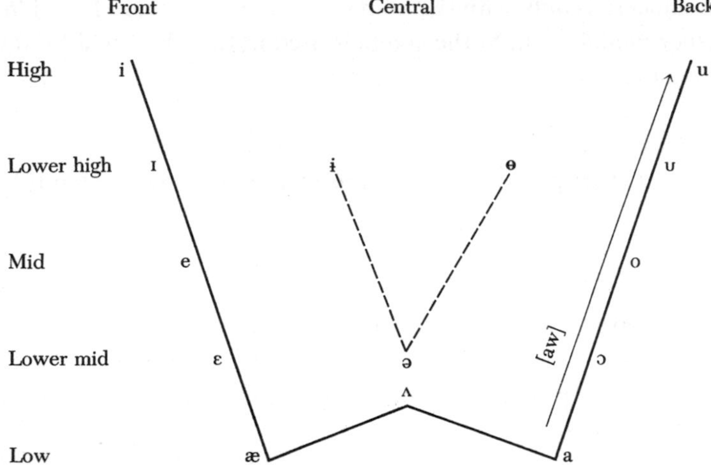


4. [ts] as in ***ts*** of Hebrew ***Tsipór*** 'bird': an apicoalveolar affricate.
5. [ɲ] as in ***gn*** of French ***cognac:*** a frontopalatal nasal.
6. [y] as in ***ü*** of German ***müde*** 'tired': a rounded high front vowel.
7. [ã] as in ***and*** of French ***quand*** 'when': a nasalized low back vowel.

E. Most popular given names, especially when not abbreviated, have one or more resonant sounds other than vowels. Some names such as ***Mary*** and ***Wayne*** are composed of only resonant sounds, whereas the names ***Joseph*** and ***Edith*** have no resonant sounds other than vowels. Names of the latter type are rare. How many resonant sounds are in your name? ______

F. The sequence of sounds on the vowel chart may be remembered by comparing it to the ***meow*** of a cat. It begins with ***m*** and makes an arc stretching from high front to low central to high back. Do you hear [miɪeɛæaɔoʊu]? ______________________

**Manner of Articulation:**

Describe the *manner of articulation* of the following sounds.

1. [m] ______ *nasal* ______
2. [æ] ______________________
3. [n] ______________________
4. [r] ______________________
5. [d] ______________________
6. [ɪ] ______________________
7. [s] ______________________
8. [k] ______________________
9. [r] ______________________
10. [ɪ] ______________________
11. [p] ______________________
12. [š] ______________________
13. [ə] ______________________
14. [n] ______________________
15. [z] ______________________

**Position of Articulation:**

Describe the *position of articulation* of the following sounds. (Consider the degree of frontness of a vowel as its position of articulation.)

1. [p] *bilabial*
2. [ə] *central*
3. [z] ______
4. [ɪ] ______
5. [š] ______
6. [n] ______
7. [f] ______
8. [ɔ] ______
9. [g] ______
10. [w] ______
11. [l] ______
12. [θ] ______

**Articulatory Description of Sounds I:**

Write the phonetic symbols of sounds defined as follows:

1. low back vowel [a]
2. apicoalveolar semivowel [ ]
3. voiceless apicoalveolar stop [ ]
4. lower high front vowel [ ]
5. voiceless dorsovelar stop [ ]
6. frontopalatal semivowel [ ]
7. mid central reduced vowel [ ]
8. apicoalveolar lateral [ ]
9. mid back vowel [ ]
10. apicoalveolar semivowel [ ]

**Articulatory Description of Sounds II:**

Give a phonetic description, such as those in the preceding exercise, for each of the sounds below. Descriptions differ for consonants and vowels. For consonants the following order is used:

1. voicing (indicated only when there is a voicing contrast)
2. position of articulation
3. manner of articulation

Vowels are described as follows:

1. tongue height
2. degree of frontness
3. "reduced" (not indicated if vowel is not reduced)
4. "vowel" (always included)

1. [f] *voiceless labiodental fricative*
2. [ə] ______
3. [n] ______
4. [ɛ] ______
5. [t] ______

6. [ɨ] ______________________________

7. [k] ______________________________

8. [s] ______________________________

Give eight words in conventional spelling as examples of these eight sounds. (Underline the letter that corresponds to the sound.) ______________________________

______________________________

**Sound Relations I:**

Compare the sounds that are represented by the underlined letters in the following pairs of related words:

describe–description
thief–thieves
absent–absence
defend–defense
choice–chosen

Describe their similarities and differences on the basis of voicing, position, and manner of articulation.

| *Sounds* | *Voice* | *Position* | *Manner* |
|---|---|---|---|
| 1. [b p] | [b] *is voiced* | *both are bilabial* | *both are stops* |
| | [p] *is voiceless* | | |
| 2. [f v] | ______ | ______ | ______ |
| | ______ | | |
| 3. [t s] | ______ | ______ | ______ |
| 4. [d s] | ______ | ______ | ______ |
| | ______ | | ______ |
| 5. [s z] | ______ | ______ | ______ |
| | ______ | | |

**Sound Relations II:**

List the similarities and differences of the following pairs of sounds. Consider voicing (when applicable), position and manner of articulation for consonants, and tongue height and degree of frontness for vowels.

| Sounds | Similarities | Differences |
|---|---|---|
| 1. [p g] | *both are stops* | [p] *is voiceless,* [g] *is voiced* |
| | | [p] *is bilabial,* [g] *is dorsovelar* |
| 2. [b t] | | |
| | | |
| 3. [n ŋ] | | |
| 4. [č ǰ] | | |
| | | |
| 5. [ž v] | | |
| | | |
| 6. [ð š] | | |
| | | |
| 7. [k s] | | |
| | | |
| 8. [g ǰ] | | |
| | | |
| 9. [i u] | | |
| 10. [e o] | | |
| 11. [ɪ ʊ] | | |
| 12. [ɪ æ] | | |

**Phonetics and Spelling:**

Write the phonetic symbol for the first consonant of the following words:

1. physics [f]
2. Thor ____
3. there ____
4. khaki ____
5. ghoul ____
6. rheumatism ____
7. cycle ____
8. compute ____
9. knee ____
10. gnome ____
11. psyche ____
12. who ____
13. ship ____
14. check ____
15. chauffeur ____
16. Zhivago ____

17. Xerxes ____
18. wrap ____
19. quay ____
20. wrath ____

**Transcription for Reading Practice:**
Transcribe these words into conventional English spelling.

1. [kæt] ____*cat*____
2. [trɪk] ____________
3. [trit] ____________
4. [tem] ____________
5. [taym] ____________
6. [hayt] ____________
7. [hol] ____________
8. [hawl] ____________
9. [rɔy] ____________
10. [bʊk] ____________
11. [ǰʌǰ] ____________
12. [rozəz] ____________
13. [čɪp] ____________
14. [čip] ____________
15. [bʌtn] ____________
16. [pæč] ____________
17. [batl] ____________
18. [yuθ] ____________
19. [klæŋ] ____________
20. [bɛt] ____________
21. [beð] ____________
22. [gəraž] ____________
23. [bʌz] ____________
24. [vɔys] ____________
25. [goldfɪš] ____________
26. [jʌst] ____________

**Transcription I:**
Transcribe these words phonetically.

1. ban ____[bæn]____
2. bang ____________
3. hung ____________
4. ham ____________
5. hail ____________
6. pale ____________
7. dread ____________
8. sting ____________
9. help ____________
10. bee ____________
11. buy ____________
12. brought ____________
13. dog ____________
14. horse ____________
15. blush ____________
16. chick ____________
17. suit ____________
18. soot ____________
19. rut ____________
20. note ____________
21. shave ____________
22. scratch ____________
23. plague ____________
24. machine ____________

25. strength ____________

26. bugs ____________

27. father ____________

28. mother ____________

29. calm ____________

30. bomb ____________

31. hearse ____________

32. hoarse ____________

33. course ____________

34. coarse ____________

35. cot ____________

36. caught ____________

37. bird ____________

38. root ____________

39. coop ____________

40. Mary ____________

41. marry ____________

42. merry ____________

43. morning ____________

44. mourning ____________

45. greasy ____________

46. house ____________

47. debt ____________

48. wash ____________

**Transcription II:**

Transcribe the following into phonetic spelling.

1. The crew slept. ____________
2. There they are! ____________
3. The motorcade passed us. ____________
4. Live a full life. ____________
5. Singing is fun. ____________
6. Harry wallowed in riches. ____________
7. The police pursued the robbers. ____________
8. The soldiers were fatigued. ____________
9. Miss America was selected yesterday. ____________
10. Having exhausted all possibilities, he finally gave up. ____________

____________

## EXERCISE 3: Distinctive Features

**Distinctive Features I:**

Look at the distinctive-feature chart of the consonants of English found on page 30 of Bolinger. Answer the following questions by comparing that chart with the phonetic chart of this chapter.

1. To which positions of articulation does [+ grave] correspond? (Give in the order of

front to back.) ______________, ______________, ______________

If [ŋ] were on the chart, would it be [+ grave]? ______________

2. To what positions of articulation do [+ diffuse] sounds belong? (Give in the order of front to back.) ______________, ______________, ______________, ______________

3. To what manners of articulation do [+ strident] sounds belong? __________, __________

Why are [θ, ð] not [+ strident]? Check the definition of ***strident*** in your text. __________

______________________________

4. To what manner of articulation do [+ continuant] sounds belong? ______________

**Distinctive Features II:**

Answer the following questions by checking the distinctive-feature chart of English in Bolinger. Find all sounds that are defined by the combination of the following sets of features.

1. [– vocalic, + consonantal, + grave, +nasal] [m], [ŋ]
2. [– vocalic, + consonantal, + nasal] ______, ______, [ŋ]
3. [– vocalic, + consonantal, + grave, + strident] ______, ______
4. [– vocalic, + consonantal, + strident] ______, ______, ______, ______, ______, ______, ______, ______

Compare the number of sounds defined in 1 and 2 and in 3 and 4. Note that 1 and 3 have one feature more than 2 and 4. Does the addition of a feature increase or decrease the number of sounds defined? ______________ This fact, that generalizations may be represented by fewer symbols than the same number of unrelated sounds, is one of the advantages of using distinctive features in descriptions, even though for specific sounds they are more cumbersome than the phonetic symbols of the first part of this chapter.

**Distinctive Features in Pairs:**

The first pair of each set of phonemes below is different from the second in one or two features. After determining common features in each pair of a set, compare the two pairs and find the feature(s) that separate(s) them. Mark the + or – distinction in the space provided as shown on line 1. Doing this exercise will increase your awareness of the differences between phonemes and groups of phonemes.[2]

1. b, d/v, ð *– continuant* *– continuant* / *+ continuant* *+ continuant*

[2] We are indebted to Professor Meri Lehtinen of the University of Minnesota for the form of this exercise.

2. p, t/v, s ______ ______ / ______ ______

______ ______ ______ ______

3. p, t/č, k ______ ______ ______ ______
4. t, č/p, k ______ ______ ______ ______
5. f, θ/v, ð ______ ______ ______ ______
6. p, b/f, v ______ ______ ______ ______

______ ______ ______ ______

7. m/n ______ ______
8. š, č/ž, ǰ ______ ______ ______ ______
9. č, ǰ/s, z ______ ______ ______ ______

______ ______ ______ ______

10. p, b/k, g ______ ______ ______ ______

## EXERCISE 4: Intonation

**Intonation:**

The major characteristics of intonation are range, direction, height, abruptness, and pattern. Apply these terms to the following examples:

A. How would a cheerleader's emotional expression of the results of a game differ in intonation if she were to report the following?

   1. We won 48 to 13. ______
   2. We lost 13 to 12. ______

B. Using Bolinger's notation, write the following sentences showing pitch direction.

   1. He is hungry. Aren't you? ______
   2. Where did you find it? In my room? ______

   ______

   3. *Q*. Where did you find it? *A*. In my room. ______

   ______

C. Which characteristic is used to distinguish these two sentences in speech?

   1. If you are happy when you see me, smile!
   2. If you are happy, when you see me smile!

   ______

D. In the sentence ***I won't play chess with you,*** which characteristic of intonation is used to express the desire

1. not to play chess, but another game. ____________________

2. not to play with you, but with anyone else. ____________________

E. Show the intonation pattern of ***on the bus***

1. as a command. ____________________

2. as a reply to the question ***Where did you hear that?*** ____________________

4

# Structure in Language: The Units of Sound

## EXERCISE 1: The Allophone

It may be claimed that no two representations of a sound are ever exactly alike. Although this is technically correct, as one can see by examining sound spectrograms (electronic visual reproductions of sounds), we perceive like sounds as the same sound. But these like sounds may be construed as different sounds by the speakers of another language. Two such like sounds are the /k/ in ***keep*** and ***cool.*** The first is frontopalatal, phonetically represented as [c]; the second is dorsovelar, symbolized as [k]. The various sounds perceived as one sound in any given language are the *allophones* of the sound. The "one" sound is the *phoneme.* The phoneme /k/[1] has the two allophones [c] and [k] in ***keep*** and ***cool.*** Let us consider the major articulatory variations of the phoneme /k/.

Consider the following words: ***cat, keep, cool, stack, scat!, act,*** and ***tack.*** In order to perceive the similarities and differences of the allophones more clearly, a feature grid will be used. The symbols used in the grid will denote the following:

+ the feature in the column is *present* in that row
– the feature in the column is *absent* in that row

Check your pronunciation of the words with the phonetic transcription given on the chart. Most of the features are quite apparent. A few minutes of concentration on the variations in pronunciation will aid you in mastering the notion of allophones. You might find that your own speech is not represented here. In any case, the questions that follow are based on this chart.

**Some Allophones of /k/ in English:**

A. On the chart above, are all cases of initial /k/ aspirated? ____________________

Final /k/? ____________________

B. Are all aspirated sounds released? ____________________ Are all released sounds aspirated? ____________________

[1] Virgules / / indicate phonemic transcription, as brackets [ ] indicate phonetic transcription.

**Major Allophones of /k/**

| Word | Phonetic representation of /k/ | Aspirated[2] | Released[3] | Fronto-palatal [c] | Dorso-velar [k] |
|---|---|---|---|---|---|
| ***cat*** | [cʰæt] | + | + | + | − |
| ***keep*** | [cʰip] | + | + | + | − |
| ***cool*** | [kʰul] | + | + | − | + |
| ***stack*** | [stæk˥] | − | − | − | + |
| ***scat!*** | [sc˥æt] | − | + | + | − |
| ***act*** | [æk˥t] | − | − | − | + |
| ***tack*** | [tæk˥] | − | − | − | + |

[2] *Aspirated* means that the sound is released with an outrush of air. If you hold a lighted match a couple of inches in front of your mouth, it will be blown out when you pronounce ***pin.*** The aspirated /p/ in pin is symbolized [pʰ].

[3] In *released* sounds, the articulator is sharply withdrawn from the point of articulation. In this case the dorsum of the tongue is withdrawn from the velum. Compare the release of /k/ in ***scat*** and ***act.*** The released sound is symbolized by [⌜], the unreleased by [⌝]. Aspirated sounds, for example [kʰ], are released.

C. Is the frontopalatal allophone [c] used before a front or a back vowel? ______

D. When is the dorsovelar allophone [k] used? ______

E. Are there any cases of final [c]? ______

F. Aside from intonation, one of the ways the speech of nonnative speakers differs from that of native speakers is in the use of allophones. When we hear a foreign accent, we recognize differences, but they are difficult to pinpoint. Native speakers are not generally aware of the allophones that cause this difference. On the basis of the above information, explain why you would hear an accent in the word [tæcʰ] for ***tack.*** This is the pronunciation of the word for 'lone' in Persian. Examine the distribution of [cʰ]. Does it appear in the final position of any word on the chart? ______

______

______

G. Examine the aspiration of the initial /k/ in the following sets of words:

| I | II |
|---|---|
| cáncel | canál |
| cátalogue | catástrophe |
| call | collíde |
| cóntract | contráct |
| cóllege | collégiate |
| córporate | coóperative |
| kiln | kinétic |

The /k/'s in column II are followed by reduced vowels. Are they aspirated? ________

Under what condition do you find initial unaspirated stops? ________________

________________________________________

H. Just as no initial /k/ before a full vowel (column I in G) is unaspirated, no /k/ following /s/ is aspirated. Each position, initial and medial, has its own characteristics. These two positions are said to be in *complementary distribution.* Find the distribution of the two allophones of the phoneme /l/ given below by examining the sets of words in which they occur.

| [l] | [ɫ] |
|---|---|
| lip | bulk |
| loot | full |
| link | milk |
| lie | cool |

Distribution: ________________ ________________

I. Consider [tæk⌝] and [tæk⌜]. Can final /k/ be released? ________________

Unreleased? ________________ When two allophones can fill the same position, they are said to be in *free variation.* Allophones are either in complementary distribution or in free variation.

J. Given the phonetic representations for /p/, fill in the "aspirated" and "released" columns for the words ***pin, pun, spin, spun,*** and ***nip.***

**Major Allophones of /p/**

| Word | Phonetic representation of /p/ | Aspirated | Released |
|---|---|---|---|
| ***pin*** | [pʰɪn] | + | + |
| ***pun*** | [pʰʌn] | | |
| ***spin*** | [sp⌜ɪn] | | |
| ***spun*** | [sp⌜ʌn] | | |
| ***nip*** | [nɪp⌜] | | |
| ***nip!*** | [nipʰ] | + | + |

1. In what position (initial, medial, or final) do the possibilities of aspirated, unaspirated, released, and unreleased allophones of /p/ occur? ________________

   These allophones are said to be in ________________ ________________.
   (See I.)

2. On the other hand, no [pʰ] follows /s/ and no word begins with [p⌜]. They are said to be in ________________ ________________. (See H.)

K. What practical applications to foreign language learning does the study of allophones have? ________________________________________________

________________________________________________

________________________________________________

________________________________________________

________________________________________________

________________________________________________

________________________________________________

________________________________________________

## EXERCISE 2: The Phoneme

**Determining Vowel Phonemes:**

The study of phonemics includes features other than just the ones touched on in the previous exercise. It also includes features such as length and nasalization—any feature, in fact, that *could* be distinctive in a speech sound whether or not it happens to be distinctive in English. If, on studying the environment of a sound (such as /p/ before a full vowel in English), we discover that the feature of aspiration is automatic, then that feature is non-distinctive: it does not serve to tell one phoneme from another. What the linguist does is to state the rule by which the feature can be predicted (*x* sound in *y* environment always has *z* feature) and then eliminate it from the description of the phoneme in question. He must then look for some other feature or features that characterize that phoneme. The following exercise illustrates this technique by applying it to the vowels of Persian. You are to decide whether such features as length and stress are needed to characterize them—that is, are needed in making a phonemic transcription of the Persian vowels. The solution should become obvious as you answer the questions. (The dot following the vowel means extra length. The consonant and vowel sounds are phonetic—those described in the previous chapter—plus [x], which is a voiceless dorsovelar fricative as in German ***Bach.*** The stress in a word of more than one syllable is indicated by ′ above the vowel in the stressed syllable.)

| | | | | | | | |
|---|---|---|---|---|---|---|---|
| 1. | i·n | 'this' | u·d | 'lute' | | |
| | ɛsm | 'name' | ɔmr | 'life' (time) | | |
| | æz | 'from' | a·z | 'greed' | | |
| 2. | bi·d | 'willow' | bu·d | 'was' | xu·d | 'helmet' |
| | sɛr | 'insensible' | sɔr | 'slide' | xɔd | 'self' |
| | sær | 'head' | na·m | 'name' | | |

| | | | | |
|---|---|---|---|---|
| 3. | si· | 'thirty' | bu· | 'smell' |
| | sɛ | 'three' | dɔ | 'two' |
| | dæ | 'ten' | ba· | 'with' |
| 4. | ni·st | 'isn't' | gu·št | 'meat' |
| | zɛšt | 'ugly' | kɔšt | 'killed' |
| | dæšt | 'plain' | ka·št | 'planted' |
| 5. | di·vá·r | 'wall' | ku·zɛ́ | 'jug' |
| | pɛsǽr | 'son' | mɔtɔ́r | 'engine' |
| | sæfí·d | 'white' | ta·zɛ́ | 'fresh' |
| 6. | kæbí·r | 'great' | æknú·n | 'now' |
| | na·mɛ́ | 'letter' | šɔtɔ́r | 'camel' |
| | ægǽr | 'if' | kɛtá·b | 'book' |

A. Find minimal pairs (pairs of words that are similar in all respects but one) to distinguish the following Persian vowel phones from each other. The difference in meaning is attributable to that single difference in sound. The two sounds are thereby established as separate phonemes.

| | | |
|---|---|---|
| [i· u·] | [bi·d] | [bu·d] |
| [ɛ ɔ] | __________ | __________ |
| [æ a·] | __________ | __________ |
| [i· ɛ] | __________ | __________ |
| [ɛ æ] | __________ | __________ |
| [u· ɔ] | __________ | __________ |
| [ɔ a·] | __________ | __________ |

B. Which vowels are consistently long? ________ ________ ________

C. Which ones are consistently short? ________ ________ ________

D. Look at group 4. Is vowel length affected by final consonant clusters? ________

E. In group 5, all six vowels appear in an unstressed position (the first syllable). In group 6, all six vowels appear in a stressed position. Does stress affect the length of the vowels? ________

F. Is the stress predictable from the data given? ________ If so, give the rule.

________________________________

G. Is length predictable? ________ If so, give the rule. ________

________________________________

H. If stress and length are predictable, is it necessary to write them? ________

I. Write the simplified, phonemic vowels of Persian in the chart below.

| | Front | Back |
|---|---|---|
| High | | |
| Mid | | |
| Low | | |

J. Group 5 would appear as follows phonemically:

| | |
|---|---|
| /divar/ | /kuze/ |
| /pɛsær/ | /mɔtɔr/ |
| /sæfid/ | /taze/ |

Write group 6 phonemically.

| | |
|---|---|
| ________________ | ________________ |
| ________________ | ________________ |
| ________________ | ________________ |

## EXERCISE 3: Segmental Phonemes of English

**Minimal Pairs:**

For the following sets of segmental phonemes of English, find pairs of words that are similar in all features but the sounds noted here. Find two pairs of words; one pair should contrast the initial position, another the final. Write them phonetically. The sounds are in the order of decreasing frequency of occurrence in English. If you cannot find examples, go on to the next pair. The pair /t r/ is illustrated here.

| *Pairs* | *Initial* | *Final* |
|---|---|---|
| 1. /t r/ | [tʌn], [rʌn] | [tut], [tur] |
| 2. /r n/ | | |
| 3. /n s/ | | |
| 4. /s l/ | | |
| 5. /l d/ | | |
| 6. /d h/ | | (no example) |
| 7. /h m/ | | (no example) |
| 8. /m k/ | | |
| 9. /k ð/ | | |

10. /ð z/ __________ __________

11. /z v/ __________ __________

12. /v f/ __________ __________

13. /f b/ __________ __________

14. /b p/ __________ __________

15. /p ŋ/ (no example) __________

16. /ŋ g/ (no example) __________

17. /g š/ __________ __________

18. /š č/ __________ __________

19. /č θ/ __________ __________

20. /θ ǰ/ __________ __________

21. /ǰ ž/ (no example) __________

22. /i ɪ/ __________ __________

23. /ɪ e/ __________ __________

24. /e ɛ/ __________ __________

25. /ɛ æ/ __________ __________

26. /æ ʌ/ __________ __________

27. /ʌ a/ __________ __________

28. /a ɔ/ __________ __________

29. /ɔ o/ __________ __________

30. /o ʊ/ __________ __________

31. /ʊ u/ __________ __________

## EXERCISE 4: Particle, Wave, and Field in Phonology

According to the tagmemic theory, phonemes are *particles.* A string of phonemes—syllables and parts of syllables—may be considered as a *wave.* These strings of phonemes combine in characteristic patterns, some of which will be considered below for English. The contrastive relationships among particles are displayed by the phonetic chart in Chapter 3. Such a relationship is called a *field* relationship.

**The Syllable—A Wave Phenomenon:**

The exercises in the rest of this section will be limited to English monosyllables. The monosyllable is a frequent form in English.

Give two English words in phonemic transcription that exemplify each of the following monosyllable types:

C = consonants (/p t k b d g č ǰ f v s š z ž m n ŋ l h/)
S = semivowels = semiconsonants (/y r w/)
V = all vowels

VC /ʌp/, /it/

CVC ______

CV ______

CVS ______

SVC ______

VS ______

SVS ______

SV ______

CVCC ______

V ______

SVSC ______

VSS ______

VSC ______

CVSC ______

CSVC ______

**The CVC Pattern in English:**

Each of these patterns is further broken down according to positions of articulation. Let us consider the possible CVC words in English. For the sake of simplicity, let us use one symbol for a group of related sounds as follows:

B = bilabials and labiodentals (/p b f v m/)
I = interdentals (/θ ð/)
A = apicoalveolars (/t d s z l n r/)
F = frontopalatals (/š ž č ǰ y/)
D = dorsovelars (/k g ŋ w/)
G = glottal (/h/)
V = vowels (/i ɪ e ɛ æ ʌ a ɔ o ʊ u/)

Note that the semivowels /r y w/ are distributed in A, F, and D respectively. Thus, CVC also covers SVC, CVS, and SVS. Since in English /ž/ and /ŋ/ do not occur initially and /h/ does not occur finally, the theoretically possible number of CVC words is 22 × 11 × 23 =

5566 English words. Of the 10,000 most frequently used words examined in Ernest Horn's *A Basic Writing Vocabulary,* 307 words are reported by Roberts to be of the CVC type.[4] This number is only 6 per cent of the number of permissible words. Some of the permissible words exist but are rare in English. The following words may be found in larger dictionaries: ***dap, duff, fid, gib, jus, beck, lall, luff, mel, motte, raff, rick, shim,*** and ***sudd.***

Give three English words to fit each CVC pattern below. The symbols are those which were defined above.

DVA ________ *cat, witch, gun* ________

BVA ________________________________

IVA ________________________________

AVD ________________________________

BVF ________________________________

AVA ________________________________

FVA ________________________________

GVA ________________________________

FVD ________________________________

AVB ________________________________

DVB ________________________________

IVF ________________________________

GVD ________________________________

IVB ________________________________

DVF ________________________________

There are thirty-six such possible sets. In Roberts' analysis no examples for eleven of the sets are found. Can you find any words that fit any of the following patterns, IVI, IVG, AVF, AVG, FVI, FVG, DVI, DVG, GVB, GVI, GVG? There are 568 words that fit these patterns. Check some of your hunches. You might find that some of the words that you considered non-words are actually words. They are often found in crossword puzzles. (An example of IVI is ***Thoth.***) ________________________________

________________________________

**Initial Consonant Clusters—Two Consonants:**

In the chart below give examples of words that begin with the phoneme at the left followed by the phoneme above each column. If you find no words that fit, draw a line in the appropriate intersection. Place fairly common foreign words in parentheses.

[4] Roberts, *op. cit.,* Table 4, p. 50.

| | l | r | w | y | Others |
|---|---|---|---|---|---|
| p | *please* | *pray* | (*pueblo*) | *pure* | |
| b | | | | | |
| t | | | | | |
| d | | | | | |
| k | | | | | |
| g | | | | | |
| f | | | | | |
| v | | | | | |
| θ | | | | | |
| s | | | | | |
| š | | | | | |
| h | | | | | |
| m | | | | | |

A. In the words above how did you spell /kl-/ ________________, /kr-/ ________________, /kw-/ ________________, /ky-/ ________________, and /fr-/ ________________?

How else might the last one be spelled? ________________________________

B. From the chart above determine which consonant phonemes occur before /l/ ________________________________, before /r/ ________________________________, before /w/ ________________________, and before /y/ ________________________.
The last one differs from one dialect to another on the basis of pronunciation of words such as ***stupid*** (/styúpɨd/ or /stúpɨd/).

**Initial Consonant Clusters—Three Consonants:**

Complete the chart below as you did in the previous exercise. Ø in the first column indicates that you are to add no consonants. (These are words with two-consonant initials, which share some features with the others.)

A. How did you spell /skØ-/ ________________________, /skl-/ ________________________, /skr-/ ________________, /skw-/ ________________, and /sky-/ ________________?

B. Using the chart below, do the following: in the cases where three-consonant clusters occur, describe (name) the first phoneme /________/, describe the voicing and manner of articulation of the second ________________________________________,

| | Ø | l | r | w | y | Others |
|---|---|---|---|---|---|---|
| sp | *speak* | *splash* | *spray* | —— | *spew* | |
| st | | | | | | |
| sk | | | | | | |
| sf | | | | | | |
| sm | | | | | | |
| sn | | | | | | |

and describe manners of articulation of the third consonant ____________.

C. Write five words that begin with /sn-/. ____________

____________

Do they have any semantic notions in common? In Brightland and Gildon's *A Grammar of English Tongue,*[5] published in 1711, we find this interesting quip: /sn-/ "is an ending [sic] that generally implies the nose, or something belonging to it, which are deriv'd from it, and have a great Relation to it; as, *snout, sneeze, snore, snort, sneer, snicker, snot, snivil, snite, snuff, snuffle, snaffle, snarl, snudge,* to hold your Nose into your Bosom." What does your list show, if anything? ____________

**Summary of Initial Consonants and Consonant Clusters:**

Match the phonemes on the left with the feature on the right that is most appropriate. Place the letter of the definition of the feature to the left of the series of phonemes.[6]

| | |
|---|---|
| ____ /r l w y/ | A. never occur initially; all other consonants do |
| ____ /w r t k p y l m n f/ | B. never cluster initially as *either member* of a cluster |
| ____ /p h f s t g k θ b d v m š/ | C. occur as the first member of a cluster |
| ____ /p f t k m/ | D. occur as the second member of a cluster |
| ____ /ž ŋ/ | E. occur as either first or second members of a cluster |
| ____ /w r l y n/ | F. occur only as second members of clusters |
| ____ /č ǰ ð z ž ŋ/ | G. the only phonemes that occur as third members of clusters |

**"Fuzzy Borders" Between Syllables:**

The "fuzzy borders" between syllables have been the cause of some changes in words. For example, the word ***apron*** in Middle English was ***napron. A napron*** was interpreted as

[5] P. 127.

[6] Roberts, *op. cit.*, p. 60.

***an apron.*** Below are listed a few phrases that might lead to misunderstanding. Add a few similar expressions to the list and identify the features by which these can be distinguished.

a gray train/a great rain ______ (*released vs. unreleased* /t/) ______

I scream / ice cream ____________________

a tall / at all ____________________

a name / an aim ____________________

____________ ____________________

____________ ____________________

____________ ____________________

# 5

# Structure in Language: The Higher Levels

## EXERCISE 1: Morphemes

**Morphemes I:**

Separate the following words into their morphemes by placing a slash between them. Some are composed of only one morpheme. The first has been completed.

1. *aw/ful*
2. breakfast
3. crystallization
4. deformity
5. evangelical
6. forgetfulness
7. gyroscope
8. honesty
9. insincere
10. jargon
11. knockabout
12. lovely
13. miraculous
14. nowhere
15. obstinate
16. periodical
17. query
18. restaurant
19. satisfied
20. trimmings

A. How would you divide ***apparently?*** It may be divided as ***apparent/ly*** or as ***appar/ent/ly.*** What is the rationale for dividing it the second way? ________________

____________________________________________________

Can you find other words that change in the same way as do ***appear*** and ***appar-?***

____________________________________________________

Are there examples to establish ***-ent-*** as a morpheme? ________________

____________________________________________________

B. Some linguists analyze ***made*** as ***make*** + past. If this kind of analysis is used, what information about the words, besides that found in Bolinger, is needed in order to decide what a morpheme is? ________________

____________________________________________________

C. In the word ***their,*** one might say that ***thei*** is a morpheme (as in ***they***) and ***-r*** is a morpheme (as in ***your***). Comment on this justification of ***their*** as two morphemes.

______________________________________________

______________________________________________

**Morphemes II:**

Divide the words in the following sentences into their morphemes by placing a slash between each morpheme. The sentences are from Bolinger's discussion of the morpheme. Read them through first.

1. *The/ organ/ic/ function/ of/ language/ is/ to/ carry/ mean/ing.*
2. The apparently meaningful bits that are smaller than words are termed morphemes.
3. What are words?
4. A word is evidently something that is not to be broken up.
5. The morpheme is semi-finished material from which words are made.
6. Semi-finished means second-hand.
7. Practically all words that are not imported bodily from some other language are made up of old words or their parts.
8. The only thing a morpheme is good for is to be melted down and recast in a word.
9. The meanings of morphemes can vary as widely as their forms.
10. Almost no morpheme is perfectly stable in meaning.
11. When morphemes are put together to form new words, the meanings are almost never simply additive.

## EXERCISE 2: Source Morphemes and System Morphemes

Separate the source morphemes from the system morphemes in sentences 3, 4, 6, 8, and 9 of the preceding exercise. List each morpheme only once.

| *Source Morphemes* | | *System Morphemes* | |
|---|---|---|---|
| ________ | ________ | ________ | ________ |
| ________ | ________ | ________ | ________ |
| ________ | ________ | ________ | ________ |
| ________ | ________ | ________ | ________ |
| ________ | ________ | ________ | ________ |
| ________ | ________ | ________ | ________ |
| ________ | ________ | ________ | ________ |
| ________ | ________ | ________ | ________ |
| ________ | ________ | ________ | ________ |
| ________ | ________ | ________ | ________ |

| | | | |
|---|---|---|---|
| ________ | ________ | ________ | ________ |
| ________ | ________ | ________ | ________ |
| ________ | ________ | ________ | ________ |

A. Which group is more numerous? ________

B. Which group occurs more frequently? ________

C. Would you expect a different result for A and B if the corpus were much larger? ________

________

________

## EXERCISE 3: Allomorphs

**Allomorphs I:**

Transcribe phonemically the singular and plural allomorphs of the following words that occur in your own speech:

| *Word* | *Singular Allomorph* | *Plural Allomorph* |
|---|---|---|
| 1. life | */layf/* | */layv/-* |
| 2. thief | ________ | ________ |
| 3. path | ________ | ________ |
| 4. knife | ________ | ________ |
| 5. booth | ________ | ________ |
| 6. wolf | ________ | ________ |
| 7. leaf | ________ | ________ |
| 8. sheaf | ________ | ________ |
| 9. loaf | ________ | ________ |
| 10. sheath | ________ | ________ |
| 11. house | ________ | ________ |
| 12. truth | ________ | ________ |

**Allomorphs II:**

Which negative prefix (***ir-***, ***il-***, ***im-***, ***in-***) is used with each of the following words?

| *Prefix* | *Word* | *Prefix* | *Word* | *Prefix* | *Word* |
|---|---|---|---|---|---|
| 1. *ir-* | relevant | 5. ______ | adequate | 9. ______ | possible |
| 2. ______ | logical | 6. ______ | movable | 10. ______ | admissible |
| 3. ______ | modest | 7. ______ | legal | 11. ______ | reversible |
| 4. ______ | equitable | 8. ______ | regular | 12. ______ | literate |

With which sound or position of articulation is each form of the prefix used? ______________

______________________________________________________________________

______________________________________________________________________

## EXERCISE 4: Morpheme Identification

**Modern Hebrew:**

Determine the morphemes in the following list of Hebrew words. Proceed by isolating the one that means 'wrote'.

1. katávti 'I wrote'
2. katávta 'you (masculine singular) wrote'
3. katávt 'you (feminine singular) wrote'
4. katáv 'he wrote'
5. katvá 'she wrote'
6. katávnu 'we wrote'
7. kətavtém 'you (masculine plural) wrote'
8. kətavtén 'you (feminine plural) wrote'
9. katvú 'they wrote'

A. What are the suffixes for the following words?

| | | | |
|---|---|---|---|
| ________ | I | ________ | we |
| ________ | you (m. s.) | ________ | you (m. pl.) |
| ________ | you (f. s.) | ________ | you (f. pl.) |
| ________ | he | ________ | they |
| ________ | she | | |

B. What are the three allomorphs of *wrote*? ______________________________

______________________________________________________________________

C. Given the Hebrew word ***yašáv*** 'he sat,' translate the following:

| | |
|---|---|
| she sat ______________ | they sat ______________ |
| you (m. pl.) sat ______________ | yašávnu ______________ |
| I sat ______________ | yašávt ______________ |

**Classical Arabic:**

1. yáktubu 'he writes'
2. yaktúbuhu 'he writes it (m.)'
3. yaktúbuha 'he writes it (f.)'
4. yáktubu lahu 'he writes to him'
5. yáktubu laha 'he writes to her'
6. yaktúbuhu laha 'he writes it (m.) to her'

7. yaktúbuhu lahu 'he writes it (m.) to him'
8. yaktúbuhu lahum 'he writes it (m.) to them (m.)'
9. yaktúbuhu lii 'he writes it (m.) to me'
10. yaktúbuhu lana 'he writes it (m.) to us'
11. yaktúbuhu laka 'he writes it (m.) to you (m. s.)'
12. yaktúbuhu laki 'he writes it (m.) to you (f. s.)'
13. yaktúbuhu lakum 'he writes it (m.) to you (m. pl.)'
14. yaktúbuhu lakúnna 'he writes it (m.) to you (f. pl.)'
15. yaktúbuhu lahúnna 'he writes it (m.) to them (f.)'

A. Write the morphemes for the following words:

| | | | |
|---|---|---|---|
| ____________ | me | ____________ | us |
| ____________ | you (m. s.) | ____________ | you (m. pl.) |
| ____________ | you (f. s.) | ____________ | you (f. pl.) |
| ____________ | him (it) | ____________ | them (f.) |
| ____________ | her (it) | ____________ | to (give the allophones) |

B. Is stress predictable? If so, give the rule. (Omit lakúnna and lahúnna.)

________________________________________

________________________________________

C. Given the word ***yúrsilu*** 'he sends,' translate the following:

yursíluhu ________________________

yursíluha lahu ________________________

yursíluhu lakunna ________________________

He sends it (m.) to us. ________________________

He sends her to them (f.). ________________________

## EXERCISE 5: Word Classes

**Clues to Word Classes:**

Some of the underlined words in the following paragraph may not be familiar to you. You will, however, know what part of speech each word is. As you read, look for the cues that help you determine the part of speech.

In the morning, after you get out of the rack, you will scrub the deck, the bulkheads, and the overhead before leaving the billet. You will clean the portholes, and sweep the ladder. After head-calls, you will go through the hatch, put your cover on your gourd, make sure you are wearing clean skivvies, and run to the messhall. You are not allowed to get chow from the reefer in the galley or to get pogibates at the gedunk. After you leave the messhall, the smokinglamp will be lit if there are no fights with the Squids and no one is fatmouthing. All sickbay commandos will report to the Louie or the Gunner. Don't listen to scuttlebut. I am the only one with the skinny.[1]

[1] From a paper by Merle N. Schneidewind, "Navy Slang."

A. What part of speech are most of the underlined words? ______

B. List the clues that you had for determining this. Consider word ending and word position in relation to verbs or modifiers. ______

______

______

______

______

______

**Nouns:**

Add one or more of the suffixes in the list below to each numbered word to create new nouns. In some cases the form of the new noun is quite different from its elements; for example, ***pope + cy = papacy.***

| | | | | |
|---|---|---|---|---|
| -age | -cy | -ics | -ist | -ness |
| -al | -ee | -ing | -ity | -or |
| -an | -ence | -ion | -let | -ship |
| -ance | -er | -ions | -ling | -ster |
| -ce | -ian | -ism | -ment | -th |

1. distinct *+ ion, + ness*
2. elegant ______
3. lenient ______
4. senile ______
5. fresh ______
6. young ______
7. democrat ______
8. member ______
9. library ______
10. magic ______
11. violin ______
12. gang ______
13. lecture ______
14. alcohol ______
15. marry ______
16. refer ______
17. accept ______
18. write ______
19. build ______
20. train ______
21. dismiss ______
22. retire ______
23. elect ______
24. dear [dar] ______
25. home [ham] ______
26. warm ______
27. communicate ______
28. phoneme ______

Check your list and answer the following questions.

A. Which suffixes are added to adjectives to make nouns? ______________________

______________________________________________

B. List the suffixes that may be added to verbs to make nouns. ______________________

______________________________________________

C. Which suffixes may be added to nouns to create new nouns? ______________________

______________________________________________

D. What is the common form of 'unableness'? ______________________

______________________________________________

**Verbs:**

Below is a list of fifteen transitive verbs. Match them with the Noun Phrases found on the right to produce grammatical and acceptable sentences. You will note that although all the verbs are transitive, there are certain syntactic and semantic restrictions on what each one may be paired with. Match each verb with the appropriate numbers. (People differ in their attitudes as to the acceptability of some sentences.)

| | |
|---|---|
| I consider *1, 3, 5, 6, 7, 10, 11, 13* | 1. his abilities as a musician. |
| I know *1, 6, 10, 13* | 2. the daylight out of him. |
| I admire ______ | 3. him impossible to comprehend. |
| I find ______ | 4. very little fish. |
| I keep ______ | 5. her trustworthy. |
| We prefer ______ | 6. her to be trustworthy. |
| You terrify ______ | 7. him president. |
| You eat ______ | 8. it in the garage. |
| I force ______ | 9. him stealing bread. |
| We'll try ______ | 10. him to be a scholar. |
| We'll elect ______ | 11. fighting policemen. |
| We caught ______ | 12. myself to eat liver. |
| We avoid ______ | 13. the truth. |
| I want ______ | 14. to persuade him to stay. |
| I take ______ | 15. no credit for this. |

What is the difference in syntactic requirements between ***consider*** and ***know?*** (Consider the choices with 5, 6, 7, and 10.) ______________________________

______________________________

______________________________

**Semantic Compatibility:**

In the passage below, called "Political Speech," the choice of words to fill the blanks is rather predictable if the context is known. However, if the context is unknown and one fills the blanks with random words of the proper parts of speech, the passage becomes nonsensical and sometimes funny. Games such as "Mad Libs" depend on this principle of semantic incompatibility for their humor. In the passage below, ask someone to provide you with words of the particular parts of speech that you name (these are written below the lines). Do not let him see the paragraph until he has finished. How do you account for the fact that if this exercise were done by a number of people who saw the passage as they filled in the words, they would agree on their choice of many of the words? ______________

______________________________

POLITICAL SPEECH

Ladies and gentlemen, on this ______ (*adjective*) occasion it is a privilege to address such a ______ (*adjective*) looking group of ______ (*plural noun*). I can tell from your smiling ______ (*plural noun*) that you will support my ______ (*adjective*) program in the coming election. I promise that, if elected there will be a ______ (*noun*) in every ______ (*noun*). And two ______ (*plural noun*) in every garage. I want to warn you against my ______ (*adjective*) opponent, Mr. ______ (*name of person in room*). This man is nothing but a ______ (*adjective*) ______ (*noun*). He has a ______ (*adjective*) character and is working ______ (*noun*) in glove with the criminal element. If elected, I promise to eliminate vice. I will keep the ______ (*plural noun*) off the city's streets. I will keep crooks from dipping their ______ (*plural noun*) in the public till. I promise you ______ (*adjective*) government, ______ (*adjective*) taxes, and ______ (*adjective*) schools.[2]

[2]Roger Price and Leonard Stern, *Son of Mad Libs* (Los Angeles: Price/Stern/Sloan Publishers, 1959). Copyright 1959 by Price/Stern/Sloan Publishers, Inc. Reprinted by permission of the publisher.

## EXERCISE 6: Syntax

**Syntactic Differences:**

Of the three sentences given for each set below, one sentence is syntactically different from the other two. Circle the letter before the sentence that is different. Be ready to explain your choice in each case. Consider the following example:

A. She was driven to the airport.
B. She was flown to Cuba.
C. She was opposed to the plan.

C is different because one can say that "X drove her to the airport," "X flew her to Cuba," but not "X opposed her to the plan." By considering such rearrangements, you should be able to do the rest.

1. A. He reads well.
   B. He writes well.
   C. He seems well.
2. A. Mary is anxious to graduate.
   B. Mary is eager to eat.
   C. Mary is easy to tease.
3. A. The boy fell into a puddle.
   B. The tadpole turned into a frog.
   C. The family moved into a house.
4. A. John impresses Bill as incompetent.
   B. John regards Bill as incompetent.
   C. John identifies Bill as incompetent.
5. A. She decided to play.
   B. She wanted to sleep.
   C. She ran to school.
6. A. They're afraid to run.
   B. They're able to play.
   C. They're ready to use.
7. A. The doctor's house was surprising.
   B. The doctor's arrival was surprising.
   C. The doctor's departure was surprising.
8. A. She's going to drive me to work.
   B. She's going to drive me to drink.
   C. She's going to drive me to school.
9. A. The king's banishment was unjust.
   B. The committee's appointment was unjust.
   C. The patient's complaint was unjust.

10. A. John promised his mother to drive carefully.
    B. John persuaded his mother to drive carefully.
    C. John expected his mother to drive carefully.

**Syntactic Ambiguities:**

The following sentences are ambiguous as they stand. Rewrite them to remove the ambiguity, preserving one of the meanings. For example, in ***The jockey dismounted from the horse with a smile,*** the ambiguity is removed if ***with a smile*** is replaced by an adjective and the adjective is placed between ***the*** and ***jockey,*** as in ***The smiling jockey dismounted from the horse.***

1. John was angry at the time. ______________________________

______________________________

2. Mary likes music better than Susan. ______________________________

______________________________

3. John and Mary visited me. ______________________________

______________________________

4. My father drag races with red and gold convertibles. ______________________________

______________________________

5. That girl's cooking made me sick. ______________________________

______________________________

6. John enjoys entertaining women. ______________________________

______________________________

7. The dress comes in pink, yellow, and green on white. ______________________________

______________________________

8. Draw more simple designs. ______________________________

______________________________

9. He composed music for a play that is hard to understand. ______________________________

______________________________

10. Certain reactions to given stimuli are inherent in the human animal. ______________________________

______________________________

______________________________

11. The boy feels strange. ______________________________

______________________________

12. They're ready to eat. ______________________________

______________________________

13. John was injured by the tractor in the field. ______________________________

______________________________

14. It was too hard for me to cut. ______________________________

______________________________

**Tagmemes and Syntagmemes:**

Give two examples of each of the following syntactic strings, or *syntagmemes.*

1. Noun-as-subject and verb-as-predicate

   Example: *Infants cry.* ______________________________

2. Noun-as-subject, verb-as-predicate, and noun-as-object

   Example: *Children drink milk.* ______________________________

   ______________________________

3. Noun-as-subject, linking-verb-as-predicate, and adjective-as-complement

   Example: *Astronauts remain young.* ______________________________

   ______________________________

4. Noun-as-subject, verb-as-predicate, noun-as-indirect-object, and noun-as-direct-object

   Example: *The barber gave the man a haircut.* ______________________________

   ______________________________

5. Interrogative-pronoun-as-complement, linking-verb-as-predicate, noun-as-subject

   Example: *Who are those children?* ______________________________

   ______________________________

6. Give another example of a syntagmeme in English. ______________________________

   ______________________________

   ______________________________

**Phrasing:**

Replace each numbered unit in the sentence below with a phrase or a clause. Write your answers on the corresponding lines.

The dog chased my car.
1 2 3

1. ______________________________

2. ______________________________

3. ______________________________

The new sentence is: ______________________________

______________________________

**Embedding:**

Identify the embedded sentences in the following sentence:

"An underground magazine called *Metanoia,* conceived by several former university students, has evolved from a one-page Xerox sheet to a polished thirty-five-page magazine in less than a year."

Begin with the sentence ***A magazine has evolved from a sheet to a magazine in less than a year.***

1. *The magazine is called* Metanoia.
2. ______________________________
3. ______________________________
4. ______________________________
5. ______________________________
6. ______________________________
7. ______________________________
8. ______________________________
9. ______________________________

# The Evolution of Language: Courses, Forces, Sounds, and Spellings

## EXERCISE 1: Indo-European Languages

The names of the languages listed below are found in your desk dictionary (*Standard College Dictionary, Webster's Seventh New Collegiate Dictionary,* and others). Not all of these languages are of Indo-European origin, nor are they all spoken today. Consult your dictionary and give the subfamily of those languages which are of Indo-European origin. Place an X before the names of languages no longer spoken. The ten commonly recognized subfamilies of Indo-European are: Albanian, Armenian, Balto-Slavic, Celtic, Germanic, Hellenic or Greek, Hittite or Anatolian, Indo-Iranian, Italic or Romance, and Tocharian.

| | | | | | |
|---|---|---|---|---|---|
| ____ | Albanian | *Albanian* | ____ | Hindi | ____ |
| *X* | Aramaic | ____ | ____ | Hindustani | ____ |
| ____ | Armenian | ____ | ____ | Hittite | ____ |
| ____ | Basque | ____ | ____ | Hottentot | ____ |
| ____ | Bengali | ____ | ____ | Hungarian | ____ |
| ____ | Bulgarian | ____ | ____ | Italian | ____ |
| ____ | Czech | ____ | ____ | Latin | ____ |
| ____ | Dutch | ____ | ____ | Norwegian | ____ |
| ____ | English | ____ | ____ | Pahlavi or Pahlevi | ____ |
| ____ | Estonian | ____ | ____ | Persian | ____ |
| ____ | Finnish | ____ | ____ | Polish | ____ |
| ____ | Flemish | ____ | ____ | Portuguese | ____ |
| ____ | French | ____ | ____ | Prussian | ____ |
| ____ | Gothic | ____ | ____ | Russian | ____ |
| ____ | Greek | ____ | ____ | Sanskrit | ____ |

____ Slovak ____________________ ____ Urdu ____________________

____ Spanish ____________________ ____ Walloon ____________________

____ Tocharian ____________________ ____ Welsh ____________________

____ Turkish ____________________

Write the names of the Indo-European languages in the preceding exercise under the proper subfamilies below. (You might check your answers against the chart of Indo-European languages found with the listing of Indo-European languages in *Webster's Seventh New Collegiate Dictionary.*)

| *Albanian* | *Armenian* | *Balto-Slavic* | *Celtic* | *Germanic* |
|---|---|---|---|---|
| ________ | ________ | ________ | ________ | ________ |
| ________ | ________ | ________ | ________ | ________ |
| ________ | ________ | ________ | ________ | ________ |
| ________ | ________ | ________ | ________ | ________ |
| ________ | ________ | ________ | ________ | ________ |
| ________ | ________ | ________ | ________ | ________ |

| *Greek* | *Hittite* | *Indo-Iranian* | *Italic* | *Tocharian* |
|---|---|---|---|---|
| ________ | ________ | ________ | ________ | ________ |
| ________ | ________ | ________ | ________ | ________ |
| ________ | ________ | ________ | ________ | ________ |
| ________ | ________ | ________ | ________ | ________ |
| ________ | ________ | ________ | ________ | ________ |
| ________ | ________ | ________ | ________ | ________ |
| ________ | ________ | ________ | ________ | ________ |

## EXERCISE 2: The Comparative Method

**The Comparative Method I:**

By comparing the sounds, words, and syntax of different languages or dialects, we arrive at clues to their relationship to each other; in addition, we learn something about the earlier forms of the languages. A form that is shared by most of the languages being considered, particularly those which are geographically separated, is very likely an early form. An innovative, or later, form is systematically dissimilar to others. Consider the following words in three geographically and temporally separated Germanic languages, and answer the questions that follow.

| *Old English* | | *Gothic* | *Old High German* |
|---|---|---|---|
| pund | 'pound' | pund | pfund |
| tīen | 'ten' | taihun | zehan |
| cūþ | 'known' | kunþs | chund |

N.B. *c* = [k], *z* = [ts], *ch* = [kx] or [x].

A. Considering the pronunciation of the initial consonant in each case, the words with the innovating forms are: ______________, ______________, and ______________.

They are all in the ____________________ dialect.

B. What are the earlier or "proto" forms of the initial consonants, as far as this limited amount of data shows? ______________, ______________, and ______________.

**The Comparative Method II:**

A list of words from four old Germanic dialects is given below.[1] Assuming that the innovation is a change from stops to fricatives, arrange these in the order of increasing change from the oldest form. (The spelling *ch* represents a voiceless dorsovelar fricative [x].)

| (*English*) | *1* | *2* | *3* | *4* |
|---|---|---|---|---|
| 'I' | ich | ich | ich | ik |
| 'make' | machen | machen | machen | maken |
| 'village' | dorf | dorp | dorf | dorp |
| 'that' | das | dat | das | dat |
| 'apple' | appel | appel | apfel | appel |
| 'pound' | pund | (p)fund | pfund | pund |

(Not affected by the innovation) *4*, ____, ____, ____ (Most affected by the innovation).

**The Comparative Method III:**

Here are five words in the older Germanic languages all meaning 'to raise.' Arrange them on the basis of similarity and degree of innovation on a tree diagram in the space provided on the following page, and compare your results with the diagram on page 87 of Bolinger. The Gothic form given is the oldest form.

| | |
|---|---|
| heffen | Old High German |
| hebbian | Old Saxon |
| hafjan | Gothic |
| hebban | Old English |
| hefja | Old Icelandic |

[1] We are indebted to Professor Stephen Schwartz of the University of California at Los Angeles for these examples.

## EXERCISE 3: Cumulative Change

**A Sixteenth-Century Text:**

Read the following passage from *The French Schoolemaister,* written in the sixteenth century by Claudius Desainliens (alias Claude Hollyband), and answer the questions that follow. The conversation is between Fraunces (Francis), a schoolboy, and Margerite (Margaret), the maid, and later between Fraunces and his father. You should be able to read this Early Modern English text without much difficulty. A brief lexicon is provided at the end of the selection.

## READING: The Daily Life of Elizabethan England[2]

*Margaret:* Ho Fraunces rise, and get you to schoole: you shalbe beaten, for it is past seven: make yourself readie quickly, say your prayers, then you shall have your breakfast.

[*F.*] Margerite, geeue mee my hosen: dispatche I pray you: where is my doublet? bryng my garters, and my shooes: geeue mee that shooyng horne.

[*M.*] Take first a cleane shirte, for yours is fowle.

[*F.*] Make hast then, for I doo tarie too long.

[*M.*] It is moyst yet, tary a little that I may drie it by the fier.

[*F.*] I cannot tarye so longe: go your way, I will none of it.

[*M.*] Your mother will chide mee if you go to schoole without your cleane shirt.

[*F.*] I had rather thou shouldst be shent, than I should be either chid or beaten: Where haue you layde my girdle and my inckhorne? Where is my gyrkin of Spanish leather? Where be my sockes of linnen, of wollen, of clothe. Where is my cap, my hat, my coate, my cloake, my kaape, my gowne, my gloves, my mythayns, my pumpes, my mayles, my slippers, my handkarchief, my poyntes, my sachell, my penknife, and my bookes. Where is

[2] A. W. Pollard, "Claudius Hollyband and his *French Schoolmaster* and *French Littleton,*" *Bibliographical Society Transactions* XIII (1915), pp. 226–28.

all my geare? I haue nothyng ready: I will tell my father: I will cause you to be beaten: Peter, bring me some water to wash my hands and my face. I will have no river water, for it is troubled: geue me well, or Fountayne water: take the ewre, and powre uppon my handes: powre high.

[*M.*] Can you not wash in the baason? Shall you haue alwayes a seruaunt at your tayle? You are to wanton.

[*F.*] Wilt thou that I wash my mouthe and my face where I haue washed my handes, as they doo in many houses in England? Geue mee a towell: mayden. Now geue me my breakefast, for I am readie: make haste.

[M.] Haue you saluted your Father and your Mother? Have you forgotten that?

[*F.*] Where is he?

[*M.*] He is in the shoppe.

[*F.*] God geeue you good morow my father, and all your companie: father geeue mee your blessyng if it please you.

[*Father.*] Are you up? is it time to rise at eight of the clock? You shall be whipt: go, and kneele downe, and say your prayers: God blesse thee. . . . Now goe, and haue mee recommended vnto your maister and maistress, and tell them that I pray them to come tomorow to dinner with mee: that will keepe you from beating. . . . learne well, to the end that you may render vnto mee your lesson when you are come againe from schoole.

[*F.*] Well father.

**Lexicon:**

| | |
|---|---|
| *hosen* | close-fitting leg covering or tights fastened to the doublet |
| *doublet* | man's close-fitting garment, with or without sleeves, covering the body from the neck to the waist or a little below |
| *tary* | to linger |
| *shent* | harmed or disgraced |
| *girdle* | belt or sash |
| *pumpes* | low-heeled, slipperlike shoes |
| *mayles* | bag |
| *inckhorne* | ink container |
| *gyrkin* | jerkin, a close-fitting waistcoat |
| *kaape* | cape |
| *poyntes* | strings or ribbons fastening the hosen to the doublet |
| *geare* | apparel |
| *ewre* | ewer, wide-mouthed pitcher or jar |
| *baason* | basin |

A. List five words in the first paragraph that are spelled differently today. ____________

____________________________________________

B. At first reading you might consider Fraunces a woman for asking for his ***hosen, garters,***

***girdle,*** and ***gowne.*** List a few other words that are no longer used in the same sense as in the text. Describe the difference in meaning in each case. ____________________

______________________________________________________________________

______________________________________________________________________

C. Find three sentences or phrases that have a different syntax in present-day English. An example of archaic syntax is the position of ***not*** in "Can you not wash in the baason?"

1. ____________________________________________________________

2. ____________________________________________________________

3. ____________________________________________________________

D. Translate into contemporary English the passage in the last paragraph that starts with "Now, goe . . . ," and continue to the end of the paragraph. ____________________

______________________________________________________________________

______________________________________________________________________

______________________________________________________________________

______________________________________________________________________

## EXERCISE 4: Borrowing

**Borrowing I—General:**

English has borrowed from many languages. By referring to your desk dictionary, identify the immediate etymological source of the following words. Specify the dictionary used.

______________________________________________________________________

| *Word* | *Etymological Source* | *Word* | *Etymological Source* |
|---|---|---|---|
| air | ____________ | custom | ____________ |
| babel | ____________ | czar | ____________ |
| barbecue | ____________ | delivery | ____________ |
| blouse | ____________ | furlough | ____________ |
| booby | ____________ | geisha | ____________ |
| buffalo | ____________ | guerrilla | ____________ |
| bungalow | ____________ | gull | ____________ |
| canasta | ____________ | gusto | ____________ |
| cocoa | ____________ | hallelujah | ____________ |
| cola | ____________ | halo | ____________ |

| Word | Etymological Source | Word | Etymological Source |
|---|---|---|---|
| hustle | ________________ | raccoon | ________________ |
| ill | ________________ | robot | ________________ |
| judo | ________________ | safari | ________________ |
| kabob | ________________ | shanghai | ________________ |
| kamikaze | ________________ | shebang | ________________ |
| khaki | ________________ | slim | ________________ |
| kiosk | ________________ | sofa | ________________ |
| mammoth | ________________ | spy | ________________ |
| marimba | ________________ | tonic | ________________ |
| mohair | ________________ | traffic | ________________ |
| mugwump | ________________ | tycoon | ________________ |
| oil | ________________ | typhoon | ________________ |
| okra | ________________ | uvula | ________________ |
| orangutan | ________________ | veneer | ________________ |
| pajama | ________________ | veranda | ________________ |
| penguin | ________________ | vizier | ________________ |
| persimmon | ________________ | wing | ________________ |
| polo | ________________ | yacht | ________________ |
| posse | ________________ | yogurt | ________________ |
| punch (drink) | ________________ | zebra | ________________ |

**Borrowing II—Words of French Origin in English:**

Vocabulary in language accommodates the needs of the times; when hula-hoops were popular, the name was common. As objects or concepts lose popularity, the words representing them become archaic and eventually drop out of the language. When a concept or an object is borrowed from another culture, its name is often taken as well. Such words become part of the language and literature of the borrowing nation. A language that has affected the English language greatly since the Norman invasion is French. The extent of influence has not been uniform throughout the centuries. When England became English again, paradoxically, it acquired the greatest number of its French loan words. The Renaissance was a second period of great borrowing. These early influences can be seen by examining a modern literary work, selecting those words which are French, and identifying the periods of heaviest borrowing as well as the types of words borrowed during each period. The types of words borrowed often reflect the relationship of the two cultures to each other.

One hundred words of French origin have been taken from the short story "Pretty Mouth and Green My Eyes" by J. D. Salinger. The date of the earliest occurrence of these words in a text may be found in the Oxford English Dictionary (O.E.D.), as well as in the partially completed Middle English Dictionary (M.E.D.). The words and their earliest literary occurrence are given in the accompanying table. The alphabetical items from A to I are essentially from the M.E.D. figures. In words of more than one morpheme, the date of borrowing of the elements rather than the date of coining of the specific words has been given.[3]

**Survey of 100 French Loan Words Found in the Short Story "Pretty Mouth and Green My Eyes" by J. D. Salinger**

| *Word* | *Earliest Literary Occurrence* | *Word* | *Earliest Literary Occurrence* |
|---|---|---|---|
| actual | 1315 | corner | 1292 |
| advice | 1297 | countenance | 1250 |
| alert | 1598 | course | 1300 |
| annoyed | 1250 | credit | 1542 |
| apartment | 1641 | damn | 1280 |
| appeared | 1250 | deference | 1647 |
| army | 1386 | delivery | 1350 |
| arrangement | 1375 | developed | 1656 |
| attorney | 1291 | difference | 1340 |
| average | 1500 | discovered | 1380 |
| avoid | 1382 | distance | 1290 |
| balanced | 1592 | exhaling | 1616 |
| barge | 1300 | extent | 1292 |
| bastard | 1250 | face | 1290 |
| beautiful | 1325 | fault | 1290 |
| blue | 1300 | favor | 1340 |
| briefly | 1300 | foreign | 1290 |
| brush | 1377 | gaiety | 1634 |
| case | 1225 | greasiest | 1514 |
| certainly | 1297 | guy | 1350 |
| chambermaid | 1230 | helmet | 1450 |
| chance | 1297 | honest | 1300 |
| chiefly | 1300 | hotel | 1644 |
| cigarette | 1842 | hours | 1225 |
| clear | 1297 | humanly | 1398 |
| close | 1280 | lampshade | 1200 |
| closet | 1370 | large | 1175 |
| conversation | 1340 | madame | 1670 |
| cord | 1300 | maintain | 1250 |

[3] We are indebted to William Z. Pentelovitch, from whose paper, "A History of French Influence on the English Language," this information is taken.

| Word | *Earliest Literary Occurrence* | Word | *Earliest Literary Occurrence* |
|---|---|---|---|
| married | 1297 | size | 1300 |
| matter | 1330 | stayed | 1586 |
| minor | 1297 | stew | 1386 |
| minute | 1370 | story | 1225 |
| mountain | 1205 | stuff | 1330 |
| move | 1290 | supporting | 1421 |
| net | 1520 | sure | 1340 |
| nice | 1290 | surface | 1611 |
| notice | 1483 | tanked | 1660 |
| page | 1300 | taste | 1292 |
| part | 1050 | train | 1330 |
| particular | 1386 | trial | 1526 |
| party | 1290 | trifle | 1225 |
| passing | 1330 | trots | 1300 |
| plaintiff | 1278 | try | 1292 |
| policeman | 1714 | use | 1225 |
| poop | 1489 | very | 1250 |
| quart | 1325 | violet | 1330 |
| reason | 1225 | voice | 1300 |
| second | 1300 | wait | 1200 |
| sign | 1225 | war | 1154 |

A. Determine the number of words in the list that entered the language during each fifty-year period from 1050 to 1900, and plot them on the graph on page 68.

B. When is the period of greatest borrowing? ______________________________

C. What events in the history of England account for this extensive borrowing? (For a detailed explanation, see the reading in Chapter 8.) ______________________________

______________________________

______________________________

______________________________

D. What are the next two major peaks? How do you account for these according to the history of England? Might the rise of the printing press have affected the first of these peaks? How? ______________________________

______________________________

______________________________

______________________________

______________________________

| Date | Number of Words Entered |
|---|---|
| 1051–1100 | |
| 1101–1150 | |
| 1151–1200 | |
| 1201–1250 | |
| 1251–1300 | |
| 1301–1350 | |
| 1351–1400 | |
| 1401–1450 | |
| 1451–1500 | |
| 1501–1550 | |
| 1551–1600 | |
| 1601–1650 | |
| 1651–1700 | |
| 1701–1750 | |
| 1751–1800 | |
| 1801–1850 | |
| 1851–1900 | |

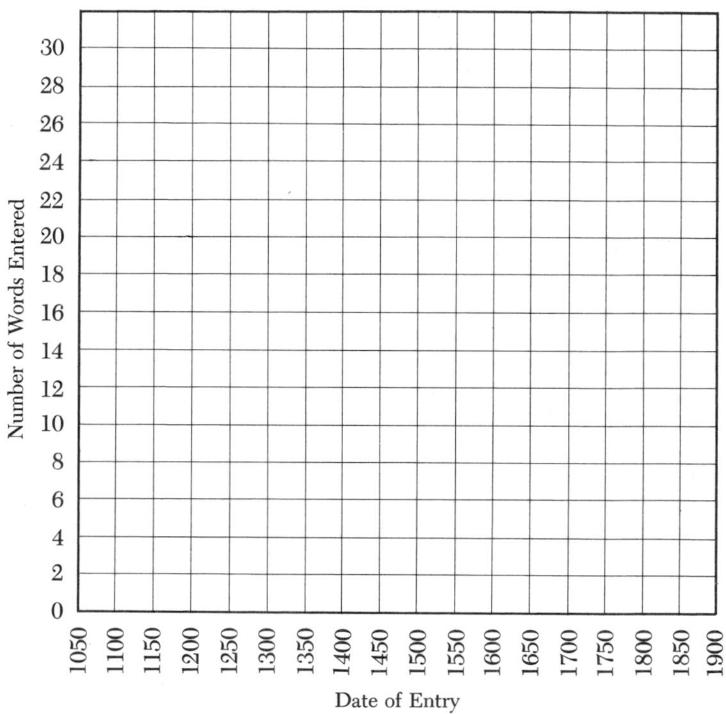


E. Jespersen's account of the influx of French words at different periods is as follows:[4]

| | | | |
|---|---|---|---|
| Before 1050 | 2 | 1451–1500 | 76 |
| 1051–1100 | 2 | 1501–1550 | 84 |
| 1101–1150 | 1 | 1551–1600 | 91 |
| 1151–1200 | 15 | 1601–1650 | 69 |
| 1201–1250 | 64 | 1651–1700 | 34 |
| 1251–1300 | 127 | 1701–1750 | 24 |
| 1301–1350 | 120 | 1751–1800 | 16 |
| 1351–1400 | 180 | 1801–1850 | 23 |
| 1401–1450 | 70 | 1851–1900 | 2 |
| | 581 | | 1000 |

[4] Otto Jespersen, *Growth and Structure of the English Language* (New York: D. Appleton & Company, 1923), p. 94.

Plot these figures on your graph. Since this list is for 1000 words, you will need to divide the figures by ten to make them correspond to the figures on the graph.

F. You may wish to add to your chart information found in the "Chronology of French Loan Words" by A. C. Baugh.[5]

G. How do the charts compare with each other? How might you explain the discrepancies?

______________________________________________

______________________________________________

______________________________________________

______________________________________________

**Borrowing III—Words of Latin Origin in English:**

After French, Latin is the language that has affected English vocabulary to the greatest degree. Latin terms have been borrowed throughout the history of English; each period, however, has a characteristic flavor. Aside from household words such as ***kitchen, dish,*** and ***cheese,*** Old English period borrowings may be characterized by the terms of the institutions of the church. Besides religious terms such as ***redeemer*** and scientific terms such as ***medicine,*** the Middle English borrowings are generally legal and scholastic terms. The majority of the Modern English borrowings from Latin are generally referred to as *learned terms*. Here are three groups of words; each group contains words from the same period of borrowing. Determine the period of borrowing of each and place Old English, Middle English, or Modern English in the space provided above each group of words.

| *Period* | ____________ | ____________ | ____________ |
|---|---|---|---|
| | abbot | client | data |
| | gospel | subpoena | edition |
| | deacon | scribe | modern |
| | pope | conviction | urban |
| | psalm | index | education |
| | nun | library | delirium |

## EXERCISE 5: Inner Forces of Change

**The Changes in Sounds:**

Whereas the changes observed so far are due to cultural contacts, there are other changes that occur within a language and do not depend on any contact with other languages. These changes are: loss (***sherf*** for ***sheriff***), assimilation (***grampa*** for ***grandpa***), dissimilation (***purple*** for ***purpre***), metathesis (***revelant*** for ***relevant***), and addition (***ellum*** for ***elm***). The following is a list of words displaying these changes. Place L, As, D, M, or Ad beside each word that displays any of these processes.

[5] In *Modern Language Notes*, Vol. 50 (Feb. 1935), p. 90.

| | | | |
|---|---|---|---|
| *L* | 1. probly for probably | ______ | 10. larnyx for larynx |
| ______ | 2. sebm for seven | ______ | 11. scant, historically from skammt |
| ______ | 3. athalete for athlete | ______ | 12. ran, historically from arn |
| ______ | 4. sump'n for something | ______ | 13. Cuber for Cuba |
| ______ | 5. gimmi for give me | ______ | 14. nucular for nuclear |
| ______ | 6. panacake for pancake | ______ | 15. bird from Old English bridd |
| ______ | 7. ekscape for escape | ______ | 16. captol for capitol |
| ______ | 8. punkin for pumpkin | ______ | 17. acrosst for across |
| ______ | 9. idear for idea | ______ | 18. thorol for thorough |

## EXERCISE 6: Spelling Pronunciation

**Spelling Pronunciation:**

The pronunciation of the following words is commonly different from what the spelling would suggest. A foreign speaker's attempt at explicitly pronouncing each morpheme of words of more than one morpheme would lead him to a spelling pronunciation. After looking up the pronunciation of these words in the dictionary, transcribe in phonemic script your own pronunciation and the common spelling pronunciation.

| *Word* | *Your Pronunciation* | *Spelling Pronunciation* |
|---|---|---|
| 1. ballet | ______ | ______ |
| 2. bases (pl. of basis) | ______ | ______ |
| 3. cupboard | ______ | ______ |
| 4. forehead | ______ | ______ |
| 5. handkerchief | ______ | ______ |
| 6. lethe | ______ | ______ |
| 7. necklace | ______ | ______ |
| 8. palm | ______ | ______ |
| 9. perusal | ______ | ______ |
| 10. subtle | ______ | ______ |
| 11. toward | ______ | ______ |

# The Evolution of Language: Meanings, Interpretations, and Adjustments

## EXERCISE 1: Meaning Brings About Changes in Form

**Blends:**

The words ***bash, smash, glimmer, flimmer, clash,*** and ***flare*** are considered blends by the Oxford English Dictionary, which gives the following etymological sources and dates:

| | | |
|---|---|---|
| bat (1205) | + mash (1000) | yields bash (1641) |
| smack (1746) | + mash (1000) | yields smash (1778) |
| gleam (1000) | + shimmer (1100) | yields glimmer (1400) |
| flame (1377) | + glimmer (1400) | yields flimmer (1880) |
| clap (1375) | + crash (1400) | yields clash (1500) |
| flame (1377) | + glare (1400) | yields flare (1500) |

Consulting your desk dictionary, find the sources of the following blends. In cases where the dictionary does not provide the answer, your own ingenuity will be your guide; for example, knowing ***motel,*** you should have no difficulty in discovering the blend in ***boatel.***

1. alcoholiday ___*alcohol*___ + ___*holiday*___
2. brunch ________ + ________
3. boatel ________ + ________
4. chortle ________ + ________
5. cinemactress ________ + ________
6. dumbfound ________ + ________
7. fantabulous ________ + ________
8. guesstimate ________ + ________
9. medicare ________ + ________
10. motel ________ + ________

11. sexational ______________ + ______________

12. simulcast ______________ + ______________

13. transistor ______________ + ______________

14. travelogue ______________ + ______________

15. Stewardess to passengers on UAL flight: "I hope you have a pleasant ***flip.***"

______________ + ______________

16. Their French work ***slagged*** all week. ______________ + ______________

*Neo-suffixation:*

17. cheeseburger ______________ + ______________

18. dictaphone ______________ + ______________

19. gaseteria ______________ + ______________

*Phrase blend:*

20. long awaited for ______________ + ______________

21. keep silent ______________ + ______________

22. Feymond's study has shown that Chrétien was ***good to his word.***

______________ + ______________

23. Newspaper correspondent on TV program: "Peter has ***hit it in a nutshell.***"

______________ + ______________

24. He didn't say anything that ***commits himself.*** ______________ +

______________

25. Bertrand Russell's ***second-hand man.*** ______________ + ______________

*Spelling Blends:* (Consult your dictionary and guess.)

26. rhyme (historical) ______________ + ______________

27. compair (contemporary) ______________ + ______________

Caution: In a conversation you might hear the word ***submerse,*** which seems to be a blend of ***submerge*** and ***immerse.*** When you check the dictionary, you find that ***submerse*** is not a blend but comes from the past participle of Latin ***submergere*** (***submersus***), which is of course related to ***submerge.***

**Malapropisms:**

In the following sentences replace the underlined word with the intended word. The first has been completed as an example.

1. The convict paced within the <u>confounds</u> of his cell. *confines*

2. Johnny Logan's "I remember the name, but I can't replace the face." ____________

3. Babe Ruth's "Look at that guy out there in left field. He is in a transom." ____________

4. His antisocial behavior results from lack of attention during his formidable years. ____________

5. When I grow up, I want to be a TV pronouncer. ____________

6. Dreyfus' vanishment from France by the French army was unjust. ____________

7. He left enough leave-way for the reader to interpret the passage as he pleased. ____________

8. Mozart was a child progeny. ____________

9. The flagrance of her perfume filled the room. ____________

10. I found the Oriental dishes very palpable. ____________

## EXERCISE 2: Changes Result from Differences in Point of View

**Folk Etymology:**

Folk etymology is also called *popular* or *false* etymology. It has existed as long as man has been interested in the etymology of words he has encountered. For example, early Roman grammarians related the Latin ***bellum*** 'war' to ***bellus*** 'beautiful' because war is *not* beautiful.[1] At times fictitious etymologies are given to strengthen a notion. Carlyle related the word ***king*** to 'one who can' associating it with the German word ***können*** 'to be capable.'[2] Ruskin would remind wives that their place was at home, since ***wife*** meant 'she who weaves.'[3] In many cases of folk etymology, the spelling of the word changes to accommodate the new sense that it is to bear. Note the change in spelling as you look up the following words. By referring to your dictionary, determine the earlier etymology of the words on the left, and underline the correct one on the right.

| | | |
|---|---|---|
| 1. hangnail | aching nail | hanging nail |
| 2. female | a male's companion | little woman |
| 3. shamefaced | bound by shame | face reflecting felt shame |
| 4. crayfish | crawling fish | crab |
| 5. greyhound | a hound | grey-colored hound |
| 6. Jordan almond | imported almond | garden almond |
| 7. Jerusalem artichoke | girasol | imported vegetable |

[1] John T. Waterman, *Perspectives in Linguistics* (Chicago: University of Chicago Press, 1963), p. 10.

[2] Simeon Potter, *Our Language*, as quoted in Wallace L. Anderson and Norman C. Stageberg, eds., *Introductory Readings on Language* (New York: Holt, Rinehart and Winston, 1962), p. 115.

[3] *Ibid.*, p. 115.

| | | |
|---|---|---|
| 8. acorn | corn | nut |
| 9. chaise longue | lounge chair | long chair |
| 10. couch grass | alive grass | synthetic sofa cover |

**Fusion:**

Underline the words or phrases below that demonstrate fusion. Specify the context in the space to the right of each phrase you underline. In making your decision, apply the four criteria mentioned by Bolinger: speed, vowel reduction, regularizing of inflection, and reluctance to separate the words.

1. law and order ______ *as used in politics* ______
2. law and authority ______________________
3. black and white ______________________
4. silver and black ______________________
5. black and blue ______________________
6. bread and butter ______________________
7. butter and jam ______________________
8. life and happiness ______________________
9. life and death ______________________
10. assault and battery ______________________
11. generator and battery ______________________
12. mother-in-laws ______________________
13. fathers-in-law ______________________
14. forecasted ______________________
15. drug addict ______________________

To which stage in the child's acquisition of language (see Chapter 1) can fusion be compared? ______________________

**Connotation:**

By resorting to a thesaurus or a synonym list (such as *Webster's New Dictionary of Synonyms*), find words that might be applied to the same person by two other individuals, one viewing the person or trait favorably, the other unfavorably. As you complete these, consider whether the words have always had a positive or negative connotation. The etymological information in the dictionary will be helpful in most cases.

| (favorable) | Trait (neutral) | (unfavorable) |
|---|---|---|
| *progressive* | liberal | *pinko* |
| | careful | |
| | saves money | |
| | loves his country | |
| | reserved | |
| | independent | |
| | resolute | |
| | levelheaded | |
| | phlegmatic | |

**Expansion and Restriction:**

*Expansion,* the widening of the scope of meaning, is also called *generalization. Restriction,* a narrowing of scope of meaning, is also called *specialization.* The word ***dog*** (Middle English ***dogge***) once referred only to dogs of native breed, whereas ***hound*** (Old English ***hund,*** akin to German ***Hund***) was the general term for all dogs. The word ***dog*** has generalized while ***hound*** has specialized. With the aid of your desk dictionary, determine which of the two processes each of the following words has undergone. Place an E or an R before each of the words to denote the process. In the space on the right, specify the earlier meaning.

| | *Earlier Meaning* |
|---|---|
| 1. *R* meat | *all foods* |
| 2. ____ layman | |
| 3. ____ deer | |
| 4. ____ assassin | |
| 5. ____ cattle | |
| 6. ____ diaper | |
| 7. ____ zest | |
| 8. ____ fee | |
| 9. ____ wealth | |
| 10. ____ meander | |
| 11. ____ doctor | |

12. ____ affection ____________________

13. ____ bonfire ____________________

14. ____ mansion ____________________

15. ____ thing ____________________

16. ____ fable ____________________

**Bifurcation:**

A. Group I contains a list of words that are related to the words in II. They not only look alike but also are of the same origin. Place each word in I beside the etymologically related word in II and in the space on the right give the form that they both go back to.

I.

| | | |
|---|---|---|
| chamber | host | pauper |
| chart | hostel | poison |
| dike | hotel | real |
| frail | leal | royal |
| glamour | legal | shatter |
| hospitality | major | skirt |

II. 1. poor *pauper, both from Latin* ***pauper***

2. fragile ____________________

3. shirt ____________________

4. camera ____________________

5. scatter ____________________

6. ditch ____________________

7. regal ____________________

8. mayor ____________________

9. guest ____________________

10. grammar ____________________

11. card ____________________

12. loyal ____________________

13. potion ____________________

14. hospital ____________________

B. The adjectives ***swollen*** and ***swelled*** are variations of the past participles of the verb ***to swell,*** but as both forms have come to be used, they have developed independent meanings.

swollen–swelled *A swollen head is an injured head. A swelled head refers to one who overestimates his own worth.*

Other pairs are: struck–stricken, broke–broken.
Give another pair of adjectives that display the same process. Describe the difference in meaning. ____________________

____________________

____________________

____________________

**Metaphor:**

The words ***egregious, dependent,*** and ***precocious*** are of metaphorical origin in Latin with the meanings of 'outside the herd,' 'hanging from,' and 'unripe' respectively. Specify the metaphors in the following metaphorical expressions.

1. blanket legislation *covers the whole of an issue as a blanket covers the bed*
2. a bright boy ____________________
3. a dull speaker ____________________
4. a sharp rebuke ____________________
5. wage ceiling ____________________
6. cold war ____________________
7. grasp a meaning ____________________
8. an aircraft sweeps over enemy territory ____________________
9. foot of a mountain ____________________
10. wage freeze ____________________
11. goose step ____________________
12. rat race ____________________
13. road bottleneck ____________________

**Euphemism:**

With the aid of a dictionary and a thesaurus, determine a few delicate words or expressions that are often used to replace the words below. In some cases the words below are themselves euphemisms. ***Bathroom*** has a long history of euphemisms, among them ***siege-house, bog-house, Sir John, Aunt Jones,*** and ***throne room.***[4]

1. death ____________________
2. cemetery ____________________
3. corpse ____________________

[4] Gilles L. Delisle, "A Quick Glance at Some Taboos."

4. defecate ______
5. pregnant ______
6. an old person ______
7. war ______
8. insane ______
9. bathroom ______
10. damn ______
11. copulate ______
12. poor ______

Can you name a field or activity that does not use euphemisms? ______

**Hyperbole:**

A. Check the sports section of a newspaper. What terms are used to express one team's defeating another? Specify the sport. ______

______

______

B. Add a few examples to the following words, which mean very little more than ***very.***

***awfully, terribly*** ______

______

C. Certain nouns have ready-made adjectives that always occur with them in some people's speech. These adjectives not only do not add any sense; they usually detract from the full force of the noun. Give some adjectives that are commonly heard with the following nouns.

1. *basic* essentials
2. ______ necessity
3. ______ pain
4. ______ silence
5. ______ clear
6. ______ circumstances
7. ______ shame

D. Do the same with the following adjectives.

1. ______ naked
2. ______ absurd
3. ______ wet

4. ____________________ new

5. ____________________ dry

6. ____________________ old

**Conflict of Homonyms:**[5]

1. In the Scottish dialect, the common word for ***ear*** is ***lug.*** The word ***near*** (Old English ***neora***), which existed in Standard English until the eighteenth century, was used as the word for ***kidney.*** Since we still have both ***ear*** and ***near*** in Modern English, why did one of them have to change when they referred to an ear and a kidney? Note that in the Scottish dialect ***ear*** was replaced and in the standard English ***near*** was replaced. (Consider the parts of speech.)

   ____________________________________________________________

   ____________________________________________________________

   What phonetic fact might have served to intensify the need for a change? (Consider ***a napron–an apron,*** discussed earlier.) ______________________________

   ____________________________________________________________

   ____________________________________________________________

2. A case in which both conflicting terms were dropped is that of the Old English ***lǣn*** 'a loan' and ***lēan*** 'reward.' As the two words came to be pronounced alike in the Middle English period, both were dropped; the first was replaced by the Old Norse cognate ***lān,*** which developed into Modern English ***loan,*** and the second was replaced by the words ***reward*** or ***recompense.*** What factor besides homonymy probably enhanced this change? (Consider the meanings of the words.) ______________________________

   ____________________________________________________________

**Conflict of Synonyms:**

The present meaning of the first word in each set below was shared by other members of the group at one time. But when there is a distinction in form, language makes use of it with a distinction in meaning. Specify what has happened to the meaning of each word.

1. animal, deer (German ***Tier***), beast ______________________________

   ____________________________________________________________

2. chair, stool (German ***Stuhl***) ______________________________

   ____________________________________________________________

3. girl, maid ______________________________

   ____________________________________________________________

[5] All examples from Edna Rees Williams, *The Conflict of Homonyms in English* (New Haven, Conn.: Yale University Press, 1944), pp. 47–55, 72.

4. bird, fowl (German **Vogel**) ______________________________

______________________________

5. boy, knave ______________________________

______________________________

**Analogy and Analysis:**

A. Suppose the following words came into English usage. Not having heard the plural of the nouns or the past of the verbs, you would probably form the plural and the past in a way that most other speakers of English would. Write the plural or the past beside each of the following words:

| *Word* | | *Plural* | *Past* |
|---|---|---|---|
| bront | 'spider' | ____________ | |
| wug | 'silver jug' | ____________ | |
| laysh | 'joy' | ____________ | |
| mank | 'to hunt' | | ____________ |
| gade | 'to worry' | | ____________ |
| ludge | 'to move' | | ____________ |

For the noun plurals, you probably selected an allomorph of the plural morpheme, namely, /s z əz/; for the past, the choice was among the past allomorphs /t d əd/. Survivals such as the historical plural forms in ***oxen, brethren, geese, mice,*** and ***sheep,*** or new verbs that change the internal vowel to form the past and the past participle as in ***sink-sank-sunk*** are not prevalent nowadays. What is the most prevalent ending for the past participle? Test the fictitious verbs above. ______________________________

______________________________

It is interesting that most readers would agree on the pronunciation of the fictitious terms. Why? What process is involved? ______________________________

______________________________

B. Many disciplines combine morphemes available from the classical languages of Greek and Latin to create needed terms for specialized concepts and objects in their fields. In medicine one finds the following terms: ***polyhemia, polygenesis, polyotia, polystichia,*** and ***polyrrhea.***[6] The Greek roots ***poly*** 'many,' ***haima*** 'blood,' ***genesis*** 'development,' ***ot-*** 'ear,' ***stichos*** 'a row,' and ***rhein*** 'flow' have been used in forming the meanings below. Match the definitions on the right with the terminology on the left by placing the correct letter in the appropriate space.

[6] C. L. Taber, *Taber's Cyclopedic Medical Dictionary* (Philadelphia: F. A. Davis Company, 1957).

| | |
|---|---|
| ____ polygenesis | A. abnormal increase in the amount of blood |
| ____ polyotia | B. theory that two or more branches of the human race evolved independently of each other. |
| ____ polyrrhea | C. the state of having more than two ears |
| ____ polyhemia | D. condition in which there are more than two rows of eyelashes |
| ____ polystichia | E. excessive secretion of fluid |

Given the above terminology, and the root ***phagein*** 'to eat,' find the term used to describe 'the condition of eating abnormally large amounts of food at a meal.'

______________________________

Check your answer against what is found in your desk dictionary.

## EXERCISE 3: Language Adjusts

**Compensatory Change:**

If the Old English sentences that follow were to be translated into Modern English following the Old English word order, most would be ungrammatical, and one would be misleading. If we were to disregard the endings and translate ***glædne giefend lufað God*** as 'A cheerful giver loves God,' the sense would be changed. Endings such as ***-ne*** of ***glædne,*** the ***-e*** of ***Gode,*** the ***-es*** of ***Godes,*** and the lack of ending in ***God,*** as well as the variations of the Modern English 'the' (***sē*** and ***þām***), signaled the relation of words to each other in Old English. Such relationships in Modern English are usually shown by position; that is, the common sentence pattern is subject, verb, object, as, for example, ***God loves a cheerful giver.*** Relationships among words are also shown by the use of prepositions, as in ***He gave me it*** vs. ***He gave it to me.*** Some personal pronouns in English (***he, his, him***) preserve the earlier means of showing relation by inflection. The possessive ***s*** inflection still remains in nouns (***God's***). Also note that sentence 8 has three negatives; the multiple number only serves to intensify the negation. Study the structures of the following ten sentences with the aid of the glosses below each word.

| *Old English* | *Modern English* |
|---|---|
| 1. ***glædne giefend lufað God.***<br>cheerful giver loves God<br>(object) (subject) | *God loves a cheerful giver.* |
| 2. ***ealle his þing gegaderude***<br>all his things gathered | ______________ |
| ***sē gingra sunu.***<br>the younger son | ______________ |

3. ***hē him lēof wæs.*** ____________________
he to them dear was

4. ***ich bēo mid ēow ealle*** ____________________
I (shall) be with you all

***dagas op worulde geendunge.*** ____________________
days up to of the world end

5. ***mē þæt riht ne þinceð.*** ____________________
to me that right not seems

6. ***Godes yrre bær.*** ____________________
God's anger he bore

7. ***hwī wepest þū Paul?*** ____________________
why weep you Paul

8. ***ne ēow nan man ne nemne*** ____________________
nor you no one not (shall) call

***lāreowas.*** ____________________
masters

9. ***hē Gode þancode.*** ____________________
he to God thanked

10. ***ic forgiefe þām þēowum.*** ____________________
I forgive to the servants

A. In the space provided above translate each Old English sentence into Modern English.

B. Is the word order of any of the Old English sentences acceptable in Modern English? Specify. ____________________

C. If the sentences ***I saw the boy*** and ***George tore the boy's book*** are combined into ***I saw the boy whose book George tore,*** the subject-verb-object order of the second sentence is reflected in the combined sentence as object-subject-verb. Give two other examples of such inverted order. ____________________

____________________

____________________

D. Some evidence that Modern English speakers think of the first position as the subject position and the third position as the object position can be seen in the following sentences: ***He was given a gift*** and ***That is him.***[7] The first is the passive of ***Somebody gave him a gift,*** which might be rephrased as ***A gift was given (to) him,*** but not as ****Him was given a gift.***[8] The sentence ***That is him,*** although common, is not accepted by the

[7] For a more detailed explanation, see S. Robertson and F. G. Cassidy, *The Development of Modern English* (Englewood Cliffs, N. J.: Prentice-Hall, 1954), pp. 285–91.

[8] In syntax the asterisk marks utterances regarded as ungrammatical.

purist, who would demand ***That is he*** or the less jarring ***He is the one.*** Note that ***He*** is in the first position and ***him*** in the third position. How would you explain the anomalous ***Me and him went*** and ***between you and I?*** Does it mean that these speakers do not have the first-position-as-subject and third-position-as-object in their grammar?

______________________________________________

______________________________________________

**Compensatory Change in Spelling:**

When the accent sign ˆ occurs over a French vowel, it often signifies the loss of a following ***s*** from an older form. In 1–8 give the English cognate which has preserved the following ***s.*** Give the Spanish and Latin cognate in 9 and 10.

1. fête *fest, feast*
2. île (in spelling) ______________
3. forêt ______________
4. conquête ______________
5. bête ______________
6. hôtel ______________
7. hôte ______________
8. côte ______________
9. même (Spanish) ______________
10. nôtre (Latin) ______________

8

# The Evolution of Language: Views and Measurements

## *READING:* A Brief History of the English Language[1]

IMPORTANCE OF STUDYING ENGLISH HISTORICALLY

. . . Our English language is . . . such a curious mixture from many sources that a brief sketch of its biography is really essential to an understanding of its structure today. Moreover there is an interesting parallel to be drawn between the development of the language and the vicissitudes of the people speaking it. If we trace the history of English, we shall observe historical relationships which also obtain in the histories of other languages.

THE ROMAN PERIOD

Under the later Roman emperors, as everyone knows, Britain was a Roman province with a flourishing colonial culture. The population was predominantly Celtic, to be sure, and spoke a language akin to modern Welsh. The native dialect no doubt persisted in the countryside, but the cities grew up about former Roman camps and included many Roman families, patrician and plebeian, who used Latin habitually. They did so even when they intermarried with the British or employed them as workers and slaves. All the amenities of Latin culture were enjoyed in the cities of this distant province: baths, forums or market places, comfortable villas with plumbing and tessellated floors, schools of rhetoric, theaters, and libraries. The Roman army was famous for making itself at home and mingling with native populations everywhere, with or without official formalities. It deserves indeed much of the credit for spreading Vulgar Latin as an international language among the common people of the ancient world. Cultured Britons were Roman citizens and used the recognized dominant language of the empire with slight modifications. In due time they were adopting the new religion, Christianity, which was rapidly becoming the chief Roman faith in the fourth century.

THE ANGLO-SAXONS

The ancestor of the English language appeared first in Albion when some tribes from Northern Germany, the Angles, Saxons, and Jutes, began to harry the shores and invade

[1] From *The Gift of Tongues* by Margaret Schlauch. Copyright 1942 by Margaret Schlauch. Reprinted by permission of The Viking Press, Inc. and George Allen & Unwin, Ltd.

the island. This happened in the middle of the fifth century A.D. The raids were part of a larger diffuse movement known to historians as the *Völkerwanderung* or folk migrations. From the shores of the Black Sea to the coasts of Britain, the northern boundaries of the *Imperium Romanum* were harassed by restless Germanic peoples: Ostrogoths, Visigoths, Vandals, Franks, Langobards, Burgundians, and the so-called Anglo-Saxons, who sought foothold within the provinces. Roman resistance was weakened for many reasons, and the Germanic peoples were able to establish themselves in the heart of some of the most fertile sections. The struggle was at its height when the Angles and Saxons began the invasion of Britain. The mother cities, Rome and Constantinople, could give no help. More than that: Rome was obliged to call on the British provincial army to give aid on the continent. So Britain was doubly exposed. By the year 500 the Germanic invaders were established. There was an end of the sophisticated urban culture of the Romans, with their debates and theaters, their laws, government, army, and incipient Christian Church.

The newcomers were pagans, worshipers of Woden and other Teutonic gods. Their organization was tribal rather than urban. They were described by contemporaries as tall, blond, and blue-eyed. In the early days of the "Germanic peril" it had been the fashion for Roman matrons to dye their hair or wear wigs in imitation of barbaric blondness. By this time, however, the threat had become grim earnest; no mere subject for coiffeurs' modes.

The languages spoken by all the Germanic tribes about 450 A.D. were closely alike. They might more properly be called dialects of a General Germanic tongue shared by all, as English now is divided into dialects throughout the English-speaking world. The Germanic dialects had in turn . . . sprung from a fairly unified (lost) ancestor which we call Primitive Germanic.

### EARLY OLD ENGLISH

We have no written documents in the Anglo-Saxon or Old English of the first few hundred years. Later, when Christianity was re-established in Britain in the early seventh century, schools, books, and the art of writing followed it. From two sources the newly converted Anglo-Saxons received instruction in these amenities. The missionaries from Rome acted as pedagogues chiefly in the south, in the kingdoms of Kent, Sussex, Wessex, and Mercia. In Northumbria some excellent work was done by Irish Christian missionaries, whose influence was felt in places like Lindisfarne, Yarrow, and Whitby. The alphabet taught here shows clearly its kinship with the Old Irish characters still used in Modern Gaelic. The first blooming of Old English literature occurred in this north country in the latter seventh and the eighth centuries. To the northern English schools of writing belonged Cynewulf, Caedmon, the Venerable Bede (who, like Alcuin, wrote in Latin), and the unknown author of *Beowulf.* Epic poems were written on the native heroic pagan traditions, and Christian themes were also treated in lyrical and heroic style—all in the Northern dialect. Unfortunately this glorious promise was cut short by the violence of the Danish invasions, beginning at the end of the eighth century. Monastic schools were reduced to smoking ruins, the learned writers scattered or killed, and precious manuscripts were destroyed.

### WEST SAXON

A revival of letters occurred later, despite the persistent fierce onslaughts of the Danes, in the kingdom of Wessex under King Alfred. The king was acutely aware of the need for education among his followers. According to his own account, even the clergy had sunk into a distressing condition of illiteracy. It was his wish "that all the freeborn youth of England who have sufficient means to devote themselves thereto, be set to learning so long as they are not strong enough for any other occupation, until such time as they can well read English writing. Let those be taught Latin whom it is proposed to educate further, and promote to higher office."

The language spoken by Alfred and his court was the Wessex or West Saxon dialect of Old English. It may be compared to Modern German in many respects. It had similarly inflected nouns with four cases in the singular and plural. There were approximately half a dozen different schemes of declension. In Modern German it is necessary to know what declension a noun "belongs to" in order to give it the proper forms in a sentence (according to use or "construction"); this too was true of Old English. The similarity of pattern is clear if one compares the inflection of two cognate or related words meaning "stone," a masculine noun:

| | SINGULAR | | PLURAL | |
|---|---|---|---|---|
| | *Old Eng.* | *Germ.* | *Old Eng.* | *Germ.* |
| Nom. | *stān* | *Stein* | *stānas* | *Steine* |
| Gen. | *stānes* | *Steines* | *stāna* | *Steine* |
| Dat. | *stāne* | *Steine* | *stānum* | *Steinen* |
| Acc. | *stān* | *Stein* | *stānas* | *Steine* |

There are reasons for the differences to be noted in the plurals. However, the kinship is clear enough. Modern German is a conservative first cousin of Old English.

A Roman missionary trying to learn Anglo-Saxon for purposes of persuasion had to remember which of about six patterns to follow with every new noun acquired. It would have been felt to be a bad blunder if, for instance, he had used the "*-e*" ending of the plural of a feminine noun to make a plural for *stān*. In precisely the same way Americans who learn German are constantly in danger of falling into barbarous error if they choose the wrong pattern in inflecting a newly acquired noun. Since articles and adjectives presented forms for every case, gender, and number, and each form had to be carefully chosen so as to agree with the coming noun, the difficulty was greatly increased.

A Latin-speaking missionary might find all this entirely natural and understandable, since his native speech was also highly inflected, but he would have been puzzled by the existence of two separate and distinct declensions for all adjectives, the "strong" and the "weak." The former was used when the adjective alone preceded a noun, as in "good man"; the latter when an article or demonstrative came before the adjective, as in "the good man." Latin had no such distinction, but German had and still has:

| | STRONG SINGULAR DATIVE | WEAK SINGULAR DATIVE |
|---|---|---|
| O.E. | *gōdum menn* | *þǣm gōdan menn* |
| | "[to] good man" | "[to] the good man" |
| Germ. | *gutem Manne* | *dem guten Manne* |

#### OLD ENGLISH VERBS

In the system of verbs one can see many resemblances between Old English and German. Both languages show a large number of verbs, called "strong," which indicate changes in tense by internal vowel change. The pattern is a very ancient one based on the vowel gradations of the old parent language (Indo-European). Some words still show the basic similarity of pattern:

| | INFINITIVE | PAST | | PAST PARTICIPLE |
|---|---|---|---|---|
| O.E. | *rīdan* | *rād,* | *ridon* | *riden* |
| Germ. | *reiten* | | *ritt* | *geritten* |
| Eng. | ride | rode | | ridden |
| O.E. | *bindan* | *band,* | *bundon* | *bunden* |
| Germ. | *binden* | *band* | | *gebunden* |
| Eng. | bind | | bound | bound |
| O.E. | *etan* | *æt,* | *ǣton* | *eten* |
| Germ. | *essen* | *ass* | | *gegessen* |
| Eng. | eat | ("et") ate | | eaten |

In both German and Old English too, there existed a second, larger group of verbs which used a different method for forming tenses. These "weak" verbs used a suffix instead: an added syllable containing a dental consonant. In modern German the suffix is always *-te,* but in Old English it varied. The possible forms were *-de, -ode, -te.* The past tense of Old English *dēman,* "to deem, to judge," was *dēmde,* "deemed"; of *lōcian,* "to look," it was *lōcode;* of *sēcan,* "to seek," it was *sōhte,* "sought."

#### OLD ENGLISH SOUNDS COMPARED TO MODERN GERMAN

The close relation between Old English and German is further indicated by constant relations in the sound patterns. When you encounter a strange word in the former you can often guess quite accurately what its cognate is in Modern German. Certain consonants have shifted away from the common Germanic position of an earlier day, but the kinship is still clear.*

* Bracketed characters refer to sound symbols in the International Phonetic Alphabet.

O.E. *drincan* resembles German *trinken* (drink) d: t
” *þencan* [θɛŋkʲan] resembles German *denken* (think) þ: d
” *twelf* resembles German *zwölf* (twelve) t: z[ts]
” *dēop* resembles German *tief* (deep) p: f

By applying a few simple correspondences like these you can use German to help you learn Old English, or Old English to help you learn German. Moreover, even the vowels show fairly consistent parallelism. The Old English *ā* [ɑ:] parallels Modern German *ei,* pronounced [ai], in a multitude of words: *stān, Stein* (stone); *bān, Bein* (bone); *ān, ein* (one), etc. So with the Old English diphthong *ēa* [ɛ:a] and Modern German *au* [aʊ]: *hēap, Haufen* (heap); *lēapan, laufen* (run, leap); *ēac, auch* (also, eke). It is useful to compile your own list as you proceed.

To be sure, minor changes in both languages have by now obscured some of the neat correspondences. Old English was particularly prone to assimilations of various sorts: palatalizations which changed [k] into [tʃ]—as you will note in the pair of words "church," *Kirche*—and subtle changes in vowels, also of an assimilatory character. The causes of these changes become apparent, usually, when the Old English forms are compared with others in the related Germanic dialects. For practical purposes Modern Dutch is even more useful than Modern German in showing family similarities.

A few lines of Old English, from a Biblical translation, will illustrate some of the characteristics of the language:*

Ond Pharāōnes dohter cwæđ tō hire: "Underfōh þis cild ond fēd hit mē, ond ic sylle þē þīne mēde." þæt wīf underfēng þone cnapan, ond hine fēdde ond sealde Pharāōnes dehter.

Ond hēo hine lufode ond hæfde for sunu hyre, ond nemde his naman Moises, ond cwæđ: "Forþāmþe ic hine of wætere genam."

Exodus 2:9-10

And Pharaoh's daughter quoth to her: "Receive this child and feed it (for) me, and I (shall) give thee thy meed." The woman took the boy and fed him and gave (him) to Pharaoh's daughter.

And she loved him and had (him) as her son, and named his name Moses, and quoth: "Because I took him (out) of water."

(Literal translation)

### CONNECTIONS WITH INDO-EUROPEAN

Even in this short passage there are a few words which show the more remote kinship of Old English with languages outside the closely knit Germanic family. No specialized knowledge is required in order to see these similarities:

O.E. *sunu* (son) corresponds to Russian *syn,* Sanskrit *sūnú.*
” *nama* (name) corresponds to Latin *nōmen,* Greek *onoma.*
” *dohtor* (daughter) corresponds to Greek *thugátēr,* Sanskrit *duhitá.*
” *mē* (me) corresponds to Latin *mē,* Russian *me'nʲa.*

*Note that þ, đ stand for [θ] and [ð] indiscriminately. The letter *h* stood for a rougher sound than ours today, something like [χ].

It is by resemblances such as these that the wider relationships are established among the various families called Indo-European.

### INFLUENCE OF LATIN ON OLD ENGLISH

Once the language of the Anglo-Saxons began to be written and to be studied along with Latin, it was brought into contact with the wide currents of world culture still pulsing strongly from the great center of Rome. The influence was felt in several ways. First of all, the study of classical Roman writers, which was more enthusiastic and intense than many readers may suppose, made Old English authors conscious of style and sentence structure in their own language. They began to cultivate certain effects they had admired in writers like Virgil, Ovid, and the prose historians. That is why the great prose translations and even the original works fostered in Old English by King Alfred have the air of being done by cultured, sophisticated writers, who knew very well what effect they were striving for. At times their admiration of Roman prose style led to unfelicitous imitation. When the translator of *Apollonius of Tyre* writes "all these things thus being done" (*đisum eallum đus gedōnum*) in the dative case, he is trying slavishly to follow a famous Latin construction in the ablative case: something like *hīs omnibus ita factīs.* It just doesn't fit. The effect remains foreign and awkward. But other writers combined planned intricacy and simplicity with more success. There are passages in the Alfredian translations of Bede, St. Gregory, Boethius, and Orosius which represent a happy marriage of Roman rhetoric with native English usage in sentence structure. In describing the death of Cædmon, the Old English version of Bede's history shifts from elaborate description to the direct recording of Cædmon's simple request: *"Beraþ mē hūsl tō"* (Bring me last sacrament). Nothing could be more English, including the ancient and entirely legitimate ending of a sentence with a preposition or adverb-particle. Thus while vigor of native idiom was retained, the very architecture of English was somewhat modified, at least among the cultured few at the courts and churches and schools, by association with the Roman literary heritage.

In the second place, the Old English vocabulary was enriched by a number of direct loans from Latin. The implanting of Christianity brought a number of direct transfers from one language to the other. Most have survived to this day. The list includes:

| | | | |
|---|---|---|---|
| abbot | hymn | organ | shrive |
| altar | martyr | pope | synod |
| angel | mass | priest | relic |
| candle | noon | psalm | temple |
| deacon | nun | shrine | |

Flourishing trade with Roman merchants continued the borrowings which had begun long ago on the continent when Germanic tribes first encountered salesmen from the Mediterranean. To the list above belong words like *cycene* (kitchen) from *coquīna; disc* (dish) from *discus; cīese* (cheese) from *cāseus; pund* (pound) from *pondus; mynet* ("mint" of money), from *moneta; copor* (copper) from *cuprum; tigele* (tile) from *tegula; strǣt* (street) from *strāta via;* and *ynce* (inch) from *unica.*

The debt to Roman word material was increased in another less obvious manner. For abstract learned concepts the Anglo-Saxon writers frequently coined words out of simple forms already existent in their own language. But they did this by translating literally the elements of the Latin words. . . . Thus the Old English vocabulary was increased under Roman inspiration without sacrifice of native ingredients. German has often followed the same method of constructing new learned words out of native elements, with an eye to the Latin model. The similar method of compounding appears in these typical examples:

| *O.E.* | *German* | *English* |
|---|---|---|
| *efen-sārgian* | *mit-leiden* | com-miserate |
| *fore-sprǣc* | *Vor-wort* | pre-face |
| *mid-wyrhta* | *Mit-arbeiter* | col-laborator |
| *ofer-ferian* | *über-führen* | trans-fer |
| *wiđ-standan* | *wider-stehen* | op-pose |
| *ūt-drǣfan* | *aus-treiben* | ex-pel |

Old English writers were thus exploring the possibilities of elaborate compounding in order to express new ideas. They never went very far in this direction—not so far, say, as some modern German writers—but it is possible that the tendency might have led to unwieldy polysyllables if Old English had developed into Modern with no disturbances from without.

### INFLUENCE OF DANISH

There was one other foreign language besides Latin which exercised a measurable influence on Old English. The long-continued attacks by Danes and other Scandinavians on the English coasts were attended by some measure of success. At one time a Danish king, Knut or Canute, actually ruled the country. Large settlements were established, especially in the northern districts. They eventually remained on a peaceful footing, and the settlers merged with the English population. Before losing their identity entirely, however, they contributed a list of loan words to the English vocabulary. Most of them are so homely and practical that we may be sure that the immigrants rapidly attained neighborly status with the people they had but recently been harrying. Words borrowed at this period include "husband," "fellow," "law," "take," "store," "gate," "skill," "sky," "ransack," "call," "thrive," "skull." A personal pronoun was taken over bodily. We owe our plural forms, "they, their, them" to the Scandinavian *þeir, þeira, þeim* which gradually displaced Old English *hīe, hīera, hem* (confusingly like the singular masculine pronoun). The loans show the intimacy finally achieved by northern settlers who must have been at first bitterly resented.

### LATE OLD ENGLISH

By the end of the Old English period, then, England had what might be called a recognized literary language, already used for several hundreds of years for important creative and translated writings. By the year 1000, however, certain changes were beginning to affect the literary language. The multiplicity of endings was gradually being reduced. Cases originally kept distinct were beginning to fall together with identical terminations. You could no longer be sure, without relying more and more on context, whether a given form meant a dative singular or a dative plural. If the confusion was appearing in formal documents written by men at least semi-learned, it was no doubt far more wide-spread among the unlearned. And very soon the process of confusion or leveling was speeded up by an important political event.

### THE NORMAN CONQUEST

In 1066, as every school child knows, England was invaded and conquered by William, Duke of Normandy, commonly called "the Bastard." He used as pretext a doubtful claim to the English crown after the death of Edward the Confessor, "last of the Saxon Kings." The army attendant upon William was chiefly composed of Normans, men speaking a provincial dialect of French but related by blood to the Danes. Their forefathers, most of them, had migrated from Scandinavia and conquered the land of Normandy even as they themselves were now proposing to conquer England. Their success meant more than a mere change in dynastic rule for the inhabitants of Britain. The old local kingdoms and tribal organizations were swept away— such as had survived the period of unified Danish rule. In their stead the whole of England, excluding Scotland and Wales, was placed under a single complex feudal system of administration.

### FEUDALISM IN ENGLAND

Feudalism of course was a highly stratified organization of society. In France there were already many ranks or orders of men, from the lowly unfree serf, up through free traders and workers, landless knights, land-owning knights, little barons, big barons, and recognized kings. Military service and other obligations were the basis of land ownership. Rights and prerogatives were at times vague or conflicting, and hence gave rise to fierce combats. Feudal France was divided into great duchies, each with a hereditary overlord at his head. Roughly speaking the dialects of medieval French corresponded to these feudal divisions. Within the confines of each duchy there was not a great deal of difference between the language of the lower and the higher orders, except insofar as differences of interest and preoccupation tended to mark off the stores of words used. The husbandman talked about agricultural matters, using more or less simple sentences studded with the technical terms of his job; the knight employed a more aristocratic vocabulary referring to tournaments, etiquette, literature, and art (within limits!), terms of inheritance, and the techniques of warfare; but in general they spoke the same dialect within the same region. The regional dialect divisions were probably much more noticeable than class divisions, apart from limited items of specialized vocabulary.

### BILINGUAL ENGLAND

When William of Normandy transferred this feudal organization to England, the linguistic situation became more complex. At once the lowest orders were doubly marked, not only by inferior economic position but also by the use of a separate, despised tongue.

Since the Church, which conducted most of the schooling of the time, was also taken over by Norman-French bishops, abbots, and other prelates, instruction in English practically ceased. Most of the native speakers became necessarily illiterate and remained so for several generations. The recording of English came to an abrupt stop almost everywhere. While English thus remained unrecorded in writing and uncorrected by formal teaching, it tended to change more rapidly than it had been doing before 1066. The leveling of forms, now accelerated, produced a greatly simplified grammar. Many of the distinctions of Old English were lost in the process. Earlier writers like Sir Walter Scott have probably exaggerated the cleavage between Norman French and English, and the length of time it endured. But it was sufficiently marked at least to intensify the drive towards simplicity, already noticeable in Old English.

#### EARLY MIDDLE ENGLISH

English re-emerged as a literary language in the hands of churchly writers in the latter twelfth century. These men, schooled primarily in Latin and Norman French, merely adapted the classroom spelling of these upper-class languages to the native idiom. Some few may have known a little about the Old English written before 1066, especially in places where efforts have been made to keep the old *Anglo-Saxon Chronicle* up to date under the Normans. In all cases they tried to write what they actually heard, phonetically. Where inconsistencies arose they were due to regional dialects in English itself, or to a conflict between French and traditional English orthography. In Old English, for instance, the word *hūs* for "house" was pronounced with a single long vowel [hu:s], and was so written. In the so-called Middle English period, from 1100 to 1400, it was still being pronounced as before, but under French influence the spelling became *hous* for [hu:s]. We can be fairly certain of the pronunciation because of the general consistency. Some writers, moreover, were interested enough in the problem to indicate the reasons for their spelling, and what it was supposed to represent.

#### CHANGES IN GRAMMAR

With the reduction of Old English declensions the English sentence fell increasingly into the word order habitual with us today: subject, predicate, complement. Otherwise it would have been impossible, eventually, to distinguish one part from the other. (Old English sentences had used the inverted order and delayed clausal verbs to be found in Modern German.) Almost all the nouns were attracted into the declension represented by *stān*, with a plural in *-as* later weakened into *-es*. Only a few survived in the other declensions. The vowels of unaccented endings were reduced to the obscure sound [ə], written *-e-*. The verbs retained endings not unlike those current in the time of King Alfred:

| | |
|---|---|
| *Ī singe* | *we singen** |
| *þū singest* | *yē singen* |
| *hē singeth* | *þei singen* |

* This is the Midland form of the plural. In the South it was *singeth*, in the North *singes*. The distinction is typical of many others which demarked the dialects from one another.

The adjectives retained vestiges of inflection, even slightly differentiating strong forms from weak; but the elaborate declensions of Old English adjectives were forgotten. The reduction of endings to short, unstressed syllables gave the language a trochaic and dactylic effect.

#### CHANGES IN SOUNDS

Although the consonants survived with little change, there was some shifting in the quality of the vowels. Old diphthongs were simplified and new ones arose. Old long vowels were shortened and short ones were lengthened under special conditions and for special reasons which need not be rehearsed here. In general the resulting new vowels were pronounced as in Modern Italian, Spanish, or German: in short, with the so-called "continental" values. Thus:

ā was [ɑ:] as in "father";
ē was [e:] or [ɛ:] as in "they" or "there," respectively;
ī was [i:] as in "machine";
ō was [o:] (not [oʊ]) as in "lone";
ū was [u:], sometimes written "ou," as in "rouge";
ȳ was identical with ī in pronunciation.

All vowels were intended to be spoken, except when two coming together in a sentence were elided (*thē intente* became *th' intente,* with three syllables to the second word). Diphthongs were pronounced by giving the above values to the separate parts: thus "*au*" represented [ɑ] plus [u] in one syllable. When you have grasped these few principles you can read Middle English aloud and enjoy the music of it along with the sense.

#### PERSISTENCE OF OLD ENGLISH WORDS

The earliest Middle English texts were still composed with an almost pure English vocabulary. The spelling, too, was conservative for a time, especially in the South, so that a casual glance at some of the early texts (ca. 1200) leaves the impression that Old English was still being written. A closer examination, however, shows that the simplification of forms was already far advanced at this time. Here is a short passage from a poem written in the South about 1170. It deals in a quaint medieval manner with the transitoriness of earthly happiness, yet there is a perennial appeal about its grave simplicity:

Ich æm elder þen ich wes a wintre and a lore;
Ic wælde more þanne ic dude; mi wit ah to ben more.
Wel lange ic habbe child i-beon a weorde and ech a dede;
þeh ic beo a wintre eald, to ying I eom a rede. . . .
Ylde me is bestolen on ær ic hit awyste;
Ne mihte ic iseon before me for smeche ne for miste.

(I am older than I was in winters and in lore; I have more strength than I did; my wit ought to be more. For a long time I have been a child in word and eke in deed; though

I be in winters old, too young I am in rede. Old age has stolen on me before I ever wist it; I could not see before me for the smoke and for the mist.)

Some of the lyrics retain pure English vocabulary at an even later date, because they deal with warm intimate things which we still prefer to express with the "Anglo-Saxon" part of our language.

Wynter wakeneth al my care,
Nou thise leves waxeth bare;
Oft I sike and mourne sore [sigh and mourn sorely]
When hit cometh in my thoht
Of this worldes joie, hou hit geth al to noht.

Nou hit is, an nou hit nys,
Al so hit ner were, ywys;
That moni mon seith, soth hit ys:
Al goth bote Godes wille:
Alle we shule deye, thoh us like ylle. [though it displeases us]

### FRENCH LOAN WORDS

Meanwhile, however, French was still the language of court, school, diplomacy, and Parliament. Even as late as the fourteenth century some outstanding English men of letters wrote exclusively in French. The English vocabulary could not long remain unaffected by this environment. What had at first been a mere infiltration of French words into English increased until by 1300 it was flood-tide. The new terms came from many occupations: from law, philosophy, theology, and military science; cookery, weaving, architecture, book-making; and the trade in wool, wine, and other commodities. Many of the more learned importations were long words which must have seemed by their vagueness imposing and slightly awesome to English ears. French words like *contritioún, transubstantioún, reverénce, penaúnce, obligacioún, dominacioún* must have arrived with double impressiveness: first because they referred to lofty matters of religion and government which the common man uneasily shies away from; and second because they simply sounded different from the native vocabulary. During the years when it was chiefly the language of illiterates, English had naturally veered away from the tendency to form lengthy compound abstractions out of native elements. Only a few like *rihtwysnesse* ("righteousness") and *agenbit* ("remorse") had survived. On the whole the native vocabulary had conserved best the basic non-abstract terms and hence turned now to an alien treasury for the needed terminology of learning.

The loans were conspicuous for another reason besides their length. They still preserved the French accentuation on the last syllable, in direct opposition to the English tendency to throw accents forward. Even when this English tendency began to affect the French importations, a strong secondary stress was retained on the last syllable: *con-trí-ci-oùn, ré-ve-rèn-ce, dó-mi-ná-ci-oùn.* The struggle between French and English tendencies in accentuation produced a wave-like rise and fall of stress which added even more dignity, it may well be, to the physical impressiveness of the words. The alternation of strongly stressed root syllables in native English, followed by the shrinking unstressed endings, was already contributing to the same effect. Out of these divergent sources came the iambic-trochaic movements of English which Chaucer used so brilliantly in his narrative verse.

### THE COMBINED VOCABULARY IN CHAUCER

And Chaucer illustrates, too, the aesthetic uses to be made of the new polyglot vocabulary. No one knew better than he how to juxtapose, contrast, or temporarily isolate the dual elements of fourteenth-century English. In this respect he may be compared to his own advantage with many modern poets. At one time Chaucer permits the full grandeur of the French polysyllables to roll out:

For of *fortúnes* sharpe *adversité*
The worste kynde of *ínfortúne* is this:
A man to han been in *prospérité,*
And it remembren when it passed is.

(*Troilus and Cressida,* III, 1. 1625 ff.)

This poignant comment on human felicity, paraphrased from Dante, gains in dignity from the use of the italicized Romance words. At the same time, the last line has a simplicity of everyday speech, the more effective by contrast; and the delayed verb in the archaic Old English style gives it a falling cadence which heightens the wistfulness. The same artful contrast of polysyllabic dignity and native simplicity is found in many other Chaucerian passages. In the ballade called "Fortune" he begins:

This wrecched worldes *trānsmutácioùn*
As wele or wo, now povre and now *honoúr*
Withouten ordre or wys *discrécioùn*
*Govérned* is by Fórtunès *erroúr.*

He laments the passing of a happier day when people told the truth and their word was as good as their bond:

Sometyme this world was so stedfast and stable
That mannes word was *obligácioùn. . . .*

("Lak of Stedfastnesse")

You will notice that the melody of Chaucer's lines depends on a correct rendering of the unaccented syllables. Unless the vowels are pronounced in these, the verse is harsh and unmetrical. Give due value to the unstressed vowels (including final *-e's*), however, and retain strong secondary stress at the end of French loan words, and you will have verse as musical and diversified as any in English.

In less exalted moods Chaucer often undertook to describe the lives and persons and small adventures of common folk. Here his brilliant realism was re-enforced by an appropriate vocabulary and a sentence structure echoing the cadences of ordinary speech. In drawing the picture of an elderly carpenter's young wife, with her gay amorous ways, her "likerous eye" and her "middle gent and smal" as any weasel's, he concludes gustily:

Hir mouth was sweete as bragot or the meeth, [ale or mead]
Or hoord of apples leyd in hey or heeth. [hay or heath]
Wynsynge she was, as is a joly colt,
Long as a mast, and upright as a bolt. . . .
Hir shoes were laced on hir legges hye.
She was a prymerole, a piggesnye [primrose or "pig's-
For any lord to leggen in his bedde, eye" (a flower)]
Or yet for any good yeman to wedde.

The homely details and comparisons expressed in everyday language—"sweet as apples laid in heath or hay"—are enough to make the reader's mouth water, as indeed they were intended to do. And the simple vocabulary of ordinary life is beautifully used when the same fair Alison rebuffs (but not permanently!) an amorous overture by her boarder, a handsome young student:

[She] seyde, "I wol nat kisse thee, by my fey!
Why, lat be," quod she, "lat be, Nicholas,
Or I wol crie 'out, harrow' and 'allas'!
*Do wey youre handes,* for youre curteisye!"
("Miller's Tale," *CT*, A3261 ff.)

With the English vernacular being handled in so masterful a manner, it had surely reached legal majority and could no longer be regarded as a subject dialect. Conversely, it was because English had already won recognition that Chaucer devoted his genius to it rather than French or Latin. Significantly enough, Parliament was first opened in English in 1362, and the chronicler Trevisa tells us the native language was used in the schools in 1385. Both events fell in Chaucer's lifetime.

### THE FIFTEENTH CENTURY

Soon after Chaucer's death, in the fifteenth century, there was a renewed drift towards simplification in English. Final unaccented vowels, by 1400 already reduced to a very slight murmur, were entirely lost. Still more nouns were shifted to the majority declension (with plurals in *-s*) out of the small group left in the minority declensions. More and more verbs were shifted to the weak conjugation from those still retaining the internal vowel change. For a time, of course, there was a choice of forms: Malory could decide between either "he clave" or "he clefte" in telling how one knight smote another asunder, as they were so frequently engaged in doing in the *Morte d'Arthur.* Similar fluctuations arose between "he clomb" and "he climbed"; "he halp" and "he helped." Some of the quaint surviving constructions out of Old English, such as impersonal verbs with the dative, the inflected genitive case for nouns denoting things, and the double negative, began to fall into disuse.

They persist in the fifteenth century, indeed even into the sixteenth, but they are felt increasingly to be archaic survivals.

| Where Chaucer said: | Later English has: |
|---|---|
| He *nevere* yet *no* vileynye *ne* sayde<br>In al his lif unto *no* manner wight. | He never said *any*thing villainous about *any*body<br>In all his life to *any* person. |
| *Me* [to me] were levere a thousand fold to dye. | *I'd* liefer [rather] die a thousand times over. |
| *Me* thynketh *it* acordaunt to resoun. | *It* seems reasonable *to me.* |
| Our present *worldes lyves* space. . . . | The space *of* our present life *of* [in] this world. |
| In hope to stonden in his *lady* [gen. sing. fem.] grace. . . . | In hope to stand in his *lady's* grace. |

Another important usage became increasingly prevalent in the fifteenth and early sixteenth century: the bolstering of verbs with a number of auxiliaries derived from "do" and "be." In Middle English a question was asked with the simple form of the verb in inverted position: "What say you? What think you?" For a couple of centuries after 1400 this was still done habitually, but more and more people fell into the habit of saying "What do you say? What do you think?" The "do" was colorless and merely brought about a deferment of the main verb. In effect it makes our English usage somewhat like Russian, which says "What you say? What you think?" without any inversion of the verb before the subject. In simple statements the "do" forms were used for situations where we no longer feel the need for them. An Elizabethan would say "I do greatly fear it" (an unrestricted statement). We should use the less emphatic "I fear it greatly." Compare Shakespeare's

> I *do prophesy* the election lights
> On Fortinbras; he has my dying voice—

and many other instances.

During the same period there began the gradual spread of the so-called progressive conjugation, with forms of "to be": I *am coming;* he *is sitting* down." These two special forms of English conjugation have developed an intricate etiquette, with many modifications of usage, which cause great trouble to the foreign student. One of the last distinctions he masters is the one between "I eat breakfast every morning" and "I am eating breakfast now"; between "I believe that" and "I do indeed believe that."

One of the most fateful innovations in English culture, the use of the printing press, had its effects on the language in many ways. The dialect of London, which had for over a century been gaining in currency and prestige, took an enormous spurt when it was more or less codified as the language of the press. As Caxton and his successors normalized it, roughly speaking, it became the language of officialdom, of polite letters, of the spreading commerce centered at the capital. The local dialects competed with it even less successfully than formerly. The art of reading, though still a privilege of the favored few, was extended lower into the ranks of the middle classes. With the secularizing of education later on, the mastery of the printed page was extended to still humbler folk. Boys who, like William Shakespeare, were sons of small-town merchants and craftsmen, could learn to read their Virgil and Ovid and Holy Writ even if they had no intention of entering the Church. Times had distinctly changed since the thirteenth century. It may be added that changes in society—the gradual emergence of a mercantile civilization out of feudalism—gave scope to printing which it would never have had in the earlier Middle Ages. The invention was timely in more than one sense.

All this may have been anticipated by the early printers. Their technological innovations may have been expected to facilitate the spread of culture. But they could not have foreseen that the spelling which they standardized, more or less, as the record of contemporary pronunciation, would have been perpetuated for centuries afterwards. Today, when our pronunciation has become quite different, we are still teaching our unhappy children to spell as Caxton did. Respect for the printed page has become something like fetish-worship. A few idiosyncrasies have been carefully preserved although the reason for them is no longer understood. When Caxton first set up the new business in London he brought with him Flemish workers from the Low Countries, where he himself had learned it. Now the Flemish used the spelling "gh" to represent their own voiced guttural continuant, a long-rolled-out sound [γ] unlike our English [g]. English had no such sound at the time, but the employees in Caxton's shop were accustomed to combining the two letters, and continued to do so in setting up certain English words. In words like "ghost" and "ghastly" it has persisted, one of the many mute witnesses to orthographical conservatism.

#### HUMANISM AND CLASSICAL INFLUENCES

English vocabulary continued to be diversified as printing and increased communication with the continent diversified its cultural needs and interests. The Renaissance (a term we shall not attempt to define here) brought with it widened interest in pagan classical learning. It was not so much an innovation as an extension of the already lively medieval interest in the same heritage. But linguistically the debt was expressed in a new manner. Whereas Roman words had formerly been taken over in French form, with all the modifications due to centuries of use, now the Latin vocabulary was plundered direct, at least to a much greater extent than before. Writers who knew some classical philology did not hesitate to adopt into English a number of forms unmodified except for a slightly Anglicized ending. Words like "armipotent," "obtestate," "maturity," "splendidous," "matutine," and "adjuvate" had not been in French popular use for centuries before reaching English; they were lifted directly out of classical texts with little change. Browne's *Religio Medici* furnishes many examples. Some writers went to such lengths that their language was crusted over with Latinisms.

The tendency had begun in the fifteenth century and went to absurd lengths in the sixteenth. Ben Jonson satirized it in his *Poetaster,* a play in which a character guilty of pretentious verbal concoctions is made to vomit them forth in a basin, in sight of all. The victim, named Crispinus, is supposed to stand for the playwright Marston who actually committed verbal atrocities of the sort. When the pill is administered Crispinus cries out:

| | |
|---|---|
| CRISPINUS. | Oh, I am sick— |
| HORACE. | A basin, a basin quickly, our physic works. Faint not, man. |
| CRISPINUS. | Oh—*retrograde—reciprocal—incubus.* |
| CAESAR. | What's that, Horace? |
| HORACE. | *Retrograde,* and *reciprocal, incubus* are come up. |
| GALLUS. | Thanks be to Jupiter. |
| CRISPINUS. | Oh—*glibbery—lubrical—defunct;* oh! . . . |
| TIBULLUS. | What's that? |
| HORACE. | Nothing, yet. |
| CRISPINUS. | *Magnificate.* |
| MAECENAS. | *Magnificate?* That came up somewhat hard. |

Among other words thus "brought up" are "inflate," "turgidous," "oblatrant," "furibund," "fatuate," "prorumped," and "obstupefact." The ungentle satire concludes with admonitions by Virgil to the exhausted Crispinus: among other things

You must not hunt for wild, outlandish terms,
To stuff out a peculiar dialect;
But let your *matter* run before your *words;*
And if, at any time, you chance to meet
Some Gallo-Belgic phrase, you shall not straight
Rack your poor verse to give it entertainment,
But let it pass. . . .

The critical attitude represented by Jonson was exaggerated in some cases into a fanatical purism. There were some who leaned over backwards in their attempts to avoid English neologisms out of Latin or Greek. If they went too far it was because the "ink-horn" terms of "aureate" or gilded English had become a kind of stylistic rash on the literary language. Still, many of the conscious creations of this period filled a real need, and were permanently adopted into standard speech.

Another consequence of the renewed, if not at all new, devotion to Latin was the freshened awareness of the component parts of Latin words in English. In the hands of gifted poets this resulted in a semantic rejuvenation of words. . . . Even spelling was affected by this awareness. Words pronounced still in a French manner were given a Latinized orthography which did not correspond to usage: thus "victuals" for ['vitlz] from French *vitaille.*

#### LATIN SYNTAX IN ENGLISH

Not only the English vocabulary was affected by the intensified devotion to Latin. Many attempts were made to have syntax and sentence structure conform too. There were attempts to implant long absolute constructions as an imitation of the Latin ablative absolute, and to make the sentence a tissue of intricately related clauses. The results were at times monstrous. This is one sentence committed by Sir Philip Sidney in the *Arcadia:*

> But then, Demagoras assuring himself, that now Parthenia was her own, she would never be his, and receiving as much by her own determinate answere, not more desiring his own happiness, envying Argalus, whom he saw with narrow eyes, even ready to enjoy the perfection of his desires;

strengthening his conceite with all the mischievous counsels which disdained love, and envious pride could give unto him; the wicked wretch (taking a time that Argalus was gone to his country, to fetch some of his principal friends to honor the marriage, which Parthenia had most joyfully consented unto), the wicked Demagoras (I say) desiring to speak with her, with unmerciful force (her weak arms in vain resisting), rubbed all over her face a most horrible poison: the effect whereof was such that never leper looked more ugly than she did: which done, having his men and horses ready, departed away in spite of her servants, as ready to revenge as they could be, in such an unexpected mischief.

You can amuse yourself by counting up the numbers of times you are delayed in this sentence by participial constructions in *-ing* ("assuring," "desiring," "strengthening") just when you are waiting breathlessly for the main verb. The end of the sentence (after the last colon) starts with "which done," something as close as we can get to a passive absolute construction on Latin lines; and it omits a necessary pronoun subject to "departed," since Latin verbs do not normally need to express "he" or "she" or "it" as subjects. Moreover, a number of words are used by Sidney in their original Latin sense rather than the familiar English one: "perfection" means "accomplishment, completion" as *perficere, perfectus* had meant "to complete."

### LATIN STYLE IN ENGLISH

Even those authors who tried to eschew an excessive Latin vocabulary sometimes followed Latin sentence structure and idiom very closely. Reginald Pecock begins one of his sentences thus:

> Even as grammar and divinity are 2 diverse faculties and cunnings, and therefore are unmeddled [distinct from each other], and each of them hath his proper to him bounds and marks, how far and no farther he shall stretch himself upon matters, truths, and conclusions. . . .

Every reader will notice how foreign-sounding is the expression "his proper-to-him bounds." Today we should consider it impossible to thrust a modifying phrase between "his" and the word it limits. But the phrase was so handled by Pecock, no doubt, because he was thinking of the Latin *fines sibi proprias.* The "how far" clause modifying "marks" has a Latin flavor also, recalling *quousque* clauses.

Notice too how Pecock creates new English idioms by translating literally certain Latin compounds. By "stretch himself upon," used in the non-physical sense, our author means "extend," from Latin *ex-tendere* "stretch out." In all self-conscious writers of the time there was a strong inclination to build elaborately balanced sentences, with clause counterweighing clause, in the manner of Roman rhetoricians. Pecock did this too. In formal exposition there was great use of constructions to contrast ideas "on the one hand"—"and on the other hand. . . ." In belles-lettres these elaborate balancings, both great and small, were often underscored by alliteration, making an intricate pattern of sound to correspond to the pattern of sense:

> It happened this young imp to arrive at Naples, a *p*lace of more *p*leasure than *p*rofit, and yet of more *p*rofit than *p*iety, the very *w*alls and *w*indows whereof showed it rather to be the *t*abernacle of Venus than the *t*emple of Vesta.

Thus John Lyly starts his hero Euphues on the artfully worded chronicle of his adventures. The italicized letters show how alliteration calls attention to the ideas put in antithesis. And once again we find illustration of Latin sentence structure used contrary to English idiom. It is not natural for us to say "It happened this young imp to arrive"—with "imp" presumably in an oblique (inflected) case as subject of the infinitive; nor was it probably a natural way of talking in Lyly's day. It is, however, a literal rendering of the Latin accusative with infinitive—*contigit iuvenem pervenīre.*

One more instance of non-English structure has persisted in limited scope into our day. It is the placement of adjectives after nouns on the model of both French and Latin—more particularly the former. Phrases like "lords appellants," "blood royal," "siege apostolic" are paralleled in contemporary use by surviving legal inversions: "notary public," "estates general," "body politic." Only the stereotyped inversions live on in ordinary speech, but poets avail themselves of the ability to create new ones when they are trying for an exalted effect. Thus Hart Crane, writing "wings imperious" and "junctions elegiac" is carrying on a minor Latin-Romance heritage of word order. In a phrase like "court martial" the unaccustomed inversion adds to the sense of ominous strangeness. Poets use this atmosphere to heighten desired effects deliberately.

### UNSTANDARDIZED ELIZABETHAN GRAMMAR

Attempts to stretch English on the Procrustes bed of Latin grammar delayed the achievement of a generally accepted style of vigor and simplicity. (Francis Bacon represented simplicity of a sort, but it was highly mannered.) Besides, English grammar was in a fairly unstable condition. There were conflicts of usage due to the heritage of archaisms from the Middle English period, and the competition of dialect forms from the regions outside of London, which persisted into the Elizabethan era.

The third singular present of the verb is a good example of this fluctuation. If Shakespeare, writing in London, had followed the London tradition in this he would have used the *-eth* ending always, and consistently set down "singeth, loveth, creepeth." But another ending, *-(e)s,* had been gaining popularity at the expense of *-eth.* Originally *-es* developed in the North country, but it spread southwards until in the sixteenth century it was becoming as acceptable as the native southern form. Shakespeare was able to use the two indifferently: "the bird of dawning *singeth* all night long" but "Tomorrow and tomorrow and tomorrow *Creeps* in this petty pace from day to day."

Other matters of grammar were less rigidly established in Shakespeare's day than ours. There were still strong traces of grammatical gender in the use of "he" and "she" for inanimate objects where we should say "it." Pecock, it will be noticed, spoke of each faculty having "his" proper bounds, instead of "its." Shakespeare wrote, "The corn hath rotted ere *his* youth attained a beard," and spoke of the soul as "she," as when Hamlet says to Horatio:

> Since my dear soul was mistress of *her* choice
> And could of men distinguish, *her* election
> Hath seal'd thee for *herself*. . . .

(*Hamlet,* III, ii)

The leveling of forms having proceeded with uneven tempo, there was considerable latitude of usage in inflected forms. Nominative and oblique cases of pronouns became somewhat confused; the newer usages have in many cases been approved by custom. The plays give us such forms as "My father hath no child *but I*," "When *him* we serve's away," "And damned be *him* that first cries 'Hold, enough!'" and "*Who* does he accuse?" There are also examples of compound subjects and even straight plural subjects with singular verbs, singular verbs with plural subjects, plural pronouns like "they" referring to singular indefinites like "everyone," double comparatives like "more braver"—in short, most of the hair-raising mistakes which cost students bad marks today. In formal prose there was more rigid usage than this, but the drama, closer to current speech, reflects a wider tolerance. In addition there were commonly accepted formulas which we now feel to be quaint rather than wrong. We are accustomed to think of abstract qualities such as "honor," "truth," and "courtesy" as single indivisible units: an Elizabethan, however, often made plural forms to indicate distributive use. His "Commend me to their loves," a very fair way of expressing things, simply appears odd to us, like the numerous words and phrases that have fallen into disuse: "I fain would know it," and so on.

### THE AGE OF CLASSICISM AND FORMAL RULES

In the seventeenth and eighteenth centuries there was a strong reaction away from Elizabethan laxity and in favor of formal regularity of grammatical usage. Once more Latin exerted an influence, this time for the legislation of "rules": the intricate "do's" and "dont's" to be observed if, as simple people often express it, one is to "talk grammar." The drive toward regularity and conformity in speech may be considered part and parcel of the general cultural manifestation known as "classicism," another term which we shall not attempt to define here. At least there is a certain appropriateness in the fact that grammatical relations were treated with a free and easy tolerance during an age of exploration, conquest, and colonization when plain piracy and robbery of land were being idealized; and that decorum and strict congruence were demanded as matters of taste (not only in grammar) when conquest had been organized into accepted, consolidated, and hence respectable empire. The parallelism may be worked out by students of culture in the large.

What we do know is that grammarians of the classical period set down fixed rules for the behavior of pronouns and verbs with a definiteness new in the history of English. A "good" writer could no longer put down "Between who?" even for the stage, if he intended it to be spoken by a prince like Hamlet. Such a locution was limited to low-class characters on the rare occasions when they were permitted to appear (for relief) in polite literature. When in doubt, the legislators of grammar appealed to Latin for authority. Was there some doubt about expressions such as "It is I," "It is me" or even "It am I"? The Latin rule about nominative cases as predicates after a finite form of "to be" decided the matter, and "It is I" was decreed despite a strong native tendency to say "It's me," In this period too, the fluctuating uses of "shall" and "will" were subjected to rules with complicated minor ramifications. Significantly enough, it was not a native Englishman but a French grammarian (George Mason) writing in 1622 for foreigners, who first tried to lay down the rules. In France as well as in England the dominant cultural tendencies favored regularity, probably for the same reasons. A Frenchman learning English would have been shocked at anything so chaotic as the "shall-will" conjugation, and it was natural for him, at that particular period, to try to give it a formal (if intricate) pattern.

Such an attitude affected the conservation of grammatical distinctions, too. While it regularized it also arrested leveling. For instance, the subjunctive in forms like "If I *were* you" or "If it *be* possible" had been giving way to the indicative, but a clear distinction was now reaffirmed in the precepts of eighteenth-century grammar. That codification has remained in force until our own times. Teaching has as usual had a conservative effect. If it were not for the careful preservation of these dying forms in school books, I should have begun this sentence with the words "If it was not. . . ." As it is, we tend to limit the few surviving subjunctives to formal discourse, printed or spoken.

In France an Academy had been established in order to give final, authoritative judgment on disputed questions of grammar and usage. Some writers in England advocated the establishment of a similar British Academy to legislate for the English language. It was felt in some quarters that refinement and formality should be made official. However, the project was never realized. Historians of English explain the resistance to it by citing the rugged independence of English character. This is no doubt true as far as it goes, but it is not a basic explanation. The rugged independence paradoxically manifested even in an age of conformity must itself be explained: perhaps by reference to the political interlude of the English Commonwealth, which effectively and permanently checked absolutism in government in the seventeenth century. It could not be successfully tried for any length of time after 1649. Any tendency towards absolutism in language was to some extent, therefore, checked by the changed political atmosphere resulting from the Commonwealth. Voltaire found this atmosphere to be very libertarian as compared with the French. Despite great similarities between French and English taste, there were great differences. France, lacking such a check as the experience of a republican government in the seventeenth century, showed the exaggerated effects of absolutism in both linguistic and cultural matters, down to 1789. The readjustment was the more drastic because it was so long delayed. The French Revolution, too, had its effect on the style and vocabulary of accepted speech—not only in France, but in England to a certain extent. The vogue of "simple" speech and rural dialects (one of the aspects of "romanticism") is connected with shifts in taste which heralded and accompanied the French Revolution.

### IMPERIAL EXPANSION

Meanwhile the English language had been spread far and wide over the globe, following the course of imperial expansion. India, at first settled and claimed by the French as rival colonists, fell under exclusively English sway in the eighteenth century. In North America also French claims were forced to yield throughout the entire territory represented by Canada and the Thirteen Colonies. French survived as a language only in the Quebec region of Canada. English discoveries and settlements led to the claim over Australia and New Zealand. In the nineteenth century the greater part of the continent of Africa fell under English sway, both direct and indirect. The Dutch Colony of South Africa was taken over after the Boer War; large territories like the English Sudan became British dependencies in the form of colonies of "backward" peoples; and some countries like Egypt were in practice directed by British commercial and administrative interests while maintaining formal independent statehood. Not everywhere in this far-flung territory has English been adopted as the prevalent speech. The dominions use it, of course; but in some of the colonies there has been little attempt to disseminate it beyond the circle of resident administrators, and in certain quarters (in India, for instance) it has met with conscious opposition.

The linguistic results of imperial expansion were manifold. We have already noticed the influx of foreign loan words into English from all quarters of the globe. In addition, each colonial dialect separated from the mother country has developed its own special idiosyncrasies, so that English-speaking visitors to England can be labeled, by their pronunciation, as emanating from Canada, Australia, South Africa, or "the States."

The settlement of Englishmen in India was particularly momentous for the history of linguistic science. When the dust of battle died down somewhat and peaceful contacts became possible, administrators with the gift of intellectual curiosity began to be impressed with the character of the various Indian languages belonging to the Indo-European family. When some of the bolder spirits extended their inquiry so far as to undertake the study of ancient Sanskrit, the classical literary language, they were further impressed by its affinities with the known classical languages of Europe. Sir William Jones was able to draw the proper conclusion as early as 1786: he wrote that Sanskrit, when compared to Greek and Latin,

> bears a stronger affinity, both in the roots of verbs and in the forms of grammar, than could possibly have been produced by accident; so strong, indeed, that no philologer could examine them all three without believing them to have sprung from some common source, which, perhaps, no longer exists: there is a similar reason, though not quite so forcible, for supposing that both the Gothick and the Celtick, though blended with a very different idiom, had the same origin with the Sanskrit.

Sir William was quite right. His studies may be said to have opened the door on comparative philology, encouraged the work of Rask, Bopp, Grimm, Leskien, and the other pioneers who established family relations among languages in the nineteenth century.

### CONTEMPORARY ENGLISH

In the recent past our language has shown no new tendencies of major importance. A great vowel shift has occurred since 1500, producing the modern sounds we associate with the printed symbols. The host of borrowed words is increasing daily, from all parts of the world. A supplementary list is being created from Latin and Greek roots to serve the purposes of scientific research. There is a revolt—within limits—against the rigid rules of classical grammarians. "Good" writers are again permitting themselves forms like these:

> Those two, no matter who spoke, or whom was addressed, looked at each other. (Dickens, *Our Mutual Friend.*)
>
> It depends altogether on who I get. (May Sinclair, *Mr. Waddington of Wick.*)
>
> If I were her. . . . (Middleton Murry, *The Things We Are.*)
>
> Kitty and me were to spend the day there . . . (by the bye, Mrs. Forster and me are such friends!) (Jane Austen, *Pride and Prejudice.*)
>
> Her towards whom it made/Soonest had to go. (Thomas Hardy, "In the Garden.")

Until very recently, histories of the English language usually ended with cheerful speculation on the outlook for it as a world language. There were several cogent arguments in favor of it. First, it was pointed out that it is a living language already spoken by a great number of persons all over the globe. Second, it has a comparatively simple grammar. It boasts of a rich and glorious literature which offers a strong inducement for any student to acquire mastery of it. It offers pleasure, in other words, as well as profit. And within the last few years a simplified form of it, Basic English, has been offered to beginners as a means of expediting communication through a vocabulary of 850 words, adequate for all practical purposes. By means of this list a student is able to express any ideas, and even achieve certain aesthetic values of simple poignancy, within a very short time. He learns to say "go in" for "penetrate" and "flow out" for "exude," and is thus able to meet any situation with an adequate periphrasis. (Whether he can understand the fluent replies of a native ignorant of Basic is a different question!) These are surely inducements towards the adoption of English. Mr. Ogden claimed too much when he stated that absence of an international language like Basic English is "the chief obstacle to international understanding, and consequently the chief underlying cause of war." Unhappily, much more will be needed than a single speech to end wars. Nevertheless, Basic has many supports from the point of view of pure reason. At a later date they may be discussed for practical application.

But in the present shock and roar of clashing empires, it would appear foolhardy to make any arguments or prophecies. The advantages of English, aside from its archaic spelling, still stand. But it may be some considerable time, longer than many of us had hoped, before these matters are decided by such mild individuals as professional philologists. The appeal to reason, the argument from simple practicality for all mankind, may have to wait upon history for a long time. And by then it may be that another candidate among the languages of the world may have achieved the position of outstanding advantage. We can only wait and see.

## EXERCISE 1: Periods of English

Identify the following English writings as Old English (OE), Middle English (ME), Early Modern English (EME), and Modern English (MnE) by comparing them to the samples in the text. In each case give some reason for your decision, for example spelling, inflections, word origin, syntax, or content. The first has been completed for you.

*Modern English* 1. Now, you ask what rule you anchoresses should hold. You should always, with all your might and with all your strength, keep the inner and the outer rule well for its sake. *No archaic spellings or inflections*

________________ 2. Nu aski ȝe hwat riwle ȝe ancren schullen holden. ȝe schullen allesweis mid alle mihte & mid alle strencðe wel witen þe inre, & te vttre vor hire sake. ________________

__________________ 3. Ælfred kyning hate gretan Wærferð biscep his wordum luflice & freondlice; & ðe cyðan hate ðæt me com swiðe oft on gemynd, hwelce wiotan iu wæron giond Angelcynn, ægðer ge godcundra hada ge worul(d) cundra. __________

__________________________________________

__________________ 4. King Alfred greets Bishop Warferth with his loving and friendly words; please know that it has often come to my mind what wise men, either of the religious or secular orders, have formerly been throughout England. __________

__________________________________________

__________________ 5. Whan that Aprille with his shoures soote/ The droghte of March hath perced to the roote,/ And bathed every veyne in swich licour/ Of which vertu engendred is the flour. __________

__________________________________________

__________________ 6. Wæs sē grimma gǣst Grendel hāten,/ mǣre mearcstapa, sē þe mōras hēold,/ fen ond fæsten; fīfelcynnes eard/ wonsǣlī wer weardode hwīle.

__________________________________________

__________________________________________

__________________ 7. I do beseech yee, if you beare me hard,/ Now whil'st your purpled hands do reeke and smoake,/ Fulfill your pleasure. __________

__________________________________________

__________________ 8. All this should not be taken as a sign that our lords are lazy or unenterprising. The point is that, in their view, effort is unrelated to money.

__________________________________________

__________________________________________

__________________ 9. Of which spede and welfare, and al your oþer kyngly lustes and pleasaunces, we desire highly be the sayd berers of these lettres, or oþerwhom your soueraign highnesse shal like, fully to be lerned and enfourmed. __________

__________________________________________

__________________________________________

__________________ 10. Our father which art in heauen, hallowed be thy name. Thy kingdome come. Thy will be done in earth, as it is in heauen. Give vs this day our dayly bread. __________

__________________________________________

## EXERCISE 2: Times of Borrowing

On the basis of the understanding you have gained about word borrowings of different periods, estimate the period of borrowing of the following words and check them with the table of the earliest literary occurrence of these words in Chapter 6 (pages 66 and 67). Place ME (1100–1450), EME (1450–1650), or MnE (1650–present) beside each word.

1. ________ alert
2. ________ apartment
3. ________ army
4. ________ attorney
5. ________ bastard
6. ________ chambermaid
7. ________ cigarette
8. ________ countenance
9. ________ course
10. ________ credit
11. ________ damn
12. ________ foreign
13. ________ hotel
14. ________ humanly
15. ________ madame
16. ________ net
17. ________ notice
18. ________ party
19. ________ plaintiff
20. ________ policeman
21. ________ reason
22. ________ sure
23. ________ train
24. ________ war

## EXERCISE 3: Etymological Composition of English

Many people are surprised to learn that English is a Germanic language. The Italic branch, particularly French and Latin, have had such a great influence on the vocabulary of English that the surprise is understandable. If we consider the etymological make-up of English on the basis of frequency of words used, we find that in the first decile (the 10 per cent most frequently occurring words), 83 per cent are of Anglo-Saxon (OE) origin.[2] Look at Figure 8–1,[3] and answer the questions that follow.

1. What is the most striking difference between the first and the second deciles?

   ________________________________________________

2. In the first decile, the greatest percentage of words are of Anglo-Saxon origin. Which language leads in the other deciles? ________________________
3. Which language contributes to English fairly equally in all deciles? ____________
4. How would you explain the low frequency of Latin in the first decile, but its increase in later deciles? ________________________________

   ________________________________________________

   ________________________________________________

[2] A. Hood Roberts, *A Statistical Linguistic Analysis of American English* (The Hague: Mouton & Co., 1965), p. 36.

[3] From *Ibid.*, p. 37.

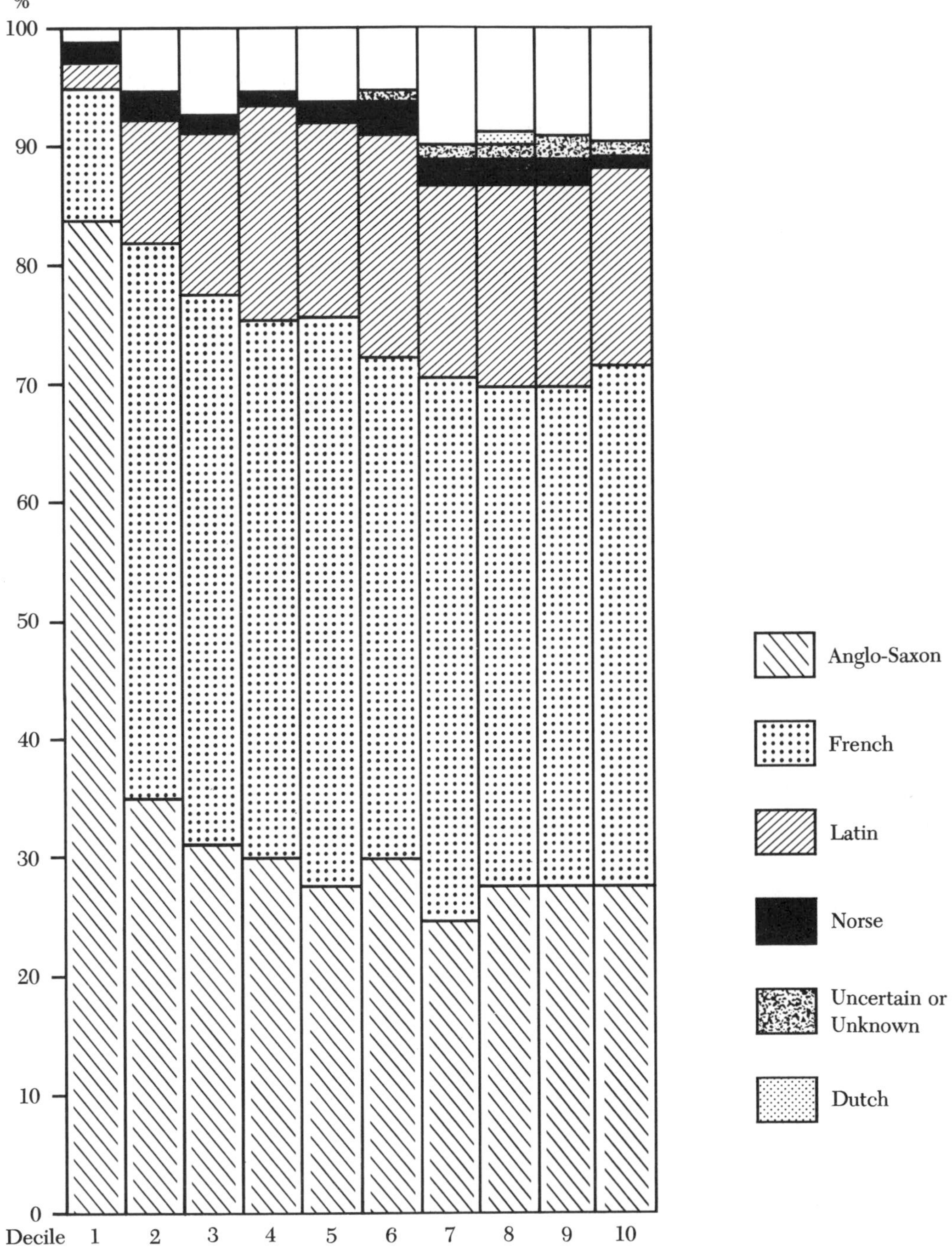


**Figure 8-1** Etymological composition of English by relative frequency and by decile.

5. Estimate the overall percentage of words from Anglo-Saxon, French, Latin, and Norse. (The first decile is the most crucial in determining such an answer; each following decile plays an increasingly smaller role.) Anglo-Saxon ________ per cent, French ________ per cent, Latin ________ per cent, Norse ________ per cent. After estimating, check your figures below.[4]

[4] Roberts (*ibid.*, p. 38) gives the following figures: Anglo-Saxon 78.1 per cent, French 15.2 per cent, Latin 3.1 per cent, Norse 2.4 per cent, others 1.2 per cent. Another analysis, quoted by Robertson and Cassidy in *The Development of Modern English* (Englewood Cliffs, N. J.: Prentice-Hall, 1954), gives a strikingly different proportion: Anglo-Saxon 61.7 per cent, French 30.9 per cent, Latin 2.9 per cent, Norse 1.7 per cent, others 2.9 per cent. P. 155.

9

# Dialect

## EXERCISE 1: Regional Dialects

Regional dialect boundaries are drawn on the basis of information gathered from speakers of the region. Field workers interview informants who learned to speak in and are still living in the area to be studied, and the resultant data is entered on maps. Map 1 is such a map. Each circle means that one speaker in that area used the form indicated. Maps 2 and 3 show a common next step: the area of predominance of a form is marked off by a line. Map 4 shows several such lines on one map, and gives some idea of how a number of lines can reinforce each other. When enough of these lines come together in the same general area, they can mark off a dialect area. That is the goal of this exercise—to use the information contained in the first four maps to draw a dialect boundary on the fifth map. The dialect boundary in question separates what traditionally has been called the Northern and the Midland speech areas, and what one dialectologist recently has tentatively redefined as Upper Northern and Lower Northern.[1] A line that shows the extent of use of a word is an *isogloss;* if it deals with a sound, it is called an *isophone.* Maps 1 and 4 deal with words, and Maps 2 and 3 with sounds.

Note that the words of Maps 1 and 4 are for the most part rural words. The project that gathered the information presented in these maps, *The Linguistic Atlas of the United States and Canada,* depended more heavily than some linguists might have wished on informants from rural areas and small towns, and the dialect boundaries drawn according to this information may be valid only away from the major population centers.

First of all, draw the isogloss of ***see*** on Map 1. You are only interested in that part of the map where the isophone of Map 2 lies. Then, combining the isoglosses and isophones from the first four maps into a group, draw the Northern-Midland (or Upper Northern-Lower Northern) dialect boundary on Map 5.

[1] Charles-James N. Bailey, "Is There a 'Midland' Dialect of American English?" a talk given at the summer meeting of the Linguistic Society of America, July, 1968.

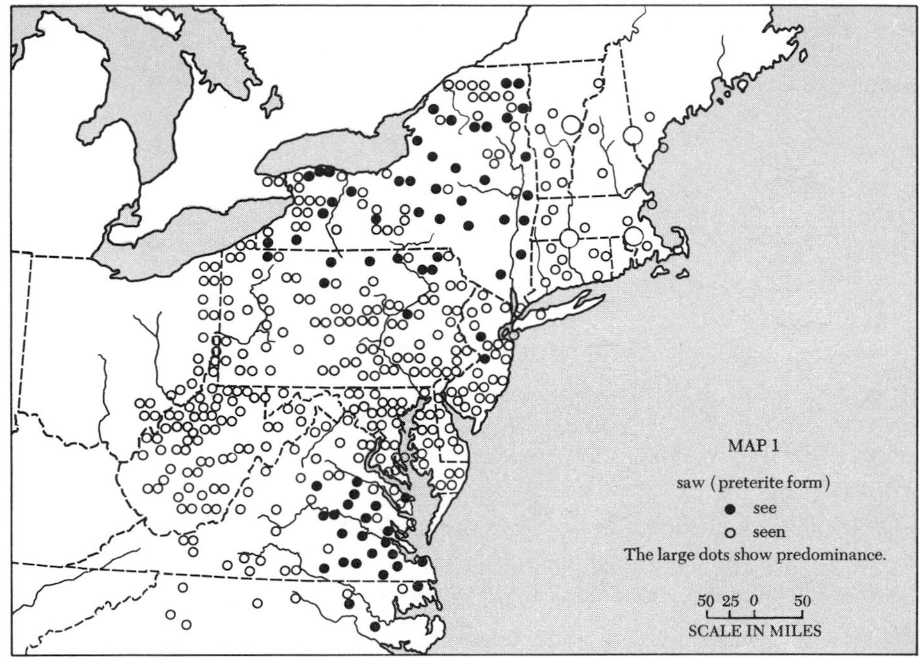


Adapted from E. Bagby Atwood, *A Survey of Verb Forms in the Eastern United States* (Ann Arbor, Mich.: University of Michigan Press, 1953), Fig. 17. Copyright 1953 by University of Michigan Press. Reprinted by permission of the publishers.

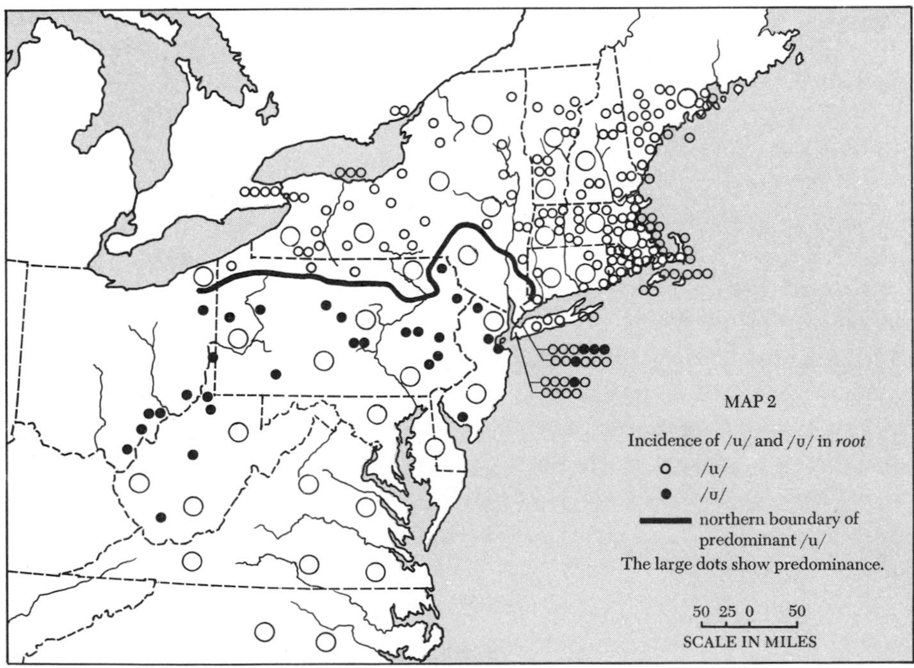


Adapted from Hans Kurath and Raven I. McDavid, Jr., *The Pronunciation of English in the Atlantic States* (Ann Arbor, Mich.: University of Michigan Press, 1961), Map 113. Copyright 1961 by University of Michigan Press. Reprinted by permission of the publishers.

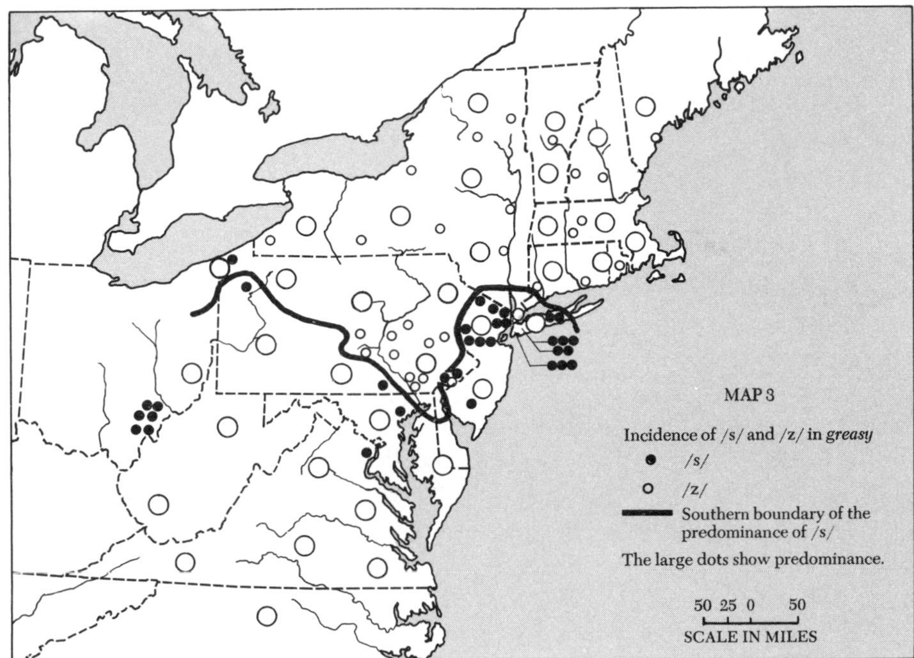


Adapted from Hans Kurath and Raven I. McDavid, Jr., *The Pronunciation of English in the Atlantic States* (Ann Arbor, Mich.: University of Michigan Press, 1961), Map 171. Copyright 1961 by University of Michigan Press. Reprinted by permission of the publishers.

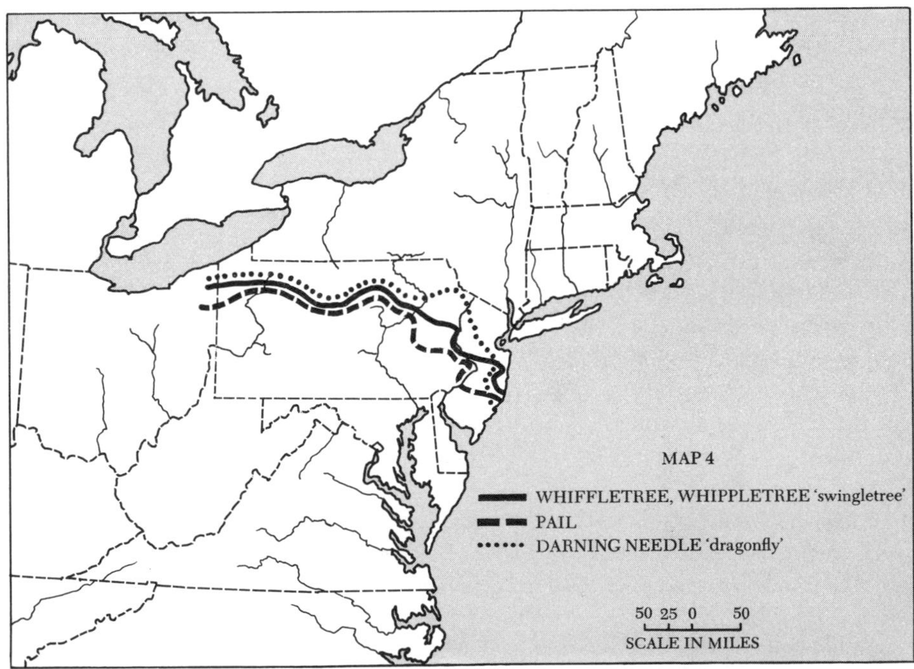


Adapted from Hans Kurath, *A Word Geography of the Eastern United States* (Ann Arbor, Mich.: University of Michigan Press, 1949), Fig. 5a. Copyright 1949 by University of Michigan Press. Reprinted by permission of the publishers.

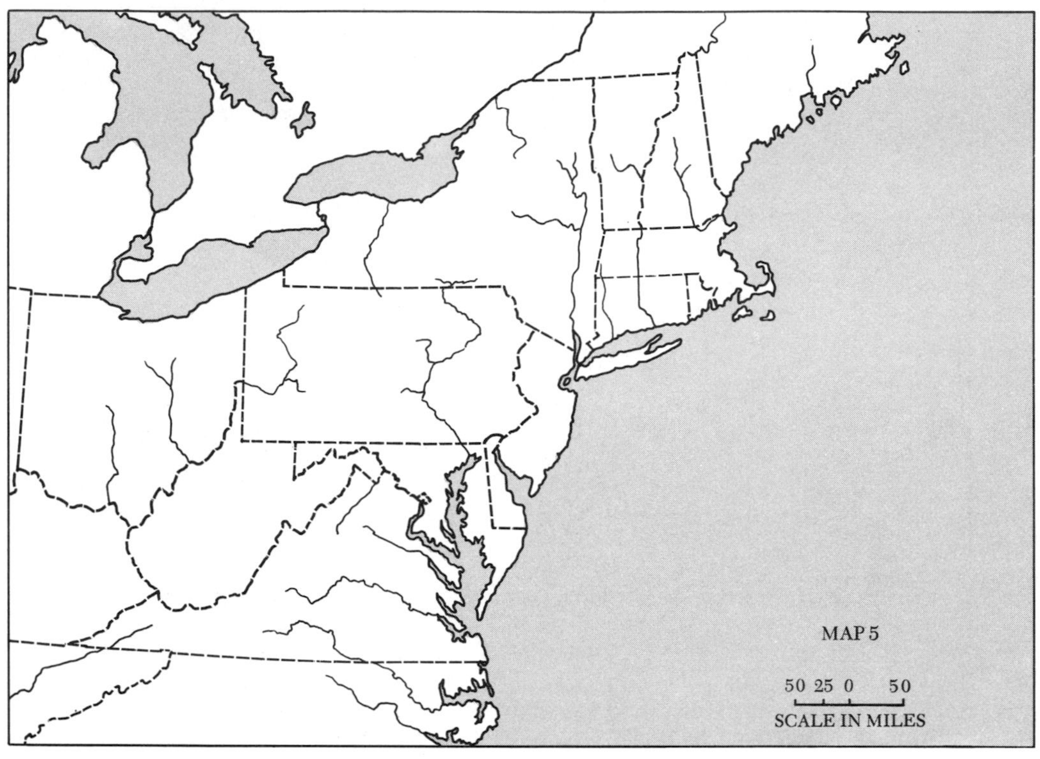


Adapted from Hans Kurath and Raven I. McDavid, Jr., *The Pronunciation of English in the Atlantic States* (Ann Arbor, Mich.: University of Michigan Press, 1961), Map 1. Copyright 1961 by University of Michigan Press. Reprinted by permission of the publishers.

## EXERCISE 2: Social Dialects

### A *Correct* Dialect?

A common opinion about language is that there is such a thing as a single correct pronunciation of a word. The manuals of "correct English" used to tell their readers what these pronunciations were. It is not an uncommon experience for English teachers to be asked what the "right" pronunciation of a word is.

Read the following summary of the regional and social variations in pronunciation of the word ***aunt.***

> ***aunt*** In the Northern, Midland, and Southern speech areas, except for Eastern New England and a part of Tidewater Virginia, /æ/ is nearly universal at all social levels. The vowel /a/ as in *pot* is predominant in most of Eastern New England, though there are instances of /æ/ everywhere. "No social prestige seems to attach to /a/ in this area; in fact, some speakers regard /a/ as old-fashioned." This pronunciation is a prestige form in Connecticut, New York City, and Philadelphia, and is found only in cultured speech there. In a part of Tidewater Virginia dominated by Richmond, /a/ is the usual pronunciation at all social levels. Elsewhere in Virginia, this pronun-

ciation is a prestige form "almost exclusively in cultivated city speech—as in Alexandria, Winchester, Charlottesville, and Roanoke. As a prestige pronunciation, it has also been adopted by better educated speakers on Albemarle Sound, N. C. The few instances of /a/ recorded in *aunt* from Charleston, S. C. southward occur in folk speech (four of the six in the speech of Negroes). Here cultured speakers avoid /a/."[2]

In the space below, answer either of the following two questions.
1. What is the correct pronunciation of ***aunt?***
2. How would you rephrase the first question so that it could be briefly and reasonably answered?

---

---

---

**An *Irregular* Dialect?**

A common myth about language in this country is that dialects other than the "establishment" dialects are erratic and disorderly, and thus lazy and inexpressive. Actually, they are consistent and patterned. Consider the following statements from one fourteen-year-old Negro boy in a Washington, D. C., poverty area.[3]

1. Every day last winter when they would come by to get me I would be busy.
2. Tomorrow morning when my mother get up I will be busy.
3. Every day, in the morning, when the others get up at my place I be busy.
4. Every day, in the morning, when you come I be busy.

He refused to substitute ***I'm busy, I will be busy, I would be busy,*** or (a dialect form) ***I busy*** for ***I be busy*** in 3 and 4. He would use these suggested substitutions knowledgeably at other times, but said he would not use them in this context.

He would not say ***I be busy right now;*** for him the correct wording was ***I'm busy right now.*** If a person saw him on the street during the week and asked him why he had not been going to church Sundays, he might say, ***Sunday I be busy.***

What does ***I be*** in ***I be busy*** in 3 and 4 mean in this dialect? Does it mean action in the present, action carried on from the past through the present, an action taking place occasionally or what?

---

---

[2] Hans Kurath and Raven I. McDavid, Jr., *The Pronunciation of English in the Atlantic States,* p. 135. Copyright 1961 by University of Michigan Press. Reprinted by permission of the publishers.

[3] Marvin D. Loflin, "A Note on the Deep Structure of Non-standard English in Washington, D. C.," *Glossa,* Vol. 1, No. 1 (1967), pp. 26–32. Reprinted by permission of the publishers.

## *READING:*

## *THE LANGUAGE OF THE GHETTO CHILD*

JOAN C. BARATZ[4]

What the psychologist who is studying the ghetto child and his learning patterns needs, among other things, is a sense of the child's language system. In this area the three major professions are the educators, the psychologists (mainly child-development types), and the linguists. The educators were the first to contribute a statement about the language difficulties of these children, a statement amounting to the fact that the children were virtually verbally destitute—they couldn't talk; if they did, it was deviant speech, filled with "errors." The next group to get into the fray, the psychologists, initially confirmed that the children didn't talk, and then added the sophisticated wrinkle that if they did talk, their speech was such that it was a deterrent to growth. The last group to come into the picture were the linguists, who, though thoroughly impressed with the sophisticated research of the psychologist, were astonished at the naiveté of his pronouncements concerning language. The linguist began to examine the language of black children and brought us to our current conception—that black children speak a well-ordered, highly structured, highly developed language system which in many aspects is different from standard English.

The linguist takes as basic that all human beings develop language. After all, there is no reason to assume that black African bush children develop a language and black inner-city Harlem children do not. Subsumed under this is that the language is a well-ordered system with a predictable sound pattern, grammatical structure, and vocabulary (in this sense, there are no "primitive" languages). The linguist assumes that any such verbal system used by a community *is* a language. The linguist also contends that children learn language in the context of their environment—that is to say, a French child learns French not because his father is in the home or his mother reads books to him but because that is the language he hears continually inside and outside the home and that is the language individuals in his environment respond to. Another assumption the linguist works with is that by the time a child is five he has developed language—he has learned the rules of his linguistic environment.

The syntax of low-income Negro children differs from standard English in many ways, but it has its own internal consistency. Unfortunately, the psychologist, not knowing the rules of Negro non-standard English, has interpreted these differences not as the result of well-learned rules but as evidence of "linguistic underdevelopment." He has been handicapped by his assumption that to develop language is synonymous with the development of the psychologist's own form of standard English. Thus he has concluded that if black children do not speak like white children they are deficient. One of the most blatant errors has been a confusion between hypotheses concerning language and hypotheses concerning cognition. For this reason, superficial differences in language structures and language styles

[4] Reprinted from *The Center Magazine,* a publication of the Center for the Study of Democratic Institutions, Vol. 2, No. 2 (January, 1969), pp. 32–33. Reprinted by permission of the publishers.

have been taken as manifestations of underlying differences in learning ability. To give one example, a child in class was asked, in a test of simple contrasts, "Why do you say they are different?" He could not answer. Then it was discovered that the use of "do you say," though grammatically correct, was inappropriate to his culture. When he was asked instead, "Why are they different?" he answered without any hesitation at all.

There is a widespread notion among psychologists that some environments are better than others for stimulating language and learning growth. This assumption is, I believe, an outgrowth of the psychologist's confusion between general language development and the acquisition of standard English, which causes him to think that he must explain a "language deficit." According to researchers of this school, among the most detrimental factors is the "inadequacy" of the ghetto mothering patterns. The ghetto mother, they say, is so taken up with survival—"subsistence behaviors"—that she is too exhausted to talk to her children. Such a notion tells us more about the psychologist's lack of knowledge about the ghetto mother than it does about her real role. It also assumes that there is a minimal amount of language that must be present for language to be learned and that Negro mothers do not give this to their children. Part of this notion is that language is only learned from one's mother and that the language learned from her is underdeveloped. It is also presumed that the mother of a black child does not know how to stimulate or reinforce her child so that learning can occur. Under that assumption is the idea that such things as reading a book and singing to a child are essential behaviors in order for language to develop. Finally, it is presumed that she encourages passive, withdrawn behavior in her children because verbal ability is not highly valued in the ghetto community.

It seems as if all these assumptions have evolved because of misconceptions of what language is and how it functions. The psychologist has constructed elaborate environmental and psychological explanations of differences in language behavior but the elaborateness is unnecessary. The assumptions have been used after the fact to explain data erroneously—they have no experiential base.

**A Dialect of Washington, D. C.:**

The data that Joan Baratz refers to in her last sentence can be explained through the hypothesis that there exist many different social *dialects*. The Center for Applied Linguistics has been studying urban dialects and dialectology. One of its projects was to tape the natural and spontaneous conversation of a number of American Negroes from Washington, D. C. This exercise is constructed around the transcript of those tapes.

The four people represented in the transcripts below all come from the same block and are of "a lower socioeconomic stratum."[5] Harry Jones (HJ) and Patricia Jones (PJ) have one son, Michael (MJ). Anita Porter (AP) and Jacqueline Drew (JD) are occasional playmates of Michael. Harry and Patricia were both thirty-nine years old in 1966, the date of the recording, and Michael and Anita were ten. Jacqueline was eleven. Sandy Barrett (SB) is a Negro research assistant, in her twenties.

[5] Bengt Loman, *Conversations in a Negro American Dialect* (Washington, D. C.: Center for Applied Linguistics, 1967), p. ix. The selections from the conversations are from pages 21–22, 56, 57, and 94. Reprinted by permission of the publishers.

The passages are reproduced here in a simplified form. Phrases in italic indicate that two people are speaking at once.

*Passage 1*

1. AP: Le' me tell you all a story.
2. Jacqueline know it.
3. JD: *I cain'.*
4. AP: *See i' was dis* man.
5. I' was a white man an' a colored man.
6. Uh, how bout da' man hear da'?
7. SB: So wha'?
8. AP: An' nis, an' nis white,
9. an' nis white man say:
10. if you go in nere, an' eat dem beans,
11. I gi' you ten thousan' dollars.
12. JD: I ma tell you . . . I ma tell . . .
13. AP: *An'so* . . . de white man wen' in *nere.*
14. JD: *Okay wait* a minute Anita.
15. AP: An' ne ghos' was . . . le' me tell i' . . .
16. an' ne . . . *an' ne ghos' was in* nere.
17. JD: *I ain' go tell you da'.*
18. I ma tell you another story about a . . . bout . . .
19. a a . . . white man,
20. a black man, an' de Chinese man.
21. AP: Da's de story I'm tellin'.
22. JD: An' mine's ain' bout no ghos'.
23. AP: An' all three o' dem men. An' so. So one
24. de white man wen' in nere firs'.
25. An' ne, an' ne ghos' scared him ou',
26. an' so he ranned ou'.
27. An' s- . . . an' so, um . . .
28. an' de Chinese man wen' in nere.
29. An' so he tried to eat dem beans
30. an' de ghos' scared him ou',
31. so de colored man wen' in nere. An' he say,
32. an' he scare', an' he was scarin' de colored man.
33. Colored man say: I mo k- . . . I mo . . .
34. No de ghos' say I ma kill you.
35. An' ne ghos' say: . . . An' ne . . . an' ne . . .
36. colored man say:
37. I ma kill you if you mess wi' dese beans.
38. Some'm like da'.

(pp. 21–22)

Keep in mind, in reading over this transcript, that many of the irregularities are not unique to this dialect, but would be apparent in the recorded spontaneous speech of most adults or children.

The main question is: In what ways is this dialect different from another English dialect such as that used on network TV? For example, how does network TV English treat the initial consonant of words like ***the, them,*** and ***there?*** Go over the passage line by line, entering in the spaces below the words that usually have [ð] in network TV English. To check the phonetic environment, include the word that precedes each of these words in the passage.

| *Line* | *Words* | *Line* | *Words* | *Line* | *Words* |
|---|---|---|---|---|---|
| *4* | *was dis* | ____ | ____________ | ____ | ____________ |
| *6* | *bout da'* | ____ | ____________ | ____ | ____________ |
| ____ | ____________ | ____ | ____________ | ____ | ____________ |
| ____ | ____________ | ____ | ____________ | ____ | ____________ |
| ____ | ____________ | ____ | ____________ | ____ | ____________ |
| ____ | ____________ | ____ | ____________ | ____ | ____________ |
| ____ | ____________ | ____ | ____________ | ____ | ____________ |
| ____ | ____________ | ____ | ____________ | ____ | ____________ |
| ____ | ____________ | ____ | ____________ | ____ | ____________ |
| ____ | ____________ | ____ | ____________ | ____ | ____________ |
| ____ | ____________ | ____ | ____________ | ____ | ____________ |

After what sounds (not letters) is a [d] found in the passage when a [ð] might be expected in network TV English? ________________________________

After what sounds is an [n] found where [ð] might be expected? ________________

Can you account for this situation in terms of articulatory phonetics? ____________

________________________________________________

Pick out the third person singular present forms that are used in the passage. Include the subject of the verb.

| *Line* | *Words* | *Line* | *Words* |
|---|---|---|---|
| 2 | *Jacqueline know* | ____ | ______________ |
| ____ | ______________ | ____ | ______________ |
| ____ | ______________ | ____ | ______________ |
| ____ | ______________ | ____ | ______________ |

In which of these cases would you expect a past tense ending in TV English?

________________________________________________

Besides these cases, there remain two forms that are different from network TV English: ***Jacqueline know*** and ***da' man hear.*** On the basis of this admittedly sketchy evidence, what recurring difference can you describe? ______

Many of the past forms in the passage are the same (except for a consonant loss) as those in the network TV dialect. List them here with their line numbers. ______

Which form is different from that of the network TV dialect? ______

Find the case where a future form is expected in the network TV dialect, but a present tense form is used. ______

What does ***ma*** mean below?

12. JD: I ma tell you, I ma tell
18. I ma tell you another . . .
34. No de ghos' say I ma kill you.
37. I ma kill you if you mess wi' dese beans.

Is there an idea of futurity expressed? ______

Can you gather the idea of necessity (***must***) from every context of ***ma*** in this passage? ______

Is there an idea of determination or at least intention? ______

You have done some work in sound changes recently. Could ***I ma kill you*** come from ***I'm going to kill you?*** By what process? ______

*Passage 2*

PJ: Well you know what Michael,
I'm not tryin' to cut you acro', cu-,
cut across you;
But you know a good thing for us to talk about
right before the presence
of doctor Lomans an' Margy,
about de way you're acting in school of lately,
which is not very nice,
an' maybe in some way they can help me an' you.

(p. 56)

*Passage 3*

PJ: an' maybe she'll give us some o' her
ideas abou' dis [dð]- some other time, . . .

(p. 57)

*Passage 4*

1. PJ: . . . An' what's wha's so bad abou' dis [dð]-
2. is the reason, . . .

(p. 57)

*Passage 5*

1. PJ: . . . Well i' seems 'o me
2. dat would have be included in de health ru'.

(p. 94)

In Passage 2 Patricia Jones is taking advantage of the presence and status of Dr. Loman and Margy Gurney (the researchers) to try to discipline her son Michael. She is a little more at ease in Passages 3 and 4. Passage 5 is taken from a relaxed conversation with her ten-year-old nephew.

Patricia Jones has worked for much of her life for white middle-class families and thus has been exposed to their ways of speaking. Can you pick out items in the first thirteen lines of Passages 2–5 that reflect this exposure? Look again at Passage 1. Does she change the word order in one phrase to an order that is closer to a standard dialect? Give the line number and write out the phrase. ______________________________

______________________________

How does she pronounce the [ð] of standard English in Passages 2, 3, and 4? Include the word that precedes [ð].

| *Line* | *Words* |
|---|---|
| *5* | *before the* |
| ____ | ______________ |
| ____ | ______________ |
| ____ | ______________ |
| ____ | ______________ |

How does this differ from the practice of Anita Porter and Jacqueline Drew? In Patricia's speech is [n] found after words ending with [n], as in their speech? ______________
Is [ð] ever found in the speech of Anita and Jacqueline?

______________________________

Jacqueline and Anita use [d] and [n] where [ð] is expected. What three sounds or sound combinations does Patricia use? ____________ ____________ ____________
The data from Passages 3 and 4 show a combination of one sound from the dialect of Anita and Jacqueline with another sound from the network TV dialect. Explain the combination.

______________________________

______________________________

How would you describe the style of the phrase ***right before the presence of*** in Passage 2? Is it elegant, natural, affected, or what? Why do you think this way of speaking was chosen?

____________________________________________

____________________________________________

Passage 5 is further from the standard English dialects than Passages 2, 3, and 4. List each difference below.

*Line* *Words*

1. Differences in [ð]:

____ ____________

____ ____________

2. Differences in verb phrase:

____ ____________

*Line* *Words*

3. Consonant loss:

____ ____________

____ ____________

____ ____________

Passage 5 is closer to the dialect of Anita and Jacqueline. Can you account for this by noting a change in the speaking situation? ____________________

____________________________________________

* * * * *

The purpose of the following essay, as Professor McDavid states in his introduction, is to "trace the chain of influence from the historical background to the sources of local speech patterns and the relationships of those speech patterns to the social order."

## *READING:*

## *CHICAGO: THE MACROCOSM*

RAVEN I. MCDAVID, JR.[6]

Northern Illinois—like northern Indiana, southern Michigan and southeastern Wisconsin—was first settled from the Inland Northern dialect region: western New England, by way of Upstate New York. In many of the small towns in Chicago's exurbia, the older families still show distinctly New England speech-traits, such as the centralized diphthongs [əʊ] and [əɪ] in *down* and *ride*, or /ʊ/ in *spoon* and *soon*. But the city of Chicago developed a more polyglot tradition from the beginning. The city was established at the time when the Erie Canal made it easy for the economic and political refugees from western Europe

[6] From "Dialect Differences and Social Differences in an Urban Society," in William Bright, ed., *Sociolinguistics, Proceedings of the UCLA Sociolinguistics Conference,* 1964 (The Hague: Mouton & Co., 1966), pp. 76–80. Reprinted by permission of the publishers. Professor McDavid ascribes much of the information of his essay to Professor Lee Pederson of Emory University in Atlanta.

to reach the American heartland. The Irish brought reliable labor for the new railroads and a continuing tradition of lively politics; the Germans contributed their interest in beer, education, art, music and finance. Almost immediately Chicago also became a magnet for the younger sons of the agricultural settlements in southern Illinois and southern Indiana—Midlanders, whose speech patterns derived from western Pennsylvania. Scandinavians followed Germans and Irish; toward the end of the Nineteenth Century the population of the metropolitan area was swelled by mass peasant immigration from Southern and Eastern Europe—the strong backs and putatively weak brains on which Chicago's mighty steel industry was built. When this immigration tailed off during World War I, a new supply of basic labor was sought in the Southern Negro. Negro immigration has increased until Chicago is possibly the largest Negro city in the world. More recently the Negroes have been joined by Latin Americans (Mexicans, Cubans, Puerto Ricans), and last by rural whites from the Southern Appalachians. In response partly to the pressure of the increasing non-white population, partly to easy credit and slick promotion, Chicago whites like those in other cities have spread into the suburbs, many of which are at least informally restricted to a single economic and social (sometimes even an ethnic or religious) group.

In Chicago as in most large cities, the development of social dialects has been a by-product of what might be called differential acculturation: differences in the facility and speed with which representatives of various social groups develop the ability to live alongside each other as individuals, without stereotyped group identification. In favor of the trend is the traditional American principle of individual dignity, and the belief that each man should be allowed to improve his lot as far as his ability and his luck permit. Against it is the tendency of people to flock together according to their nature and common ties—whether Filipinos, Orthodox Jews, Irishmen, hipsters or college professors—a tendency abetted by those with a stake in keeping the flock from scattering and by the tendency of each group to reject the conspicuous outsider. In the early Nineteenth Century, the Pennsylvanians and downstaters, with a few generations of Americanizing under their belts, soon mingled freely with all but the wealthiest and most genealogically conscious Northerners. Acculturation was more difficult for the "clannish" Irish, Germans and Scandinavians.* The Irish were usually Roman Catholics; the Scandinavians spoke a foreign language; many Germans suffered from both handicaps, and all three groups had broken with their native cultures only recently and maintained many of their native customs. Nevertheless, all three of these groups had enough in common with the "Older American Stock"—all coming from northwestern Europe—to make some sort of symbiotic assimilation easy, though all of these older immigrant groups were to suffer during the xenophobic hysteria of 1917–19 and after.† In general they managed to participate freely in the community, while retaining their cultural societies, newspapers and even foreign-language schools.

* It is obvious that only outsiders are clannish; in-groups are merely closely knit.

† Since the Germans were the largest functioning foreign-language group, and since their position in the cultural life of the community was so high, it is almost impossible to calculate to what extent the teaching of languages and literature, and the position of the scholar, suffered as a result of these witch-hunts. The abolition of Germanic studies at the University of Texas, as a gesture of patriotism, was only one of many such acts.

The later immigrants from Southern and Eastern Europe suffered, in general, from the twin disabilities of foreign language and Roman Catholicism. Moreover, they were largely peasants and illiterate, without the strong sense of their cultural tradition that the Germans and Scandinavians had brought.* All these groups found themselves at the focus of a complicated polyhedron of forces. In an effort to help their acclimatization—and no doubt to avoid the erosion of traditional ecclesiastical allegiance—the Roman hierarchy fostered the "ethnic parish," designed specifically for a single nationality or linguistic group. Whether or not this institution served its immediate purpose, it had the side effects of further identifying foreignness and Roman Catholicism, of separating the new groups from the American Protestants, from the "native Catholics" (chiefly of Irish and German descent), and from each other, and of fostering ethnic blocs in local politics.† The blocs persist; but the common tendency of Chicagoans (as of Clevelanders) of Southern and Eastern European descent is to abandon their ancestral languages and turn their backs on their ancestral cultures, even in the first American-born generation. The notable exceptions are the Jews, with the attachment to the synagogue, to the synagogue-centered subculture, and to the family as a religious and culturally focused institution. But it is possible for an individual from any of these new immigrant groups to give up as much of his ethnic identity as he may wish, and to mingle relatively unnoticed in apartment building or housing development alongside members of the earlier established groups.

In contrast to both of these groups of European immigrants, the American Negro in Chicago is a native speaker of American English, normally of at least five generations of residence in North America (cf. McDavid, 1951); little survives of his ancestral African culture, though undoubtedly more than American Caucasoids are generally willing to admit. Early Negro settlers in Chicago were able to settle as individuals—whether freemen or manumitted or fugitive before the Civil War, or emancipated migrants afterward; furthermore, a large number of the earliest Negro immigrants were skilled craftsmen, who might expect to find a place in an expanding economy, and with some education to smooth off the rough corners of their dialects. However, even as an individual settler the Negro was more easily identified than any of the whites who had preceded him; and many Negroes exhibited traumata from slavery and mass discrimination. With the mass migrations of Negroes, other forces began to operate: the arrivals from 1915 on were largely a black peasantry, somewhat exposed to urban or small-town life but almost never actively participating in the dominant culture. Their own American cultural traditions—gastronomic, ecclesiastical and everything between—often diverged sharply from those of middle-class Chicago. Their speech, though American English, was likewise sharply different from that

* Paradoxically, one of the most successful adaptations of native cultural traditions to the opportunities of the American setting—that of the South Italians of Chicago to the public demands during Prohibition—tended to stigmatize the whole group, whether or not they actively participated in the Syndicate's version of venture capitalism.

† In the manuscript version of his *Language Loyalties in the United States*, Joshua Fishman repeatedly attacks the heavily Irish American hierarchy of the Roman church for discouraging the ethnic parish in the past generation. In contrast, the late Msgr. John L. O'Brien, director of parochial education in the Charleston diocese, was outspoken in his belief (based on his home community in Pennsylvania) that the ethnic parish tended to prevent the development of a truly Catholic church in the United States. The Irish, after all, had found their ethnicity one of their greatest obstacles to full participation in American society.

of their new neighbors. Even an educated Mississippian has a system of vowels strikingly different from the Chicago pattern. An uneducated Mississippi Negro would have had his poor sample of learning in the least favored part of the Southern tradition of separate and unequal schools; his grammar would differ more sharply from the grammar of educated speech in his region far more than would the grammar of any Northern non-standard dialect differ from the local white standard. Furthermore, the easy identification of the Negro immigrant would provoke open or tacit pressure to reinforce the tendency of living with one's kind—a situation which, for the Chicago Negro, is likely to strengthen the linguistic and cultural features alien to the dominant local dialect pattern. Finally, the displacement of unskilled labor by automation has injured the Negroes—less educated and less skilled, on the whole—more than it has other groups. The specter of a permanently unemployable Negro proletariat has begun to haunt political leaders in Chicago as in other Northern cities, with inferior educational achievement and inferior employment opportunities reinforcing each other, and in the process strengthening the linguistic differences between whites and Negroes.

Of the Latin American, it can be said that he adds a language barrier to the problem of physical identification which he often shares with the Negro. Of the displaced Southern mountaineer, it has often been observed that he is even less acculturated to urban living than the Negro or the Latin; however, his physical traits will make it easy for his children to blend into the urban landscape, if they can only survive.

What then are the effects of this linguistic melting pot on the speech of metropolitan Chicago? And—since I wear the hat of English teacher as well as that of social dialectologist—what are the implications for the schools?

First, the speech of the city proper has apparently become differentiated from that of the surrounding area, as the result of four generations of mingling of Inland Northern, Midland, and Irish, and the gradual assimilation of the descendants of continental European immigrants. The outer suburbs call the city /šikágo/, butcher /hagz/, and suffer from spring /fag/; to most of its inhabitants the city is /šikɔ́go/, quondam /hɔg/ butcher to the world, beset by Sandburg's cat-footed /fɔg/. To the city-bred, *prairie* and *gangway* and *clout* have connotations quite different from those they bear in the hinterlands.* Little if anything survives in the city of such Inland Northern speech forms as [əi] and [əʊ] in *high* and *how,* [ʊ] in *soon* and *spoon,* or /éjə/ as an oral gesture of assent. Even the second generation of Irish, lace-curtained or otherwise, have largely lost their brogue; such pronunciations as /ohérə/ for *O'Hare* Field seem to be socially rather than ethnically identifiable.†

Among the older generation with foreign-language backgrounds, one finds sporadic traces of old-country tongues, such as lack of certain consonant distinctions (e.g., /t/ and /θ/, /d/ and /ð/) that are regular in standard English. Among the younger generation of educated speakers some of the Jewish informants stand out, not only for the traditional American Jewish vocabulary, from *bar mitzvah* and *blintz* to *tsorris* and *yentz,* but for the

* Evidence on these features is basically that of Pederson's dissertation and his unpublished lexical research.

† The pronunciation /ohérə/, definitely substandard in Chicago, is however the normal one for Mayor Richard J. Daley, probably the most powerful municipal politician in the United States. To urban Chicagoans a *prairie* is a vacant lot; a *gangway* is a passage between two apartment buildings; *clout* is political influence.

dentalization or affrication of /t, d, n, s, z, r, l/. The former features have spread to other local groups, but the latter has not. The so-called Scandinavian intonation of English is rarely encountered, even among informants of Scandinavian descent; it has not been picked up by other groups as it has in Minneapolis.

Negroes born in Chicago before 1900 vary less from their Caucasoid contemporaries than the latter do among themselves, attesting to something like genuinely integrated residential patterns in the past. However, Chicago-born Negroes under 50 show many features of Southern and South Midland pronunciation, notably in the consistent use of /sikágo/ in outland fashion, in often having /griz/ and /grizi/ as verb and adjective,[°] in the frequent loss of postvocalic /r/ in *barn, beard* and the like, in contrasts between *horse* and *hoarse,* and in relatively greater length of stressed vowels. Such extralinguistic speech traits as wider spreads than Inland Northern usage offers between highest and lowest pitch or between strongest and weakest stress, or the quaver of ingratiation when speaking to someone presumed to be in authority, also survive and are generally recognized by Chicago-born whites and identified as characteristics of Negro speech. In grammar, the Chicago-born Negro who grows up in an environment of poverty and limited cultural opportunities—as most Chicago Negroes grow up—has a tendency to use forms that identify him easily and to his disadvantage, in writing as well as in speech. Most of these are forms of common verbs—absence of the third-singular present marker, as in *he do, it make;* old-fashioned preterites and participles, as *holp* "helped"; or the appearance of an *-s* marker in unexpected places as *we says, they does*—or in plurals of nouns, like *two postes* /-əz/. Many of these features of pronunciation and grammar, especially the lengthened stressed vowels, are also found among the recent immigrants from Appalachia, who have their own paralinguistic phenomena, such as strong nasalization, and a few grammatical peculiarities like the sentence-opening *used to:* "Used to, everybody in these-here hills made they own liquor." But because the recently arrived Appalachian whites are relatively few in number, because their residential patterns are not so rigorously segregated as those of the Negroes, and because they are not so readily identified as to physical type, their linguistic features do not seem to be perpetuated into the younger generation, and probably will never be.

* * * * *

## *READING:* Is There a Negro Speech Pattern?[7]

Is there a Negro speech pattern? This question has provoked a great deal of discussion in the last few years, much more than it deserves. At many meetings on educational problems of ghetto areas, time which could have been spent in constructive discussion has been

[°] *Grease* and *greasy* have been studied by Atwood, 1950 and previously by Hempl, 1896.

[7] William Labov, "Some Sources of Reading Problems for Negro Speakers of Nonstandard English," in Alexander Frazier, ed., *New Directions in Elementary English* (Champaign, Ill.: National Council of Teachers of English, 1967), pp. 143–46. Revised and reprinted with the permission of the National Council of Teachers of English and William Labov.

devoted to arguing the question as to whether Negro dialect exists. The debates have not been conducted with any large body of factual information in view, but rather in terms of what the speakers wish to be so, or what they fear might follow in the political arena.

For those who have not participated in such debates, it may be difficult to imagine how great are the pressures against the recognition, description, or even mention of Negro speech patterns. For various reasons, many teachers, principals, and civil rights leaders wish to deny that the existence of patterns of Negro speech is a linguistic and social reality in the United States today. The most careful statement of the situation as it actually exists might read as follows: *Many features of pronunciation, grammar, and lexicon are closely associated with Negro speakers—so closely as to identify the great majority of Negro people in the Northern cities by their speech alone.*

The match between this speech pattern and membership in the Negro ethnic group is of course far from complete. Many Negro speakers have none—or almost none—of these features. Many Northern whites, living in close proximity to Negroes, have these features in their own speech. But this overlap does not prevent the features from being identified with Negro speech by most listeners: we are dealing with a stereotype which provides correct identification in the great majority of cases, and therefore with a firm base in social reality. Such stereotypes are the social basis of language perception; this is merely one of many cases where listeners generalize from the variable data to categorical perception in absolute terms. Someone who uses a stigmatized form 20 to 30 percent of the time will be heard as using this form all of the time. It may be socially useful to correct these stereotypes in a certain number of individual cases, so that people learn to limit their generalizations to the precise degree that their experience warrants: but the overall tendency is based upon very regular principles of human behavior, and people will continue to identify as Negro speech the pattern which they hear from the great majority of the Negro people that they meet.

In the South, the overlap is much greater. There is good reason to think that most positive features of the Negro speech pattern have their origin in dialects spoken by both Negroes and whites in some parts of the South. Historically speaking, the Negro speech pattern that we are dealing with in Northern cities is a regional speech pattern. We might stop speaking of Negro speech, and begin using the term "Southern regional speech," if that would make the political and social situation more manageable. But if we do so, we must not deceive ourselves and come to believe that this is an accurate description of the current situation. The following points cannot be overlooked in any such discussion:

1. There are present in Negro speech patterns a small number of features which have not yet been plainly identified with any white Southern dialect: the deletion of the contracted *is*, as in *He crazy*, and the invariant *be* of *He be crazy* are the two prime examples. The persistance of these features, a number of irregular but strongly Creole patterns in the speech of young Negro children, and the historical evidence turned up by W. Stewart, all point to a possible Creole origin of Southern Negro speech patterns. This dialect may have passed through a process of "de-Creolization" before it became a regional or ethnic dialect of English.

2. For most Northern whites, the only familiar example of Southern speech is that of the Negro people they hear, and these Southern features function as markers of Negro ethnic membership, not Southern origin.

3. Many characteristic features of Southern speech have been generalized along strictly ethnic lines in Northern cities. For example, the absence of a distinction between /i/ and /e/ before nasals [*pin* equal to *pen*] has become a marker of the Negro group in New York City, so that most young Negro children of Northern and Southern background alike show this feature while no white children are affected.

4. In this merger of Northern and Southern patterns in the Northern Negro communities, a great many Southern features are being eliminated. Thus in New York and other Northern cities, we find the young Negro people do not distinguish *four* and *for, which* and *witch;* while monophthongization of *high* and *wide* is common, the extreme fronting of the initial vowel to the position of *cat* or near it, is less and less frequent; the back upglide of *ball* and *hawk,* so characteristic of many Southern areas, is rarely heard; grammatical features such as the perfective auxiliary *done* in *he done told me,* or the double modal of *might could,* are becoming increasingly rare. As a result, a speaker fresh from the South is plainly marked in the Northern Negro communities, and his speech is ridiculed. Negro speech is thus not to be identified with Southern regional speech. . . .

5. The white Southern speech which is heard in many Northern cities—Chicago, Detroit, Cleveland—is the Southern Mountain pattern of Appalachia, and this pattern does not have many of the phonological and grammatical features of Negro speech to be discussed below. . . .

6. Many of the individual features of Negro speech can be found in Northern white speech, as we will see, and even more so in the speech of educated white Southerners. But the frequency of these features, such as consonant cluster simplification, and their distribution in relation to grammatical boundaries, is radically different in Negro speech, and we are forced in many cases to infer the existence of different underlying grammatical forms and rules.

We can sum up this discussion of the Southern regional pattern by saying that we are witnessing the transformation of a regional speech pattern into a class and ethnic pattern in the Northern cities. This is not a new phenomenon; it has occurred many times in the history of English. According to H. Kökeritz and H. C. Wyld, such a process was taking place in Shakespeare's London, where regional dialects from the east and southeast opposed more conservative dialects within the city as middle class and lower class speech against aristocratic speech. We see the same process operating today in the suburbs of New York City; where the Connecticut and New Jersey patterns meet the New York City pattern, in the overlapping areas, the New York City pattern becomes associated with lower socioeconomic groups.

The existence of a Negro speech pattern must not be confused of course with the myth of a biologically, racially, exclusively Negro speech. The idea that dialect differences are due to some form of laziness or carelessness must be rejected with equal firmness. Anyone who continues to endorse such myths can be refuted easily by such subjective reaction tests as the Family Background test which we are using in our current research in Harlem. Sizable extracts from the speech of fourteen individuals are played in sequence for listeners who are asked to identify the family backgrounds of each. So far, we find no one who can even come close to a correct identification of Negro and white speakers. This result does not contradict the statement that there exists a socially based Negro speech pattern: it supports everything that I have said above on this point. The voices heard on the test are the exceptional cases: Negroes raised without any Negro friends in solidly white areas; whites raised in areas dominated by Negro cultural values; white Southerners in Gullah-speaking territory; Negroes from small Northern communities untouched by recent migrations; college educated Negroes who reject the Northern ghetto and the South alike. The speech of these individuals does not identify them as Negro or white because they do not use the speech patterns which are characteristically Negro or white for Northern listeners. The identifications made by these listeners, often in violation of actual ethnic membership categories, show that they respond to Negro speech patterns as a social reality.

★ ★ ★ ★ ★

## *READING:* Society Dialects[8]

Then there is the Society voice. Trying to duplicate the American Society accent has provided the greatest stumbling block for the parvenu. Some say you must be born with it to speak it properly and convincingly, but it is safe to say that graduates of such private schools as St. Paul's, Foxcroft, and Madeira, who may not have had the accent to begin with, can emerge with a reasonably close facsimile of it. It is a social accent that is virtually the same in all American cities, and it is actually a blend of several accents. There is much more to it than the well-known broad A. Its components are a certain New England flatness, a trace of a Southern drawl, and a surprising touch of the New York City accent that many people consider Brooklynese. Therefore, in the social voice, the word "shirt" comes out halfway between "shirt" and "shoit." Another key word is "pretty," which, in the social voice emerges sounding something like "prutty." There is also the word "circle," the first syllable of which is almost whistled through pursed lips, whereas the greeting, "Hi," is nearly always heavily diphthonged as "Haoy." This speech has been nicknamed "the Massachusetts malocclusion," since much of it is accomplished with the lower jaw thrust forward and rigid, and in a number of upper-class private schools, children are taught to speak correctly by practicing with pencils clenched between their teeth.

. . .

"My God!" said one young woman the other day. "My daughter's started talking with that Main Line accent. She's picked it up at school. She's started using Main Line words—words like 'yummy.' The other day I asked her how a certain party had been and she said,

[8]From *The Right People, a Portrait of the American Social Establishment* by Stephen Birmingham, by permission of Little, Brown & Co., Boston, 1968, pp. 9–10, 195. Copyright 1968 by Stephen Birmingham.

'Oh, Mummy, it was such a giggle!' " Children attending the Main Line's private schools—Shipley, Agnes Irwin, or Baldwin for girls; Haverford or Episcopal for boys—seem to acquire the accent and language by osmosis, if they have not already acquired it from listening to their parents. The terminology is quaintly special, one might say precious. One is not startled on the Main Line to hear a businessman conclude a deal with a cheerful "All righty-roo!" Or to depart from a party with a bright "Nightie-noodles!" to his host and hostess. As for the accent, Barbara Best calls it "Philadelphia paralysis," or "Main Line lockjaw," pointing out that it is not unlike "Massachusetts malocclusion." Mrs. Best recalls that when she first moved to the area a native said to her, "My dear, you have the most beautiful speaking voice. I can understand every word you say!"

## EXERCISE 3: Dialects for Various Occasions

Educated adult speakers of English have at their command a number of different *styles* of speech. Martin Joos writes of five styles: consultative, casual, intimate, formal, and frozen.[9] The consultative style is chosen for communication between strangers, or for discussion of serious or complicated matters. The speaker supplies background information to the listener, since the listener is not on an insider's casual or intimate basis with the speaker during the conversation. The listener participates continuously in the conversation, if by nothing more than nodding his head to show that he is listening. The following passage is in what Joos calls the consultative style. It was recorded from a phone line in Ann Arbor, Michigan.[10]

> I wanted to tell you one more thing I've been talking with Mr. D—— in the purchasing department about our typewriter (yes) that order went in March seventh however it seems that we are about eighth on the list (I see) we were up about three but it seems that for that type of typewriter we're about eighth that's for a fourteen-inch carriage with pica type (I see) now he told me that R——'s have in stock the fourteen-inch carriage typewriters with elite type (oh) and elite type varies sometimes it's quite small and sometimes it's almost as large as pica (yes I know) he suggested that we go down and get Mrs. R—— and tell her who we are and that he sent us and try the fourteen-inch typewriters and see if our stencils would work with such type (I see) and if we can use them to get them right away because they have those in stock and we won't have to wait (that's right) we're short one typewriter right now as far as having adequate facilities for the staff is concerned (yes) we're short and we want to get rid of those rentals (that's right) but they are expecting within two weeks or so to be receiving—ah—to start receiving their orders on eleven-inch machines with pica type (oh) and of course pica type has always been best for our stencils (yes) but I rather think there might be a chance that we can work with elite type (well you go over and try them and see what they're like and do that as soon as you can so that we'll not miss our chance at these).

The casual style is used among friends and acquaintances in small groups or pairs. Little background is given or necessary. There is much in-group slang and jargon. Formulas are

[9] Martin Joos, *The Five Clocks* (Bloomington, Ind.: Indiana University Research Center in Anthropology, Folklore, and Linguistics, 1962).

[10] From Charles C. Fries, *The Structure of English* (New York: Harcourt, Brace & World, 1952), pp. 50–51.

common, such as those of utterance 7 in the passage below.[11] Their function is to signal the casualness of the communication as well as to carry meaning. (The intonation of the exclamations has been marked in the following passage.)

1. [A—— I don't know whether you let B—— go out during the week do you suppose he could come over tonight while we go out to dinner]
2. [Well the difficulty is J—— that he got back in his lessons]
3. [Oh oh]
4. [And in his last report about two weeks ago he was down in two subjects his father hasn't been letting him do anything]
5. [Well that's a good idea]
6. [I'm awfully sorry]
7. [Well that's all right thanks A—— to tell you the truth I don't want awfully badly to go you know what I mean]
8. [M hm]
9. [Well how's the garden]
10. [Oh it's much worse than yours I imagine the only thing that looks decent at all is the strawberries]
11. [Yes I know but you know they're not going to be any good unless they get some sun and dry weather]
12. [No well there's still time for them isn't there]
13. [Yes I know]
14. [I've got strawberries started have you]
15. [What]
16. [Some of the berries have started on my plants]

Joos characterized the intimate style as more expressive than informative. If a husband comes home tired, this fact, known to any competent wife by his nonverbal signals, is not the meaning of his /tayrd/; he is more likely asking for a drink, or sympathy. Intimate speech finds certain grammatical details superfluous, and does not require much of the public vocabulary; a married couple or close friends gradually invent a large part of their intimate code.

Formal style is marked by a lack of participation of the audience; it is designed to inform; it is essentially dominating; it expects the listeners to remain silent till the end of the speech. What the speaker says can be arranged in sentences and paragraphs.

The sentences of the exercise below cannot show all the characteristics of each style, since they are isolated from context. But there are characteristics of vocabulary and syntax that mark the styles even at the level of sentences.

Translate the utterances below into the other styles. Some of the messages jar the ear when translated into an inappropriate style. For example, the translation of the consultative utterance of number 4 will sound strange when put into formal language. But it is still possible to translate it. The intimate style is not included in this exercise because by nature it

[11] *Ibid.*, pp. 24–25.

is private and most often ambiguous to outsiders. The frozen style has not been included here or discussed previously because it is restricted to printed material and declamation.

1. consultative *I don't understand this.*

   casual *Hey prof, that doesn't reach me.*

   formal *The subject is beyond comprehension.*

2. consultative ____

   casual ____

   formal *We request the honor of your presence for luncheon Tuesday next at 12:00.*

3. consultative *I would like two hamburgers and one order of french fries.*

   casual ____

   formal ____

4. consultative *Please fill up the gas tank.*

   casual ____

   formal ____

5. consultative *I'm completely exhausted.*

   casual ____

   formal ____

# 10

## Writing

### EXERCISE 1: Pictographs

Communication through pictures was a preliminary stage in the evolution of the symbolic representation of language; these pictures conveyed only concepts, not particular words. Some pictographs are simple reminders of a name or event.

The example given below was obtained in 1888 from the Passamaquoddy Indians in Maine. They kept records of their trade with the white man; this is a record of one such transaction.[1] Fill in the parentheses in the interpretation with the proper letters from the picture.

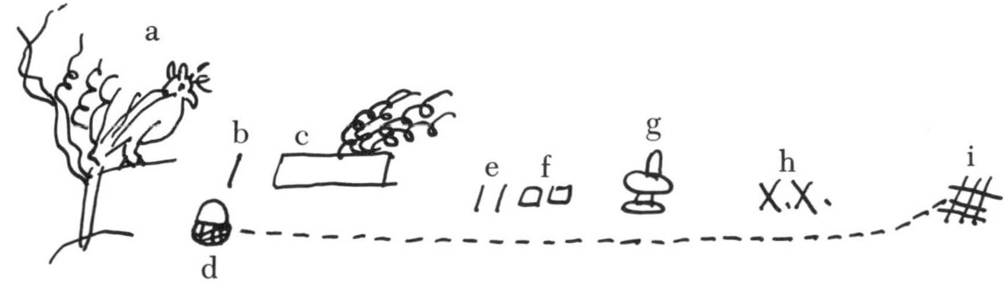


**Interpretation:** A woman called "Owl" ( ) bought one ( ) plug of smoking tobacco ( ), two ( ) quarts ( ) of kerosene for her lantern ( ), and all this is worth twenty cents ( ). To barter for this, she brings in a basket ( ) and the basket cancels the debt ( ).

### EXERCISE 2: Word Symbols

Pictographs are not *writing* symbols, since they do not symbolize language. They symbolize the information directly; language never enters the picture. One method of writing is with word symbols: each word has its symbol. Pictographs bypass language; word symbols make it possible for the exact wording of a message to be preserved. In modern English **2**, **&**, and **$** are examples of word symbols. Give a conventional word symbol for each of these words.

[1] Adapted from Garrick Mallery, *Picture Writing of the American Indians* (Tenth Annual Report of the Bureau of Ethnology, 1888–89 [Washington, D.C.: Government Printing Office, 1893]), pp. 259–61.

four ______

and ______

at . . . apiece ______

equals ______

plus ______

male, man, boy . . . ______

female, woman, girl . . . ______

Some of the word symbols in modern English writing can stand for syllables within words as well as for words. For example, the terms ***quarto, octavo,*** and ***duodecimo*** (also called ***twelvemo***) are abbreviated ***4to, 8vo,*** and ***12mo.*** Most word symbols have traditionally not been arbitrary in origin: the word symbol for ***man*** looked like a man in some way. The *Playboy* cartoons using ♂ and ♀ extend this idea. The Roman numeral ***III*** is not arbitrary. The symbol itself carries a hint of its meaning.

Devise a set of symbols for as many of the following words as you need to send a meaningful message to a classmate. Make sure they work: have the receiver write out the message he thinks you sent, and check it against your original.

***Horse*** (          ), ***breakfast*** (          ), ***brunch*** (          ), ***tree*** (          ), ***forest*** (          ) (You may find that it is sometimes convenient to make a word symbol for a manmade object, such as ***brunch,*** in more than one part.)

***Walk*** (          ) (use the same symbol for ***walks,*** if you wish), ***run*** (          ) (and ***runs***), ***read*** (          ) (and ***reads***), ***is*** (          )

***Brown*** (          ), ***big*** (          ), ***little*** (          ), ***fast*** (          )

***To*** (          ), ***around*** (          ), ***through*** (          ), ***and*** (          )

**The Message:** ____________________

____________________

____________________

**Your Classmate's Interpretation:** ____________________

____________________

____________________

What would a foreigner be able to learn about the structure of English from messages such as this, if it were all the information he had? Anything about phonology? morphology? syntax? Be as specific as you can, looking at your own message. What would a foreigner not be able to learn?

____________________

## EXERCISE 3: Rebus Writing

Most of the words in the last exercise can be symbolized by drawings, but the system is cumbersome. What could be done with ***good, bad,*** or ***would be?*** How could you handle the old political slogan "Tippecanoe and Tyler too"? A picture of a canoe tipping over might communicate the first word. Or the reader might puzzle through pictures of a tepee and a canoe, a plus sign, a picture of a tie, and a 2, in that order. This leaves out the last syllable of ***Tyler,*** but a person with some knowledge of American history would most likely be able to read it anyway. This second method of symbolizing the slogan is called rebus writing: word symbols are used to symbolize not a particular word, combining sound and meaning, but only the sounds of the word. The sounds of the word that is meant are the sounds of the word actually signified, or nearly so. This is phonetization. The writing system attaches a sound value to the sign independent of its meaning as a word. The ability to symbolize the sounds of words as well as their meanings makes writing easier; fewer symbols are needed, and more words can be successfully symbolized. Draw rebus symbols or word symbols for the following words and phrases.

would be ______________________

loggerhead ______________________

mumble ______________________

fancy ______________________

hammerhead shark ______________________

Screwtape Letters ______________________

Captain Hornblower ______________________

## EXERCISE 4: A Combination of Rebus and Word-Symbol Writing

Men of past ages devised several methods of getting around the cumbrous word-symbol writing. You have seen one, the rebus. Another system, presented in this exercise, is used in Chinese writing.

How would you write ***binge?*** Word symbols could get the idea across, but not, perhaps, the exact word. The following process, however, might succeed in catching the exact word: draw two symbols, one of a door hinge, and another of a bottle of liquor. If the reader knows by convention that the word he is trying to guess sounds like a word symbolized by the first symbol and has to do with the general semantic area of the second symbol, then he might be successful.

The Chinese use this method by combining two of their symbols into one. The symbol 工 is pronounced ***kung***[1] and means 'work.' (The number refers to the pitch phoneme of the word.) The Chinese symbol 水 means 'water.' The symbol 汞 asks the reader to determine a word that sounds like ***kung***[1] and in some way has to do with water or has some quality of water. The desired word is ***hung***[3] 'quicksilver.' Quicksilver, or mercury, runs quickly when it is spilled, like water.[2]

Devise symbols based on the above principle for the words below. First give the symbol for the word that the desired word sounds like and then the symbol for the general area of meaning.

mare ______________________

cook ______________________

rook (to gyp) ______________________

look ______________________

dead ______________________

red ______________________

lead (metal) ______________________

## EXERCISE 5: The Cherokee Syllabary

Writing systems using word symbols usually had symbols for syllables as well. The last two exercises showed how making the word symbols stand for sounds extended their usefulness. This phonetizing often led to a syllabary, a list of symbols for the syllables of a language. In the preceding exercises, you probably have already devised over thirty symbols used to stand for the sounds of words or syllables. In 1821 the Cherokee Indian Sequoya devised a syllabary of his language with eighty-five signs. His symbols are arbitrary, while most of yours are not. He attempted completeness, while your list covers only a few syllables, and you would find it difficult to complete the job for English.

Transliterate the following words written in the Cherokee syllabary.[3] The syllabary is on page 168 in *Aspects of Language*.

| *Cherokee* | *Transliteration* | *Translation* |
|---|---|---|
| ᏣᎳᎩ | ______________ | Cherokee |
| ᏏᏉᏯ | ______________ | Sequoya |
| ᏚᏂᏃᏗ | ______________ | October, harvest month |

[2]Holger Pederson, *The Discovery of Language* (Bloomington, Ind.: Indiana University Press, 1959), p. 144.
[3]The Cherokee words and translations are from John Algeo and Thomas Pyles, *Problems in the Origin and Development of the English Language*, (New York: Harcourt, Brace & World, 1966), p. 32.

| | | |
|---|---|---|
| *ᏅᏏᏚᏒᏳ* | ________________ | instantly |
| *ᎠᏓᏜ* | ________________ | war club |

Now go through the syllabary and its transliteration, and find the list of symbols Sequoya would have had to use if he had devised one symbol for each phoneme. (You must assume that the transliteration is correct.) Write the list of phonemes below.

| | | | |
|---|---|---|---|
| ______ | ______ | ______ | ______ |
| ______ | ______ | ______ | ______ |
| ______ | ______ | ______ | ______ |
| ______ | ______ | ______ | ______ |
| ______ | ______ | ______ | ______ |

## EXERCISE 6: The Hebrew Writing System

English words have a variety of morpheme endings for inflections and derivations, such as the /z/ of /dɔgz/ or the /šən/ of /ǽkšən/. Words in Semitic languages are for the most part forms with three consonants; vowels come before and after the consonants, with the function that affixes have in English. For example, Arabic ***KTB*** is a root whose basic meaning refers to writing. ***KaTaBa*** means 'he wrote,' ***aKTuBu*** 'I write,' ***yuKTaBu*** 'it is written,' ***KiTāB*** 'book,' ***KuTuB*** 'books,' ***KāTiB*** 'writer.' The classical writing system reflected the root importance of the consonants; the reader was expected to figure out the vowels from the context. We do much the same thing when we guess at poor handwriting.

1. The consonants of the Hebrew writing system are given below. Find out their values by studying the list of Hebrew words with their transliterations. The Hebrew writing is read from right to left. Ignore the vowels of the transliterations.

| | | | | | | | |
|---|---|---|---|---|---|---|---|
| צ | ____ | ם | ____ | ח | ____ | א | ____ |
| ץ | ____ | נ | ____ | ט | ____ | בּ | ____ |
| ק | ____ | ן | ____ | י | ____ | ב | ____ |
| ר | ____ | ס | ____ | כּ | ____ | ג | ____ |
| שׂ | ____ | ע | ____ | כ | ____ | ד | ____ |
| שׁ | ____ | פּ | ____ | ךְ | ____ | ה | ____ |
| תּ | ____ | פ | ____ | ל | ____ | ו | ____ |
| ת | ____ | ף | ____ | מ | ____ | ז | ____ |

| | | |
|---|---|---|
| 'father' | ['av] | אב |
| 'clothing' | [bέgεd] | בּגד |

| | | |
|---|---|---|
| 'Eve' | [xáva][4] | חוה |
| 'purity' | [tóhar] | טהר |
| 'armor' | [záyin] | זין |
| 'all of them' | [kulám] | כּלם |
| 'go' | [lɛx] | לךְ |
| 'he entered' | [nɪxnás] | נכנס |
| 'experienced' | [mnusá][4] | מנסה |
| 'he, it flew' | ['af] | עף |
| 'he, it exploded' | [patsáts] | פּצץ |
| 'beauty' | [šɛfɛr] | שׁפר |
| 'sack' | [sak] | שׂק |
| 'sub-' | [tat] | תּת |

How many symbols are there for [v]? ____ For [t]? ____ For [k]? ____ For [s]? ____

Some Hebrew letters are positional variants of the same sound. Give the positional variations of [x] ______ ______, [m] ______ ______, [n] ______ ______, [f] ______ ______, [ts] ______ ______. The symbol [x] indicates an unvoiced velar fricative.

2. There is a limit to guessing, and at times it was desirable to be able to indicate a vowel exactly. From about the ninth century B.C., three of the Hebrew letters were sometimes used as vowels. The three letters ה, ו, and י kept their customary consonant values when they were not being used as vowels.

| | | |
|---|---|---|
| [bíra] | בּירה | 'beer' |
| [ben] | בּין | 'between' |
| [bɔr] | בּור | 'well' |
| [bʊl] | בּול | 'stamp' |
| [bʊba] | בּובּה | 'doll' |

What vowels can each of these three letters stand for? ________________

3. In the eighth century A.D., other marks, placed above and below the consonant letters and called massoretic points, indicated the vowels exactly. The pronunciations below are modern Israeli pronunciations.

| | | |
|---|---|---|
| 'unleavened bread' | מַצָּה | [matsá] |
| 'universe' | תֵּבֵל | [tévɛl] |
| 'sprig' | נֵצֶר | [nétsɛr] |
| 'nephew' | אַחְיָן | ['axyán] |
| 'quarrel' | רִיב | [riv] |

Answer either of these questions: Why were the massoretic points not placed between the consonants? Why were the vowel signs not developed as early as the consonant signs?

[4] The final -[h] in the Hebrew in these two words is a survival of a *mater lectionis*, a consonant symbol used to indicate a vowel.

4. Some writers feel that the history of writing shows a movement from syllabic to alphabet writing. How far had the form of Hebrew writing of the ninth century B.C. moved?

## EXERCISE 7: English Sounds and Spellings

**The Consistency of English Spelling:**

English spelling appears chaotic and orderly by turns. For example, the phoneme /ɪ/ is spelled in a variety of ways: it occurs in the words ***hit, sieve, England, women, busy, myth,*** and ***build.***[5] The spellings are ***i, ie, e, o, u, y,*** and ***ui.*** From the following list of words, compile the spellings of the vowels and consonants that follow the list.

| | | | |
|---|---|---|---|
| hut | put | does | obey |
| veil | weight | along | dungeon |
| blood | porpoise | pain | villain |
| would | gauge | play | book |
| easily | physics | give | rough |
| rate | guard | thin | none |
| steak | wolf | ghost | trait |

/ə/ ____________________

/ʌ/ ____________________

/ʊ/ ____________________

/e/ ____________________

/g/ ____________________

/f/ ____________________

/z/ ____________________

/s/ ____________________

Which are more consistent, vowels or consonants? ____________________

[5] Robert A. Hall, Jr., *Sound and Spelling in English* (New York: Chilton Books, 1961), p. 30.

**English Spelling Reform:**

Various systems of reformed spelling have been devised as solutions to the irregularities of English spelling. The British Simplified Spelling Society published its system in 1940, and Axel Wijk published his system in 1959. Below you will find one passage spelled out twice, once according to each system. The British system is first and the Wijk system next.[6]

> We instinktivly shrink from eny chaenj in whot iz familyar; and whot kan be mor familyar dhan dhe form ov wurdz dhat we have seen and riten mor tiemz dhan we kan posibly estimaet? We taek up a book printed in Amerika, and *honor* and *center* jar upon us every tiem we kum akros dhem; nae, eeven to see *forever* in plaes of *for ever* atrakts our atenshon in an unplezant wae. But dheez ar iesolaeted kaesez; think ov dhe meny wurdz dhat wood hav to be chaenjd if eny real impruuvment wer to rezult. . . . But dhaer iz soe much misapprehenshon on dhis point, and such straenj statements ar maed, dhat it bekumz necessary to deel widh dhis objekshon in sum deetael.

> We instinctivly shrink from eny chainge in whot iz familiar; and whot can be more familiar than the form ov wurds that we hav seen and written more times than we can possibly estimate? We take up a book printed in America, and *honor* and *center* jar upon us every time we cum across them; nay, even to see *forever* in place ov *for ever* attracts our attention in an unplezant way. But theze ar isolated cases; think ov the meny wurds that wood hav to be chainged if eny real improovement wer to rezult. . . . But there iz so much misapprehension on this point, and such strainge statements ar made, that it becums necessary to deal widh this objection in sum detail.

How do these two systems treat the plural morpheme? Is it spelled according to the allomorphs of that morpheme (/-əz/, /s/, and /z/), or with just one symbol for the morpheme? In the space below, write in all the plural nouns of the passage as spelled by each system.

| *British Spelling* | *Wijk* |
|---|---|
| *wurdz* | *wurds* |
| __________ | __________ |
| __________ | __________ |
| __________ | __________ |

What is the principle that each system follows here?

________________________________________

How does each system treat the schwa (/ə/)? To find out, list the first seven words from each passage that contain a schwa. Then try to account for the spellings of schwa. (There is room for disagreement over whether some of the words are pronounced with schwa.)

| *British Spelling* | *Wijk* |
|---|---|
| __________ | __________ |
| __________ | __________ |

[6] Axel Wijk, *Regularized English* (Stockholm: Almquist & Wiksell, 1959), pp. 324–25. Copyright Almquist & Wiksell, 1959. Reprinted with permission.

| | |
|---|---|
| ______________ | ______________ |
| ______________ | ______________ |
| ______________ | ______________ |
| ______________ | ______________ |
| ______________ | ______________ |

Can you find any pattern in either of these systems?

______________________________________________

As you have discovered, neither system uses the schwa, partly because the public might be alienated from spelling reform by a new symbol. Also, the use of the schwa obscures the relationships between some words. How many letters or letter groups do the two words below have in common? (Remember that ***ti*** often stands for /š/.)______________
On the lines at the right, write the phonemic transcriptions for these words. How many phonemes do they have in common, position by position? ______________ The ordinary spellings give more clues to their relationship than do the phonemic transcriptions.

| | | | | | | | | |
|---|---|---|---|---|---|---|---|---|
| a | b | o | l | i | sh | | | ______________ |
| a | b | o | l | i | ti | o | n | ______________ |

Write out the phonemic transcriptions for the following pairs of words, and notice how the ordinary spelling gives clues to their relationships.

human ______________
humanity ______________
civil ______________
civility ______________
tutor ______________
tutorial ______________
injure ______________
injurious ______________
minister ______________
ministerial ______________
ether ______________
ethereal ______________
moral ______________
morality ______________
general ______________
generality ______________
medicine ______________
medicinal ______________

Write the phonemic transcriptions of your pronunciation of these artificial words.

kembress (as a noun)______________
kembressional ______________
condolve (verb) ______________

condolution ______________________________

hycrate (verb) ______________________________

hycratory ______________________________

The rules you followed in changing the pronunciation of the artificial and real words above are quite firmly in your mind, although they are complicated. Since we already know how to change /əbalɨš/ (in a midwestern pronunciation) to /æbəlɪšən/, we don't need the schwa or other new symbols to tell us how.

# The Evolving Approaches to Language

## EXERCISE 1: Identification of Schools of Grammar

The following passages, particularly the sections italicized for additional emphasis, are representative of the five stages in the growth of linguistics as a science. The five stages as discussed by Bolinger are *traditional grammar, historical linguistics, descriptive linguistics, structural linguistics,* and *formal linguistics.* Each of the passages below has been selected to characterize the views of one particular school. In some cases the views of two schools seem very much alike; for example, the discussion of universals by traditional grammar and by transformational, or formal, linguistics. Many of the notions of the later schools had their roots in earlier centuries; the most recent trends place emphasis on theory and scientific explanations. One of the major axioms of descriptive linguistics, proposed in the early twentieth century—to describe language as it is rather than as it ought to be—is found in the works of a grammarian of the early nineteenth century. He writes:

> Language is conventional, and not only invented, but, in its progressive advancement, *varied* for purposes of practical convenience. Hence it assumes any and every form which those who make use of it choose to give it. We are, therefore, as *rational* and *practical* grammarians compelled to submit to the necessity of the case; to take the language as it *is,* and not as it *should be,* and bow to custom.[1]

By "custom," however, he means the custom of the best speakers and writers. (See passage 1.) The notion of universals, found in the first sentences of passage 1, is accepted by the transformational grammarians. Write the name of the school most closely related to each passage below. (Italics have been added; explanatory remarks are in brackets.)

1. ___*traditional grammar*___ "Grammar may be divided into two species, universal and particular. UNIVERSAL GRAMMAR explains the principles which are common to all languages. PARTICULAR GRAMMAR applies those general principles to a particular language, modifying them according to its genius, *and the established practice of the best speakers and writers by whom it is used.*"[2]

[1] Samuel Kirkham, *English Grammar* (Rochester, N.Y.: William Alling & Co., 1835), p. 18.
[2] *Ibid.*, p. 17.

2. ______________________________ There is no scientific use in mere description of a language; *history is the only object of linguistics.*[3]

3. ______________________________ "Sound-laws have no exception" and *"No exception without a rule."*[4]

4. ______________________________ *"Language is a system whose parts can and must all be considered in their synchronic solidarity.* Since changes never affect the system as a whole but rather one or another of its elements, they can be studied only outside the system. Each alteration doubtless has its countereffect on the system, but the initial fact affected only one point; there is no inner bond between the initial fact and the effect that it may subsequently produce on the whole system. The basic difference between successive terms and coexisting terms, between partial facts and facts that affect the system, precludes making both classes of fact the subject matter of a single science."[5]

5. ______________________________ "While, according to the structure of our European languages, we always tend to look for the expression of singularity or plurality for the sake of clearness of expression, there are other languages that are entirely indifferent towards this distinction. A good example of this kind is the Kwakiutl [an American Indian language of the Pacific Northwest spoken by a people of the same name]. It is entirely immaterial to the Kwakiutl whether he says, *There is a house* or *There are houses.* The same form is used for expressing both ideas, and the idea of singularity and plurality must be understood either by the context or by the addition of a special adjective."[6]

6. ______________________________ "The writer has attempted to satisfy six requirements which seem essential for a correct [phonological] system, but which no other system that he knows of completely fulfills. (1) Range and criteria must be accurately and unambiguously defined. (2) *There must be no mentalism.* (3) The terminology must involve no logical contradictions; terms defined as variables, class names, and quality names must be consistently used in those values. (4) No material should be excluded which might prove to be of grammatical importance, and none should be included which cannot be of grammatical importance. (5) *There must be no circularity; phonological analysis is assumed for grammatical analysis, and so must not assume any part of the latter. The line of demarcation between the two must be sharp.* (6) The way should be left open for the introduction of any criteria whatsoever on the grammatical level, barring mentalism."[7]

[3]Bloomfield's paraphrase of Hermann Paul's *Prinzipien der Sprachgeschichte* in "On Recent Works in General Linguistics," *Modern Philology* (Chicago: The University of Chicago Press, 1927), p. 217.

[4]The first quote is attributed to August Leskien, 1876, the second to Karl Verner in John T. Waterman's *Perspectives in Linguistics* (Chicago: The University of Chicago Press, 1963), p. 50.

[5]Ferdinand de Saussure, *Course in General Linguistics,* trans. by Wade Baskin (New York: McGraw-Hill, 1959), p. 87.

[6]Franz Boas, *Introduction to the Handbook of American Indian Languages* (Washington: Smithsonian Institution Bureau of American Ethnology), Bulletin 40, Part 1, p. 29.

[7]Charles F. Hockett, "A System of Descriptive Phonology," in *Language,* Vol. 18 (1942), pp. 20–21.

7. ______________________________ *"The linguistic processes of the 'mind' as such are quite simply unobservable; and introspection about linguistic processes is notoriously a fire in a wooden stove.* Our only information about the 'mind' is derived from the behavior of the individual whom it inhabits. To interpret that behavior in terms of 'mind' is to commit the logical fallacy of 'explaining' a fact of unknown cause by giving that unknown cause a name, and then citing the name x as the cause of the fact. 'Mind' is indeed a summation of such x's, unknown causes of human behavior."[8]

8. ______________________________ "It is not unreasonable to insist that any linguistic theory worthy of the name be expected to give enough insight into the nature of language to afford practical suggestions as to what we may find in the grammar of a previously unstudied language. *A codification of such suggestions yields discovery procedures.*"[9]

9. ______________________________ "Trubetzkoy phonology tried to explain everything from articulatory acoustics and a minimum set of phonological laws taken as essentially valid for all languages alike, flatly contradicting the American (Boas) tradition that languages could differ from each other without limit and in unpredictable ways, and *offering too much of a phonological explanation where a sober taxonomy* [classification and labeling] *would serve as well.*"[10]

10. ______________________________ "The well-founded pessimism which derives from the difficulties to be faced in studying languages not native to the linguist may, to an unknown extent, be mitigated by (even at present far from nonexistent) advantages to be derived from approaching 'exotic' languages with a highly specific, substantively rich theory of a language justified on the basis of the not insignificant range of distinct languages for which native linguists exist or can be expected to exist quite naturally. However, the possibilities so afforded will depend very much on overcoming the incredible harm done by that still dominant, extraordinarily exaggerated, habit of thought illustrated by the slogan 'describe each language in its own terms.' It will depend very much, that is, on the realization that *the description of every aspect of a particular language must be partially determined by the knowledge we have of the nature of other languages, i.e., by the knowledge obtained about the nature of language itself.*"[11]

11. ______________________________ "A grammar of the language L is essentially a theory of L."[12]

12. ______________________________ "In summary, one fundamental contribution of what we have been calling 'Cartesian linguistics' is the observation that human language, in its normal use, is free from the control of independently identifiable external

[8]W. Freeman Twaddell, "On Defining the Phoneme," in *Language Monographs* No. 16 (1935), as reprinted in Martin Joos, *Readings in Linguistics I* (Chicago: The University of Chicago Press, 1957), p. 57.

[9]Robert E. Longacre, *Grammar Discovery Procedures* (The Hague: Mouton & Co., 1968), p. 13.

[10]Martin Joos, Epilogue to Bloch's "Phonemic Overlapping," in Martin Joos, *op. cit.*, p. 96.

[11]Footnote 6 of Paul Postal's "A Note on 'Understood Transitively,'" in *International Journal of American Linguists*, Vol. 32, No. 1 (January, 1966), p. 93.

[12]Noam Chomsky, *Syntactic Structures* (The Hague: Mouton & Co., 1964), p. 49.

stimuli or internal states and is not restricted to any practical communicative function, in contrast, for example, to the pseudo language of animals. It is thus free to serve as an instrument of free thought and self-expression. The limitless possibilities of thought and imagination are reflected in the creative aspect of language use. *The language provides finite means but infinite possibilities of expression constrained only by rules of concept formation and sentence formation, these being in part particular and idiosyncratic but in part universal, a common human endowment.*"[13]

13. ______________________________ "The best kind of a theory is one which systematizes the widest range of facts; hence a *mentalistic theory is better than a taxonomic one* because the former can handle any fact that the latter can handle whereas the latter is unable to handle many kinds of facts that the former handles easily and naturally. The differences in the facts that these theories can handle is a direct function of the difference in the conceptual machinery they contain.[14]

## EXERCISE 2: Normative Grammar—Nineteenth Century

The following sentences are samples of "false syntax" found in Samuel Kirkham's *English Grammar* of 1835. The words that Kirkham considers wrong or misplaced are italicized. Some of the same examples still appear in handbooks of English. What are your personal reactions to these sentences? Place a 1, 2, or 3 beside each sentence to denote *acceptable, questionable,* or *not acceptable.* Compare your results with those of your classmates.

1. ____ Great pains *has* been taken to reconcile the parties.
2. ____ The sincere *is* always esteemed.
3. ____ The variety of the productions of genius, like that of the operations of nature, *are* without limit.
4. ____ Time and tide *waits* for no man.
5. ____ Patience and diligence, like faith, *removes* mountains.
6. ____ Man's happiness or misery *are,* in a great measure, put into his own hands.
7. ____ The prince, as well as the people, *were* blameworthy.
8. ____ The nation was once powerful; but now *they are* feeble.
9. ____ The multitude eagerly *pursues* pleasure as *its* chief good.
10. ____ Much depends on this *rule* being observed.
11. ____ *Who* did you talk with?
12. ____ *Who* did you give the book to?

[13] Noam Chomsky, *Cartesian Linguistics* (New York: Harper & Row, 1966), p. 29.
[14] Jerrold J. Katz, "Mentalism in Linguistics," in *Language,* Vol. 40, No. 2 (1964), p. 127.

13. ____ He is a man *who* I greatly respect.

14. ____ Which of those two cords is the *longest?*

15. ____ I was at a loss to determine which was the *wiser* of the three.

16. ____ Be composed, it is *me.*

17. ____ The French language is *spoke* in every state in Europe.

18. ____ These things should be *never* separated.

19. ____ I shall work today, unless it *rains.*

20. ____ They were all well but *him.*

## EXERCISE 3: Normative Grammar—Twentieth Century

The following article by George N. Feinstein, titled "Letter from a Triple-threat Grammarian," is representative of pointers taught in rhetoric nowadays.[15] As you read it, compare Feinstein's concerns with Kirkham's. To what degree is each bound by tradition, and to what degree does clarity dictate such rules?

> Dear sir; you never past me in grammer because you was prejudice but I got this here athaletic scholarship any way. Well, the other day I finely get to writing the rule's down so as I can always study it if they ever slip my mind.
>
> 1. Each pronoun agrees with their antecedent.
> 2. Just between you and I, case is important.
> 3. Verbs has to agree with their subjects.
> 4. Watch out for irregular verbs which has crope into our language.
> 5. Don't use no double negatives.
> 6. A writer mustn't shift your point of view.
> 7. When dangling, don't use participles.
> 8. Join clauses good, like a conjunction should.
> 9. Don't write a run-on sentence you got to punctuate it.
> 10. About sentence fragments.
> 11. In letters themes reports articles and stuff like that we use commas to keep a string of items apart.
> 12. Don't use commas, which aren't necessary.
> 13. Its important to use apostrophe's right.
> 14. Don't abbrev.
> 15. Check to see if you any words out.
> 16. In my opinion I think that an author when he is writing shouldn't get into the habit of making use of too many unnecessary words that he does not really need in order to put his message across.
> 17. In the case of a business letter, check it in terms of jargon.

[15] From *College English,* Vol. 21, No. 7 (April, 1960), p. 408. Reprinted with the permission of the National Council of Teachers of English and George W. Feinstein.

18. About repetition, the repetition of a word might be real effective repetition—take, for instance, Abraham Lincoln.
19. As far as incomplete constructions, they are wrong.
20. Last but not least, lay off clichés.

## EXERCISE 4: Reed-Kellogg Diagrams[16]

Different theories of grammar have analyzed English sentences in different ways. In this series of exercises, you will study three ways of analyzing English sentences. These are the *traditional analysis,* represented by the Reed-Kellogg diagrams; the *structural analysis,* represented by Immediate Constituent (IC) analysis; and the *formal analysis,* represented by structure diagrams and transformational rules. In this and following exercises you will gain some acquaintance with these three kinds of analysis. This exercise presents the Reed-Kellogg method of diagramming sentences. This method has been popular in many high schools and grade schools since the late nineteenth century.

A. The first step is to find the noun of the subject and the verb of the predicate. In the sentences below, the nouns and verbs are underlined, and only the nouns and verbs have been diagrammed. The complete subjects of the sentences are in parentheses.

| *The sentence* | *The Rudimentary Noun + Verb Diagram* |
|---|---|
| *(Horses) run.* | *Horses \| run* |
| *(He) soon arrived.* | *He \| arrived* |
| *(The two men) left for the garage.* | *men \| left* |
| *(The teacher who came to his class late) found no one there.* | *teacher \| found* |
| *(Marcia) was irresistible whenever she used that perfume.* | *Marcia \| was* |

The following sentences are divided into subject and predicate, with the subjects in parentheses. Underline the verb in each of the predicates. (Later, you will diagram each sentence.)

1. (My car) always starts.

car | starts

[16] *Linguistics and English Grammar,* by H. A. Gleason, Jr. (New York: Holt, Rinehart and Winston, 1965), is the source for much of the information in this exercise.

2. (The cycle that had the blowout) ran into a post.

3. (They) chose him the leader.

4. (The old vacuum sitting in the closet) worked most of the time.

5. (Home) is best.

6. (The clerk at the third counter) seemed happy to cash the check.

7. (The methodical banker at the third desk, which was near the window,) lent the money on request.

8. (The new battery I put in yesterday) started the engine easily.

B. The noun is the heart of the subject. Everything else in the subject modifies the noun. Study the examples above. There, the noun of each subject is underlined. Now underline the nouns in the subjects of sentences 2 through 8 above, and then draw the rudimentary noun + verb diagrams in the spaces provided.

Make the rudimentary noun + verb diagram for each of the following sentences.

1. The old teacher went to his class.

teacher | went

2. The brown cow in the pasture grazed along the fence.

3. Most students attended the lectures.

4. The policeman at the intersection stopped my car.

5. The salesman who sold the most cars got the raise.

6. He is the best musician in town.

7. They made him dean.

C. Then sentence type subject + verb + object is one of the most common in English. It is diagrammed this way:

*Bakers | make | bread*

The first vertical line, extending below the base line, separates the noun of the subject from the verb of the predicate. The vertical line extending to the base line separates the object of the verb from the verb. In the examples below, the nouns of the subjects and the verbs of the predicates are underlined. The objects are in parentheses. The rudimentary diagrams follow.

| | |
|---|---|
| *The quarterback passed the (ball).* | *quarterback \| passed \| ball* |
| *The rancher sold the (horse).* | *rancher \| sold \| horse* |
| *We saw the (clerk) over by the counter.* | *We \| saw \| clerk* |

Draw the rudimentary diagrams of the following sentences.

1. James led the gang.

James | led | gang

2. Peter brought the party to his apartment.

3. They elected him.

4. They elected the president.

5. John hated the long walk.

D. A prepositional phrase is diagrammed below the line in this way:

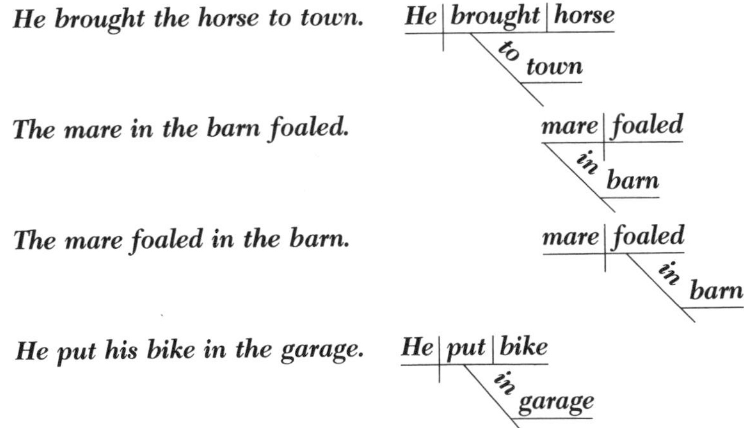


Another very common sentence type in English is subject + verb + indirect object + direct object. The Reed-Kellogg diagrams treat the indirect object like the prepositional phrase in such sentences as ***She gave the apple to him.***

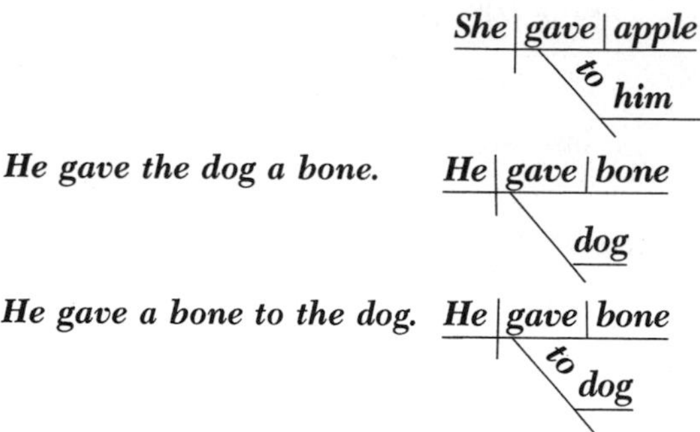


Draw the rudimentary diagrams of these sentences.

1. He brought the horse to the minister.

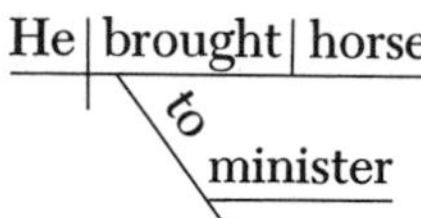


2. He brought the horse to the water.

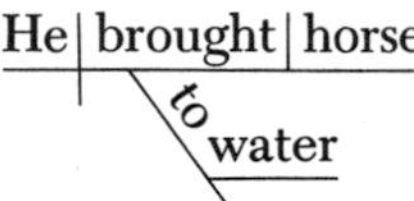


3. He offered her his hand.

4. He offered his hand to her.

5. He put the horse in the barn.

E. The Reed-Kellogg system includes a number of different sentence types under the next feature. The feature is a line slanting to the left.

*The horse seems tired.* *horse | seems \ tired*

(a) The sentence type represented above has three elements: subject, linking verb, and adjective. A linking verb is any verb except a form of ***be*** (***is, was,*** etc.) that can be substituted for ***seems*** in the preceding sentence.

(b) Another sentence type is subject + ***be*** + adjective.

***The horse is tired.*** ***horse | is \ tired***

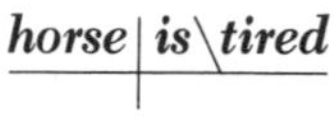

Diagram these sentences and indicate the sentence type, a or b.

1. __*a*__ The doctor appeared overworked.

doctor | appeared \ overworked

2. ____ The wind grew sluggish.

3. ____ John was busy.

(c) A third sentence type diagrammed this way is subject + ***be*** + noun, in which the noun has the same referent as the subject.

***My father is an engineer.*** ***father | is \ engineer***

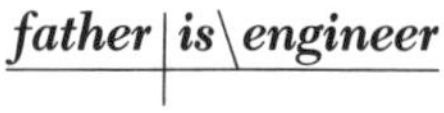

(d) A fourth sentence type is subject + linking verb + noun, in which the noun has the same referent as the subject.

***John became an architect.*** ***John | became \ architect***

Diagram these sentences and indicate the sentence type, c or d.

4. __*c*__ John was president.

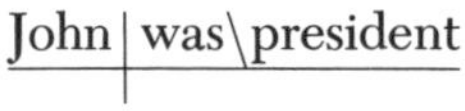

John | was \ president

5. ____ John became president.

6. ____ He remained the deputy.

7. ____ The sergeant was a specialist.

(e) Another pattern is subject + ***be*** + adverb. According to this system, a word that expresses place or time, such as ***there*** or ***then***, appearing after a form of ***be***, is an adverb.

***The man is here.***

***man | is \ here***

Diagram the following sentences, and indicate which of the five types each sentence is.

8. _*a*_ The horse in the barn appears underexercised.

horse | appears \ underexercised

in

barn

9. ____ John is outside.

10. ____ He remained the mayor in town.

11. ____ The ground under the hay is frozen.

12. ____ The grocery store is the forum of the town.

F. The next diagram feature is the line slanted to the right.

*They named him president.* — *They | named/president | him*

*The teacher considered him stupid.* — *Teacher | considered/stupid | him*

The two sentence types are noun + verb + noun + noun, in which the last two nouns have the same referent, and noun + verb + noun + adjective, in which the adjective modifies the second noun. The Reed-Kellogg system does not distinguish nouns from adjectives in these sentences. ***President*** and ***stupid*** in the sentences above are called objective complements. The word order is changed because the diagramming reflects the relationships between the words, not their order in the sentence. The relationship of ***stupid*** to ***considered*** is regarded as closer than the relationship of ***stupid*** to ***him:*** to ***consider stupid*** is thought of almost as a unit with ***him*** as object.

Diagram these sentences, and indicate whether the last word is a noun or an adjective.

1. *adj.* I thought Peter sick.

I | thought/sick | Peter

2. ____ They selected her queen.

3. ____ He called the child an idiot.

4. ____ He considered the treaty ill-timed.

G. Modifiers are slung below the horizontal line on slant lines in the Reed-Kellogg system.
***The three new coon hounds quickly found the scent.***

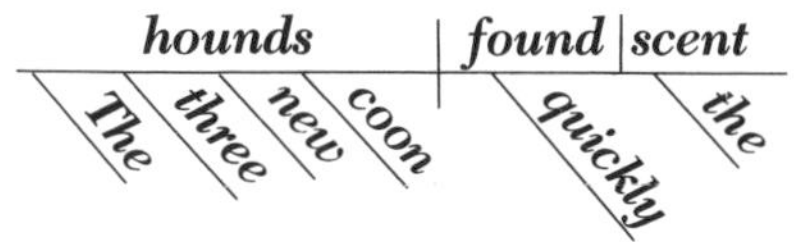

***The plot was clear before the beginning of the first commercial.***

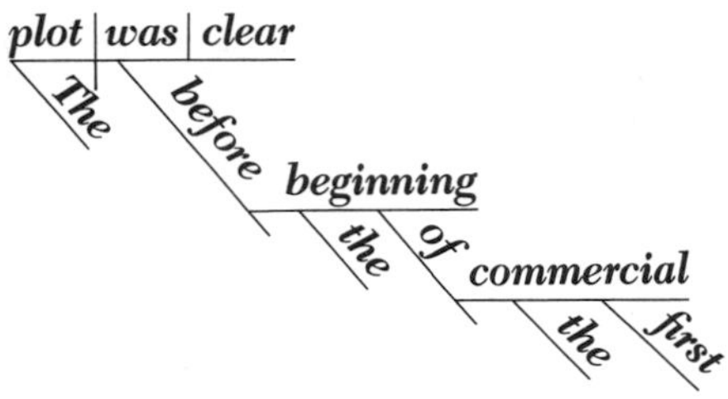


In this system of diagramming, no change is made in the diagram of the first sentence if ***quickly*** comes at the end of the sentence. Notice also that this diagram treats ***coon*** and ***the*** as modifiers of equal status. A word that is slung below a noun is called an "adjective," and a word that is slung below a verb is called an "adverb."

Diagram these sentences.

1. On Tuesday, the frustrated crowd named him their leader for the march.

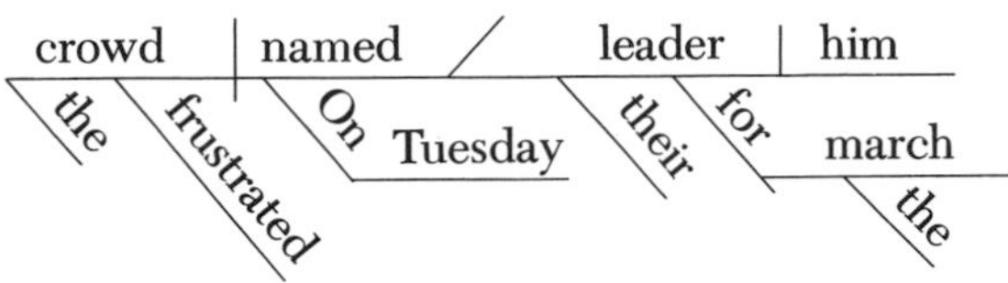


2. The old man cut some flesh from the side of the marlin.

3. He arrived on the third flight.

4. The old boy never liked her kind of food.

5. She rapidly taught him the Greek alphabet by constant repetition.

## EXERCISE 5: Analysis by Immediate Constituents[17]

One of the methods of sentence analysis used by American structuralism is called Immediate Constituent (IC) analysis: a sentence is divided into adjacent parts, then each of these parts is divided into adjacent parts, and so on until no further division is possible. This sort of analysis allows one to see the sentence in terms of layers of syntactic structures.

A. The first task is to make a division between modifiers of the sentence and the sentence itself. A sentence can be modified by either words or groups of words. (Notice that in the first Reed-Kellogg diagram below ***usually*** is represented as modifying ***comes*** only, and the diagram thus obscures the word order.)

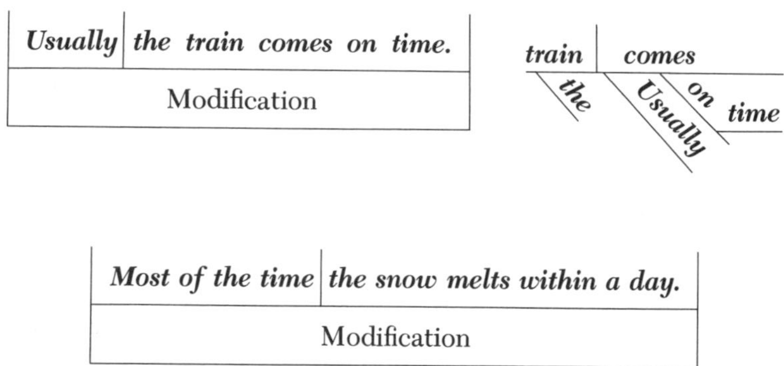


| *When the morning train comes late,* | *most of the men take the bus.* |
|---|---|
| Modification | |

Separate the sentence modifiers from the rest of the sentence below. Follow the model of the first sentence.

1. 

| When she heard that, she slammed the door. |
|---|
| Modification |

[17] *An Introductory English Grammar*, by Norman C. Stageberg (New York: Holt, Rinehart and Winston, 1965), is the model for the IC analysis in this exercise.

2. Since the car wouldn't start, I had to walk to work.

3. To make up for lost time, we skipped lunch.

B. When there is no sentence modifier, the first cut, or division, is made between the subject and the predicate. Study the examples of sentences divided into subject and predicate in the preceding exercise.

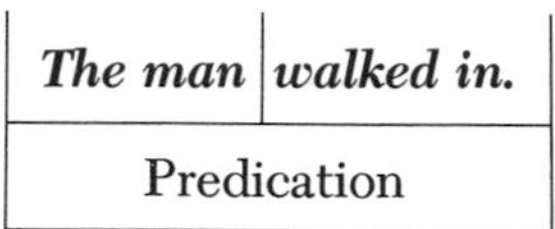


| *The old woman in the gray suit* | *walked over to the counter.* |
|---|---|
| Predication | |

| *The old man who had lost his glasses* | *had to walk into town for a new pair.* |
|---|---|
| Predication | |

Make a cut between the subject and the predicate in these sentences. You might have to cut off the sentence modifier first.

1.

| Usually | he | walked |
|---|---|---|
| | Predication | |
| Modification | | |

2. The old farmer went to the market.

3. The brown cow in the pasture walked along the fence.

4. On Tuesday, most of the students attended the lecture.

5. The salesman who sells the most cars will be given a raise this month.

6. The policeman at the intersection waved the last car through.

7. In this case, the best way to a man's heart is through his stomach.

C. The first cut in a subordinate clause is made after the conjunction that subordinates. This is called a structure of subordination.

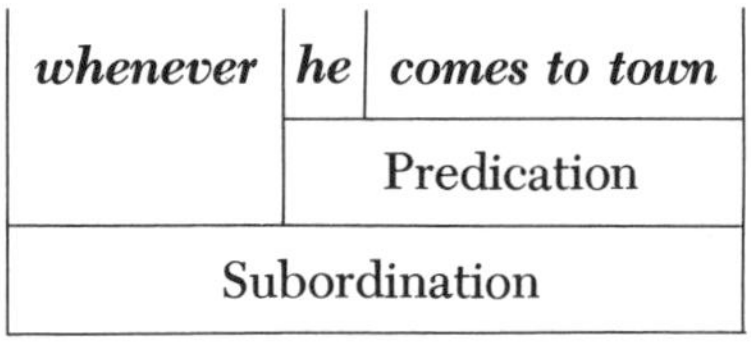

<table>
<tr><td rowspan="2">whenever</td><td>he</td><td>comes to town</td></tr>
<tr><td colspan="2">Predication</td></tr>
<tr><td colspan="3">Subordination</td></tr>
</table>

Some subordinating conjunctions are ***after, although, because, before, until, since, after, when, whenever.***

Identify the structures of predication and subordination below by making the appropriate cuts.

1. 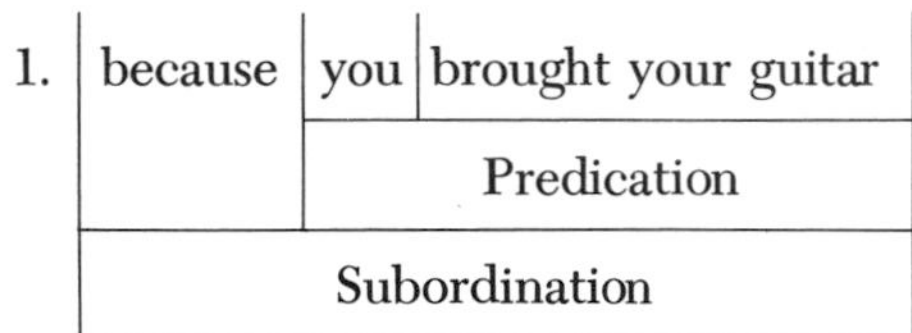


2. whenever he came into town

3. once the concert was over

D. The first cut in a prepositional phrase comes immediately after the preposition. A prepositional phrase is a structure of subordination.

| ***in*** | ***the car that Joan bought*** |
|---|---|
| Subordination | |

Make the first cut in these phrases.

1.

| under | the rug |
|---|---|
| Subordination | |

2. across the blue meadow

3. into the old white house that he had just sold

E. Make the first cut in an infinitive phrase after ***to.*** This is a structure of subordination.

<table>
<tr><td>to</td><td>come out for practice</td></tr>
<tr><td colspan="2">Subordination</td></tr>
</table>

Make the first cut in these phrases.

1.
<table>
<tr><td>to</td><td>do the right thing</td></tr>
<tr><td colspan="2">Subordination</td></tr>
</table>

2. to bring about the release

3. to hit the ball squarely

F. A noun phrase is a noun with words or groups of words modifying it. The subjects of the sentences we have studied were noun phrases. Some modifiers come after the noun, but most come before. First cut off the modifiers that come after the noun, beginning with the last, then the second last, and so on to the noun.

<table>
<tr><td>the old red car</td><td>in the garage</td><td rowspan="2">with the rusted cylinders</td></tr>
<tr><td colspan="2">Modification</td></tr>
<tr><td colspan="3">Modification</td></tr>
</table>

<table>
<tr><td rowspan="3">the old red car</td><td rowspan="2">in</td><td>the garage</td><td>with the new cement floor</td></tr>
<tr><td colspan="2">Modification</td></tr>
<tr><td colspan="3">Subordination</td></tr>
<tr><td colspan="4">Modification</td></tr>
</table>

Note that ***with the new cement floor*** does not modify ***the old car*** but ***the garage.*** The whole phrase ***in the garage with the new cement floor*** modifies ***the old red car.*** After you cut off the modifiers that come after the noun, cut off those that come before, beginning with the first modifier.

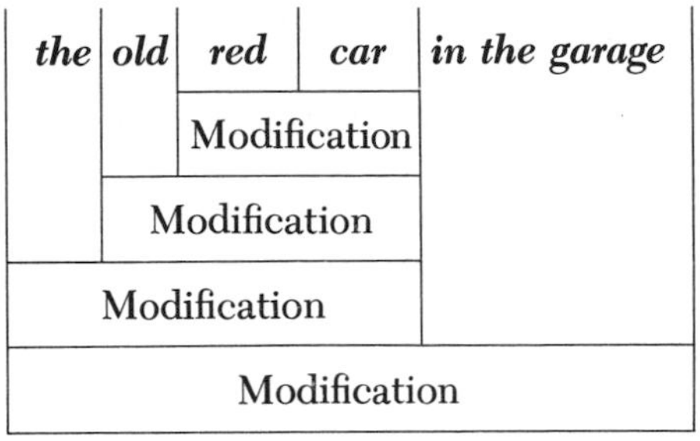

<table>
<tr><td>*the*</td><td>*old*</td><td>*red*</td><td>*car*</td><td>*in the garage*</td></tr>
<tr><td></td><td></td><td colspan="2">Modification</td><td></td></tr>
<tr><td></td><td colspan="3">Modification</td><td></td></tr>
<tr><td colspan="4">Modification</td><td></td></tr>
<tr><td colspan="5">Modification</td></tr>
</table>

Cut off all the modifiers from the main noun in each of these noun phrases.

1.

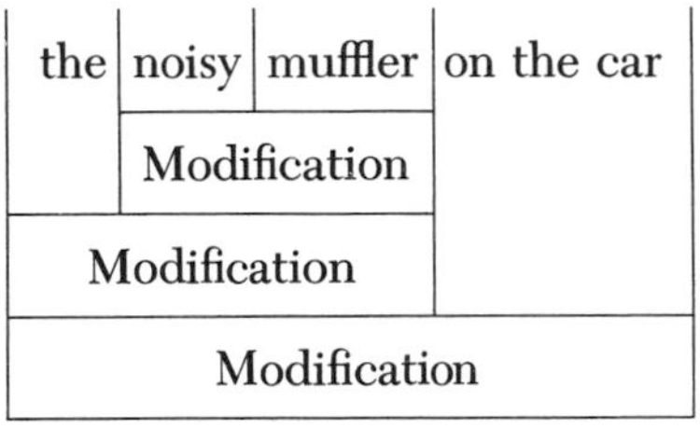

<table>
<tr><td>the</td><td>noisy</td><td>muffler</td><td>on the car</td></tr>
<tr><td></td><td colspan="2">Modification</td><td></td></tr>
<tr><td colspan="3">Modification</td><td></td></tr>
<tr><td colspan="4">Modification</td></tr>
</table>

2. the hunter who was sneaking up on the crow

3. the hunter in the red jacket who was sneaking up on the crow

4. the hunter who was sneaking up on the crow on the dead branch

G. The predicate of a sentence is a group of words related to a verb, with the verb as the heart of the predicate. Cut off the pre-verbal modifiers from the verb, beginning with the first, cutting off each by turn up to the verb.

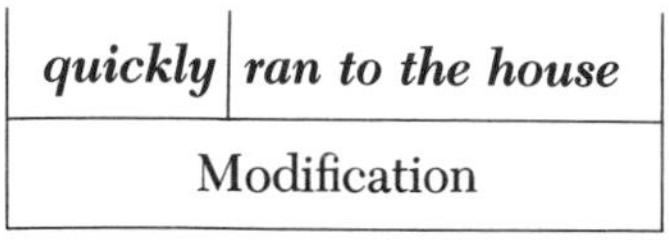

<table>
<tr><td>quickly</td><td>ran to the house</td></tr>
<tr><td colspan="2">Modification</td></tr>
</table>

Next cut off the modifiers that come after the verb, starting with the last.

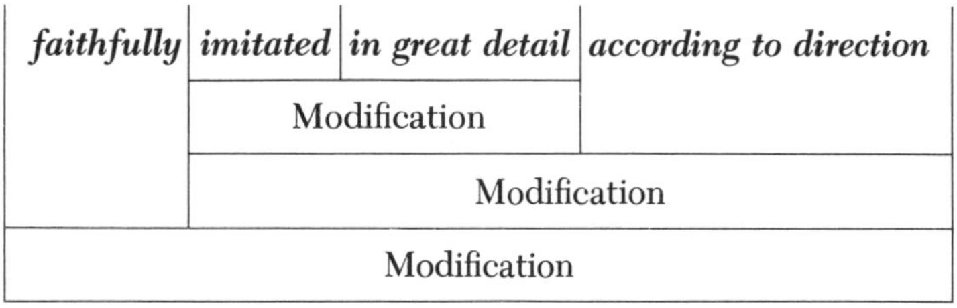

<table>
<tr><td rowspan="3">faithfully</td><td>imitated</td><td>in great detail</td><td rowspan="2">according to direction</td></tr>
<tr><td colspan="2">Modification</td></tr>
<tr><td colspan="3">Modification</td></tr>
<tr><td colspan="4">Modification</td></tr>
</table>

Make the IC cuts for the modifiers of the verbs.

1.

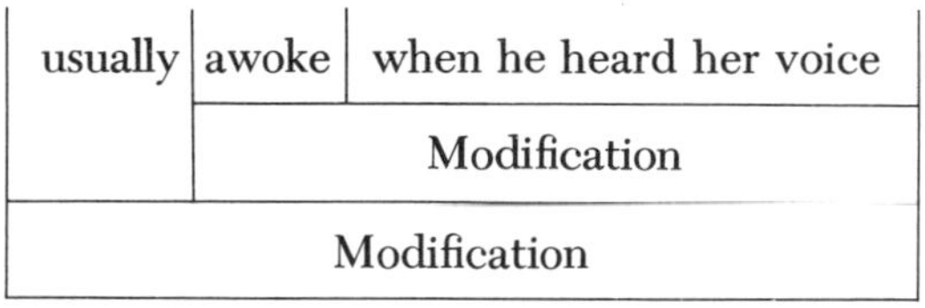

<table>
<tr><td rowspan="2">usually</td><td>awoke</td><td>when he heard her voice</td></tr>
<tr><td colspan="2">Modification</td></tr>
<tr><td colspan="3">Modification</td></tr>
</table>

2. often walked to the mailbox at his mother's request

3. sometimes went to the lake on a hot weekend

H. In the sentence ***John hit the ball***, ***the ball*** is a complement of the verb. In ***He gave John the ball***, both ***John*** and ***the ball*** are complements of the verb. A complement is a word or phrase that in some sense completes the meaning of the verb. Complements are cut off from the verb just as modifiers after the verb are cut off, beginning with the last.

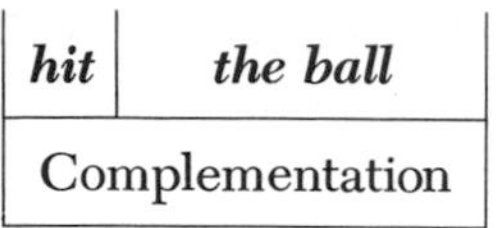


*gave* | *John* | *the ball*
Complementation
Complementation

Complements and modifiers that come after the verb are cut off in turn when they occur together.

*hit* | *the ball* | *hard*
Complementation
Modification

Make the IC cuts for verbal modifiers and complements in the following verb phrases.

1.

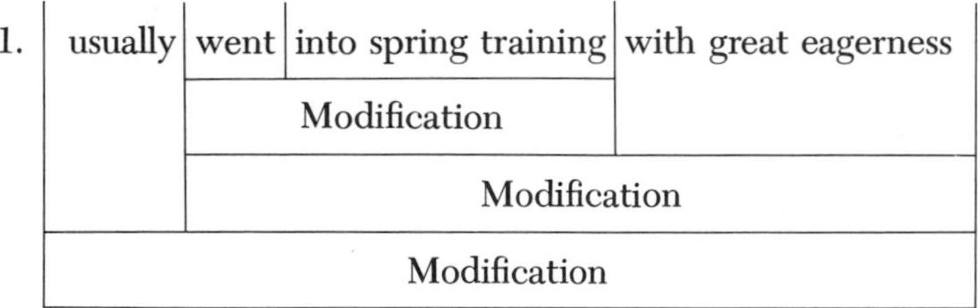


2. sullenly slouched in his chair

3. hit the ball hard to center field

I. Passive sentences are handled this way:

<table>
<tr><td rowspan="2">The bridge</td><td>was built</td><td>by engineers.</td></tr>
<tr><td colspan="2">Modification</td></tr>
<tr><td colspan="3">Predication</td></tr>
</table>

The phrase ***by engineers*** is regarded as modifying ***was built*** in some sense.

J. Questions are difficult to diagram because the constituents are not all adjacent.[18]

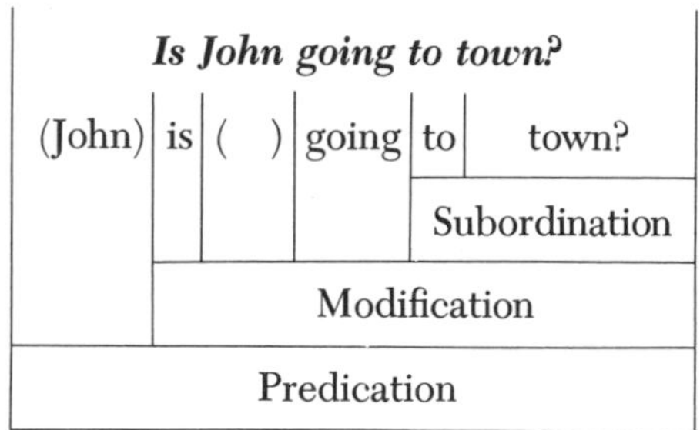


***John*** is set at the beginning in parentheses to make the diagramming a little clearer. It actually occurs at the empty parentheses, of course.

Diagram these sentences.

1.

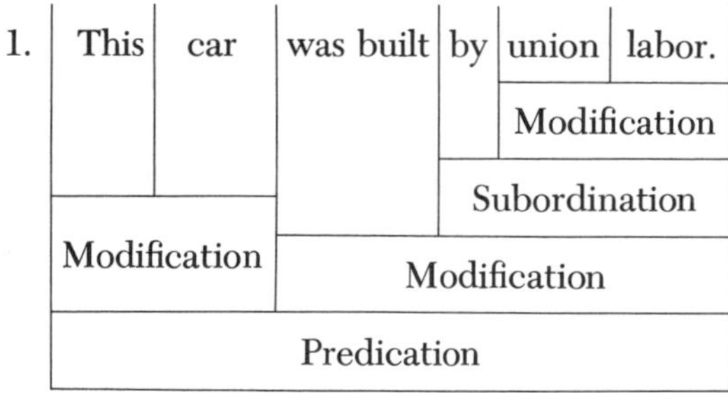


2. This car was built of steel.

[18] Charles F. Hockett diagrammed a question similarly in *A Course in Modern Linguistics* (New York: Macmillan, 1958), p. 155.

3. A good time was had by all.

4. Was the building occupied last night?

5. Is he all right?

K. Make a complete IC analysis of the following sentences. You should end up with a line between any two adjacent words (except for the verb with its auxiliaries, which are treated as units). Cut off the sentence modifier first, next cut the subject from the predicate, and then make any other cuts that apply.

1.

<table>
<tr><td>The</td><td>first</td><td>of</td><td>the</td><td>men</td><td>left</td><td>his</td><td>jacket</td><td>in</td><td>the</td><td>car.</td></tr>
<tr><td></td><td></td><td></td><td colspan="2">Modification</td><td></td><td colspan="2">Modification</td><td></td><td colspan="2">Modification</td></tr>
<tr><td colspan="2">Modification</td><td colspan="3">Subordination</td><td colspan="3">Complementation</td><td colspan="3">Subordination</td></tr>
<tr><td colspan="5">Modification</td><td colspan="6">Modification</td></tr>
<tr><td colspan="11">Predication</td></tr>
</table>

2. When you are ready, you can get the equipment from the car.

3. In the ensuing deadlock, we who were guests were advised to keep quiet.

## EXERCISE 6: Transformational-Generative Grammar (TGG)[19]

In the following brief discussion of Transformational-Generative Grammar, three generative rules, that is, phrase-structure rules, and eight transformational rules are introduced. Be sure to do each exercise before going on to the discussion that follows.

### A. Constituents of a Sentence[20]

Consider the sentence

(a) ***Columbus discovered America.***

If you were to break this sentence into two parts, you would probably break it as

***Columbus*** ***discovered America***

rather than

***Columbus discovered*** ***America.***

These two basic ***constituents, Columbus*** and ***discovered America,*** correspond to the following rule in the *phrase-structure* (PS) *rules* of TGG:

$$\text{PS 1. S} \longrightarrow \text{NP} + \text{VP}$$

PS 1 is read: a sentence (S) consists of a noun phrase (NP) followed by a verb phrase (VP). We note that the VP can also be divided into two parts, a verb (V) ***discovered,*** and an NP, ***America,*** giving the rule:

$$\text{VP} \longrightarrow \text{V} + \text{NP}$$

[19] We are indebted to Professor Larry Hutchinson of the University of Minnesota for his comments, suggestions, and guidance in the preparation of this section.

[20] In preparing this discussion we have gained many insights from Jacobs and Rosenbaum's *Grammar 1* and *Grammar 2* (Boston: Ginn and Co., 1967).

In the sentence ***Columbus died,*** the VP consists of only a verb, ***died.***

$$VP \longrightarrow V$$

We can write this rule as part of PS 2, by modifying the rule to specify that the NP may or may not occur. This option is shown by placing a parenthesis around the NP. (This convention will be followed in the rest of the chapter.)

$$\text{PS 2. } VP \longrightarrow V + (NP)$$

Do PS 1 and PS 2 hold in the following complicated sentence?

(b) ***Columbus, who was one of the most prominent explorers of the fifteenth century, discovered the land that would one day lead the other nations of the world in man's exploration of the universe.***

To answer the question, we must know more about the NP.

**B. The Noun Phrase**

Rather than listing what constituents may be considered as noun phrases, let us note some interesting properties of noun phrases. Consider what happens to the NP's of the sentence ***Columbus discovered America*** when the sentence is transformed to its passive counterpart.

***Columbus discovered America.*** $\overset{\text{passive}}{\Longrightarrow}$ ***America was discovered by Columbus.***

A transformation is symbolized by ⇒. We note that the positions of the NP's ***Columbus*** and ***America*** have been interchanged. Since only the NP's interchange, the *passive transformation* can determine the NP constituents of sentences. This is a helpful guide in the case of those sentences that undergo the passive transformation. Some sentences do not. Underline the sentences in which the passive transformation applies.

Columbus suppressed a mutiny. (A mutiny was suppressed by Columbus.)

1. Columbus died a happy man.
2. Columbus died happy.
3. Columbus greeted the Indians.
4. Columbus was a lucky man.
5. Columbus ignored the sailors.

Underline the NP's in the following sentences. If you are not sure, use the passive transformation as a guide.

1. The emotional actress divorced the movie magnate.
2. Webster's III heralded a new age of lexicography.
3. The strikers demanded better working conditions.

Now consider the sentence:

(c) ***Beauty is in the eye of the beholder.***

The passive transformation does not apply to this sentence. The NP, however, can be isolated by means of another transformation that turns the statement into a question taking "yes" or "no" as an answer, as in ***Is beauty in the eye of the beholder?*** The shift of the verb ***be*** has isolated the NP.

↑ ***Beauty (is) in the eye of the beholder.***
(NP)

Thus, the *yes-no question transformation* also identifies the NP, in this case ***beauty.*** Underline the NP's in the following sentences with the aid of the passive and the yes–no question transformation guides.

1. The clerk at the third counter was happy to cash the check.
2. His discourteous manners and unkempt look could annoy many persons.
3. Winter arrives early in Minnesota.

To apply a yes-no question transformation to the third sentence, you had to supply a form of the auxiliary ***do*** to the sentence. ***Does*** is the word that moves around the NP. Where does ***does*** belong in sentence 3? Transform the sentence to an emphatic sentence, ***Winter does arrive early in Minnesota,*** or to the negative sentence ***Winter doesn't arrive early in Minnesota.*** The position of ***does,*** and therefore the NP constituent that functions as the subject, become obvious.

There are other transformations that can be used to isolate the NP. The *cleft transformation* identifies the NP as follows:

***John lacks sincerity.*** $\overset{\text{cleft}}{\Longrightarrow}$ ***It is sincerity that John lacks.***
(NP: sincerity)

or

***John lacks sincerity.*** $\overset{\text{cleft}}{\Longrightarrow}$ ***It is John who lacks sincerity.***
(NP: John)

This transformation does not apply to NP's immediately after a form of ***be*** that is a main verb, such as

***He is the chairman*** ⟹ ****It is the chairman who he is.***

But we do have ***It is he who is the chairman,*** where the NP (***he***) is predicted. Now go back to sentence (b). Can you identify the two NP's, the VP, and the V?

### C. More about the Constituents of a Sentence

Consider the sentence:

(d) ***The police denounced the students in Lincoln Park.***

Were the students who were being denounced present in Lincoln Park or not? Did the police voice the denunciation in the park or elsewhere? The sentence would permit either of the possibilities. Sometimes we can ascertain the intention by the intonation. But it is not always helpful in resolving ambiguities. Sentence (d) may be paraphrased as sentences (c) or (f).

(e) ***The police denounced the students who were in Lincoln Park.***

(f) ***In Lincoln Park, the police denounced the students.***

Transformational grammarians claim that, since a speaker of the English language knows that sentences (e) and (f) are different from each other and yet related to (d), the grammar must account for this relationship. The explanation given is that at an abstract level, sentences (e) and (f)—that is, the different senses of (d)—are distinct. Each sentence in the abstract level then undergoes a series of transformations. As a result of these transformations, some sentences that had different structures at the abstract level come to resemble each other. In sentence (d), the different structures at the abstract level can be represented as follows:[21]

(g) ***The police denounced the students*** (***the students were in Lincoln Park***).

(h) ***The police denounced the students in Lincoln Park.***

Notice that (h) is just like our original ambiguous sentence (d). The difference is that (h) is structured so as to have only one semantic interpretation, so that ***in Lincoln Park*** only modifies the sentence ***The police denounced the students.*** It is imperative that this structure be known. The structure is shown in two ways: by means of rules such as the PS rules you have already seen, and graphically by means of tree structures that are generated by the rules. Each of these will be explained below for sentences (g) and (h).

The PS 1 rule given earlier can be expanded to include an Adverbial (Adv) such as ***in the field.*** Since the adverbial is optional—that is, it may or may not occur in any given sentence—it is placed within parentheses.

PS 1. S $\longrightarrow$ NP + VP (Adv)

Graphically, rule PS 1 generates tree structure (TS) 1 (if the Adv is selected).

TS 1

S

NP VP Adv

Adding rule PS 2, described earlier, and PS 3, which expands the NP, the tree structure becomes TS 2.

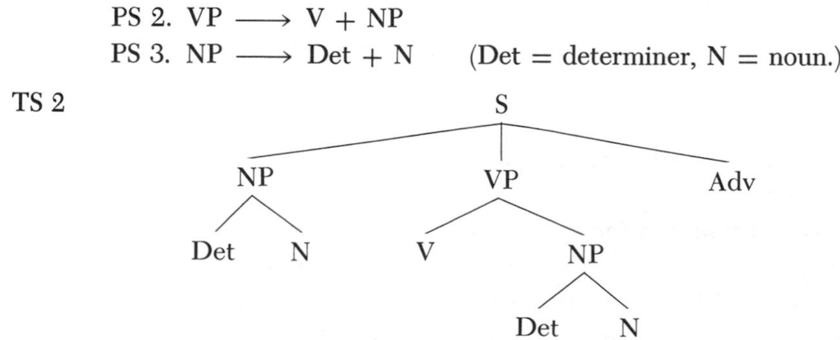


[21]Technically, the abstract level, the level that is the seat of meaning, is represented differently from what is given here. In the following representations, a number of phenomena, such as agreement, tense, etc., are included in the abstract structure for the sake of simplicity. They are properly treated by transformations.

There will be other rules in the grammar that specify that ***police*** is an N, ***denounced*** is a V, and so forth, so that the structure TS 3 will be generated.

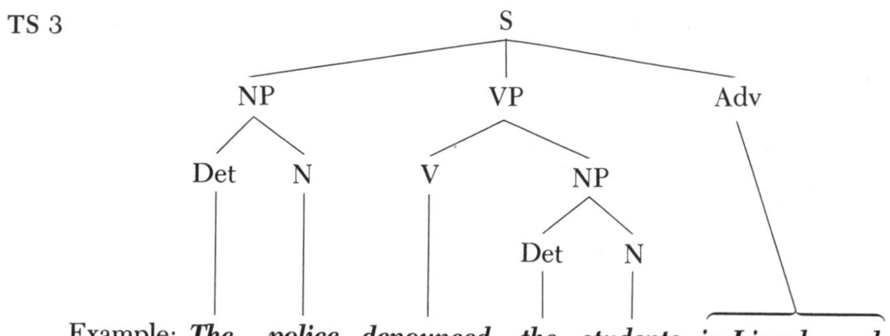


The structure of sentence (h) and similar sentences was shown by rules PS 1, PS 2, and PS 3. What is the structure of sentence (g)? In this sentence, we need to explain the fact that the police denounced the students, that the students were in Lincoln Park, and that the students who were in Lincoln Park were the ones who were denounced. The phrase-structure (PS) rules that show this relationship are as follows:

PS 1. S $\longrightarrow$ NP + VP
PS 2. VP $\longrightarrow$ V + NP

PS 3, given earlier, needs to be modified. An NP can also consist of a noun phrase (NP) followed by a sentence (S).

PS 3. NP $\longrightarrow$ NP + S

PS 3 corresponds to ***the students*** (***the students were in Lincoln Park***). We can show that it is an NP by applying one of the three guidelines for determining NP's developed in section B. If we apply the passive transformation, we note that all of the NP + S is interchanged with the other NP.

***The police denounced the students*** (***the students were in Lincoln Park***).

passive $\Downarrow$

***The students*** (***the students were in Lincoln Park***) were denounced by ***the police.***

The tree structure of sentence (g), resulting from the application of rules PS 1, PS 2, and PS 3 shown above, is found in TS 4 on page 172.

We have seen that sentence (d) is ambiguous. The transformational grammarians propose a model of description that claims that the sentence should be represented at an abstract level by as many structures as the sentence has ambiguous interpretations. The ambiguity found in sentences is then due to a coming together of some of these distinct abstract structures as transformations are applied to them. Let us now see how the two distinct abstract structures, sentences (h) and (g) and diagrams TS 3 and TS 4, come together in sentence (d).

First, we must distinguish between the structure of the abstract sentence generated by the phrase-structure rules and the structure of written and spoken sentences. We will call

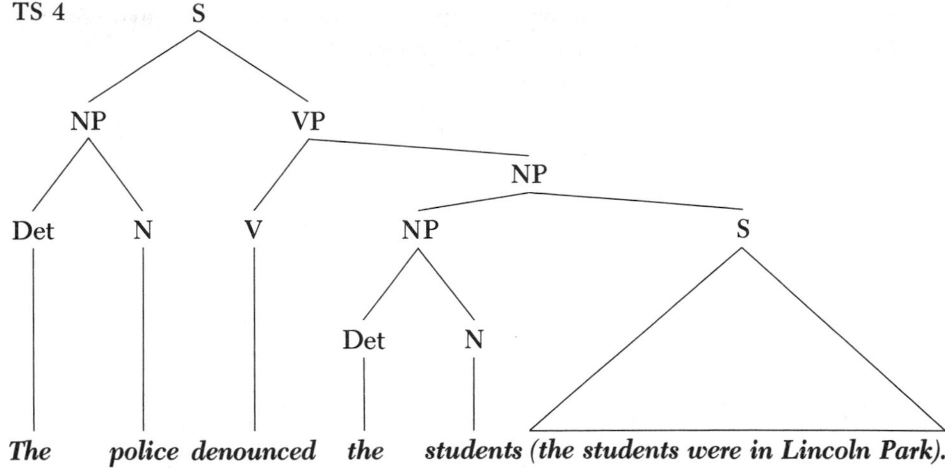


the former *deep structures* and the latter *surface structures.* More will be said about this in section G.

In sentence (g), the following changes take place from the given deep structure to the surface structure. The *relative clause transformation* changes the second identical NP, ***the students,*** to a relative pronoun, in this case ***who.***

(g) ***The police denounced the students (the students were in Lincoln Park).***

⇓ relative clause

***The police denounced the students who were in Lincoln Park.***

The result of the relative clause transformation is a sentence that occurs in English; the ***who were*** in it may be removed optionally by the *relative* ***BE*** *deletion transformation* to yield:

$\xrightarrow{\text{rel } \textbf{\textit{BE}} \text{ del}}$ ***The police denounced the students in Lincoln Park.***

This sentence is identical to (d).

Looking back at the ambiguous sentence (d), we note that its ambiguity resulted from the fact that it may be traced back to two different structures: ***in Lincoln Park*** is a reduced relative clause in (g) and an adverbial in (h). To some readers sentence (d) might not have appeared ambiguous at first. Transformational grammar forces one to recognize and account for such facts about language.

Apply the following transformations to the sentences given.

1. The students (the students were in the hall) harassed the dean.

Relative clause ______________________________

Relative ***BE*** deletion ______________________________

Passive ______________________________

Yes-no question ______________________________

2. The FBI questioned the students (the students harassed the dean).

Relative clause ______________________________

Passive ______________________________

Write the deep structure sentence and the transformations that have resulted in the following sentences.

3. ______________________________

______________ A fish was swallowed by a man.

______________ Was a fish swallowed by a man?

Draw the tree-structure diagram of the deep structure of 3.

There are at least eight interpretations of the following sentence. How many can you find?

***The seniors were told to stop demonstrating on campus.***

______________________________

______________________________

______________________________

______________________________

______________________________

______________________________

______________________________

______________________________

**D. The Adjective**

The adjective is treated as the result of a relative clause transformation. Consider the sentence:

(i) ***The police used dangerous weapons.***

with the deep structure

***The police used weapons (weapons are dangerous).***

By relative clause transformation, we obtain

***The police used weapons that are dangerous.***

By relative ***BE*** deletion transformation, we obtain

****The police used weapons dangerous.***

The *adjective transformation* changes the position of what remains of the relative clause to the front of the noun, giving us the sentence:

***The police used dangerous weapons.***

Apply the transformations listed to the following sentence.

***The soldiers brought the children (the children were hungry) to the cafeteria.***

Relative clause ____________________

Relative ***BE*** deletion ____________________

Adjective ____________________

In Bolinger's discussion of the adjective we find ****the on-the-shelf book*** and ***under-the-counter sale.*** The first arrangement is not permitted, but the second is. Why? On inspection we note that the phrase ***under-the-counter sale*** is an idiom, referring to an illegal sale, not to a sale that takes place under the counter. The contrast, then, is between the adverbial phrase ***on the shelf*** and the adjectival idiom ***under-the-counter.*** The fact that ***under-the-counter*** takes the adjective transformation emphasizes that it is an example of a fusion; that is, it is considered as one unit.

There is a second difference between the two phrases, which becomes clear when we examine the PS rules and tree diagrams of the two phrases. Other words that can be substituted for the phrases are used to clarify the difference between the two structures.

$$\text{PS 1. S} \longrightarrow \text{NP} + \text{VP}$$

$$\text{PS 2. VP} \longrightarrow \textbf{\textit{be}} + \begin{Bmatrix} \text{Adj} \\ \text{Loc} \end{Bmatrix}$$

$$\text{PS 3. NP} \longrightarrow \text{(Det)} + \text{N}$$

In PS 2, the braces are used to combine two rules into one. It means Verb Phrase (VP) consists of a form of the verb ***to be*** followed by *either* an adjective (Adj) *or* a locative (Loc) (an adverb of location).

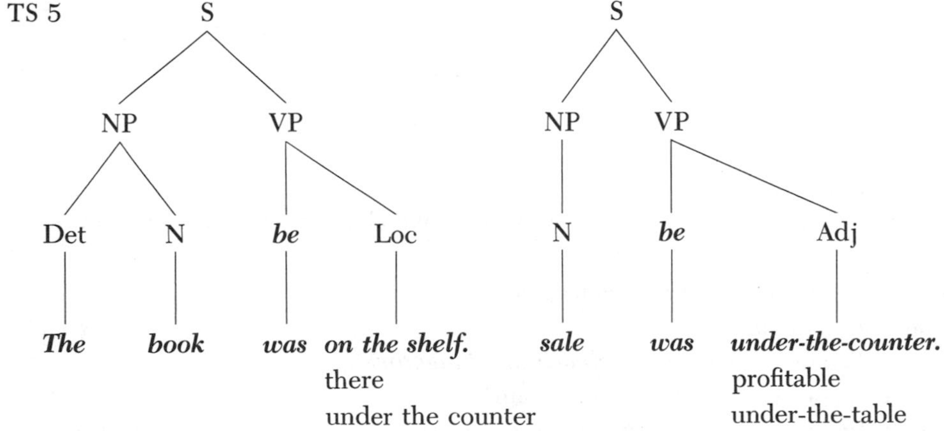


In one case we cannot use the adjective transformation since it does not apply to the Loc, an adverb—a fact that explains the starred forms ****the on the shelf book, *the there book,*** and ****the under the counter book*** (as opposed to ***the under-the-counter book***). The adjective transformation applies to the other case, forming ***under-the-counter sale, profitable sale,*** and ***under-the-table sale.***

There are numerous other examples of the latter, all having the process of fusion in common. Some others are: ***an up-and-coming young man, a tried-and-true friend, a here-is-your-hat-what-is-your-hurry hostess, an easy-come-easy-go attitude.***

Give a few more examples of phrases that accept the adjective transformation.

---

---

---

**E. More about the NP**

Let us consider another manifestation of the NP. The sentence

(j) ***It was unforgivable for the police to arrest the students***

is represented by the following derivation (application of PS rules) and tree diagram:

1. S $\longrightarrow$ NP + VP
2. VP $\longrightarrow$ ***be*** + Adj
3. NP $\longrightarrow$ N + S
4. N $\longrightarrow$ ***it***
5. S $\longrightarrow$ NP + VP
6. VP $\longrightarrow$ V + NP
7. NP $\longrightarrow$ Det + N

TS 6

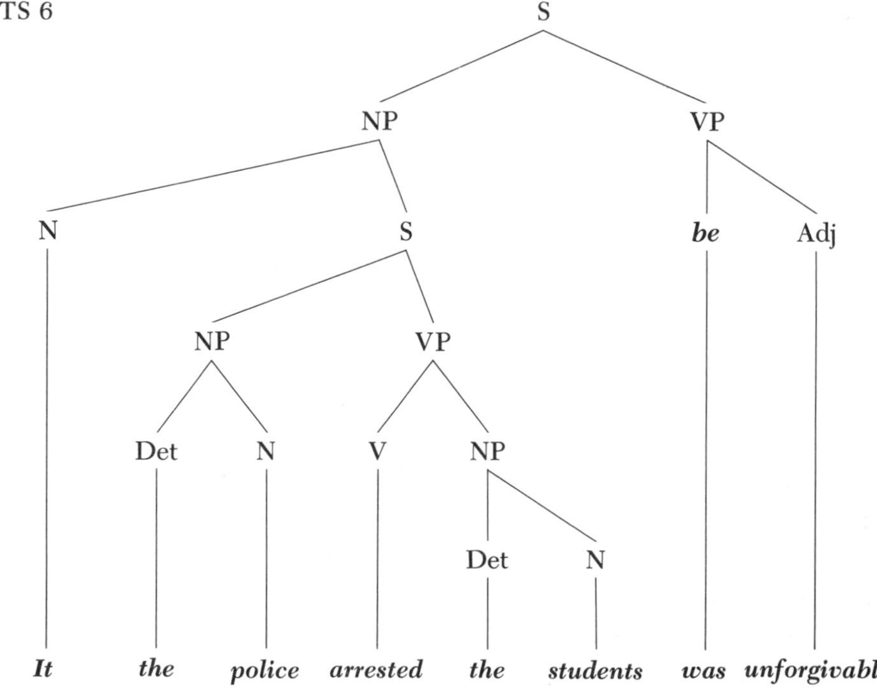

Here we find that the NP consists of an N followed by an S. We say that the S is embedded in the NP. How is the sentence represented by the tree structure related to the sentence ***It was unforgivable for the police to arrest the students***? Note the position of ***for . . . to.*** ***For*** and ***to*** surround the NP of the sentence embedded in the NP. Applying this *infinitive complementizer transformation* to the result of the tree structure diagram, we obtain

****It for the police to arrest the students was unforgivable.***

A quick inspection of the phrase-structure tree will reveal that (***for***) ***the police*** (***to***) ***arrest the students*** has been moved around ***was unforgivable*** to yield sentence (j). The moving of the S around the VP is called the *extraposition transformation.*

In the space below, draw the diagram and list the transformations applied to the sentence given to arrive at ***It was unusual for Bill to please John.*** Start with ****It*** (***Bill pleased John***) ***was unusual.***

In summary, we have seen four types of NP:

| | | |
|---|---|---|
| 1. NP $\longrightarrow$ N | | (Columbus . . .) |
| 2. NP $\longrightarrow$ Det + N | | (The mouse . . .) |
| 3. NP $\longrightarrow$ NP + S | | (The man, the man is in his office) |
| 4. NP $\longrightarrow$ N + S | | (It, the man is in his office) |

(Some other determiners (*Det*) are: ***my, no, some, any.***)

All four rules may be condensed into one rule; we will call it PS 3.

$$\text{PS 3. NP} \longrightarrow \begin{Bmatrix} \text{(Det)} + \text{N} + \text{(S)} \\ \text{NP} + \text{S} \end{Bmatrix}$$

PS 3 generates Det + N + S as well. This new structure occurs in English and corresponds to NP's such as

***The fact that the war continues is disheartening.*** ***The fact*** is Det + N and ***the war continues*** is S. Had we not included the Det + N + S possibility, the rule would have been longer. Try writing the four rules above without allowing the Det + N + S possibility. Here is another case, similar to the situation with the distinctive features in Chapter 3, in which greater generalizations require simpler rules.

**F. More about the Verb Phrase**

So far we have considered the VP's of the form:

1. ***died,*** as in ***Columbus died*** (VP ⟶ V)
2. ***discovered America,*** as in ***Columbus discovered America*** (VP ⟶ V + NP)
3. ***was easy,*** as in ***It was easy*** (VP ⟶ ***be*** + Adj)
4. ***was there,*** as in ***He was there*** (VP ⟶ ***be*** + Loc)

Consider the sentence

(k) ***Walter is the chairman.***

The VP consists of ***be*** and NP.

5. VP ⟶ ***be*** + NP

It has the following tree diagram:

TS 7

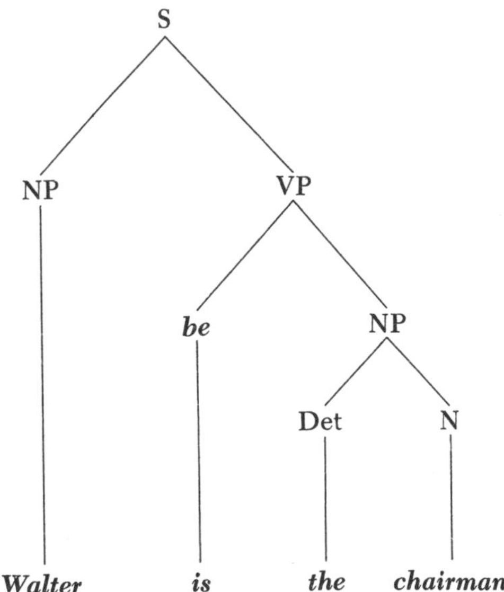


Give another example of each of the five VP types presented so far.

1. ______________________________

2. ______________________________

3. ______________________________

4. ______________________________

5. ______________________________

Rules 1–5 may be abbreviated as follows:

$$\text{PS 2. VP} \longrightarrow \begin{Bmatrix} \textit{be} + \begin{Bmatrix} \text{Adj} \\ \text{NP} \\ \text{Loc} \end{Bmatrix} \\ \\ \text{V} \quad (\text{NP}) \end{Bmatrix}$$

The structure of the VP is very complex. There is some controversy over the representation of the VP in a sentence such as ***They elected him president.*** We have not accounted for this nor for sentences such as ***John appeared nervous, John chose to leave,*** and ***John hates himself.*** Current grammatical research will hopefully shed light on these complexities.

**G. The Function of Transformations**

The transformational grammarian has as his goal not only the description of structures in language, but also the explanation of relations among structures that are known to the speakers of the language. The relations are shown by means of transformations, which are statements of relations between structures. Transformations apply to deep structures or to structures that have already undergone transformations.[22] The transformations we have examined show four qualities: change in order; deletion; addition; and substitution. An example of *change in order* is the extraposition transformation. It changed the order in ****It for the police to arrest the students was unforgivable*** to ***It was unforgivable for the police to arrest the students.*** An example of *deletion* is the relative ***BE*** deletion transformation, which changes ***the students who were in the hall*** to ***the students in the hall.*** An example of *addition* is the infinitive complementizer transformation, in which ***for . . . to*** is added around the NP of the embedded sentence. In our earlier example, it showed the relation of ****It the police arrested the students was unforgivable*** to ****It for the police to arrest the students was unforgivable.*** An example of *substitution* is the relative clause transformation. In our example, ***The police denounced the students (the students were in Lincoln Park), who*** was substituted for ***the students*** as in ***The police denounced the students who were in Lincoln Park.***

Glancing at sections C and D, where we have examples of more than one transformation applying to a string, we note that the transformations need to be ordered. Some transformations apply to strings that are generated as a result of another transformation. We further note that some transformations are *obligatory* (transposition, transformation) and some are *optional* (relative ***BE*** deletion).

[22]For full treatment of deep and surface structures, see Paul Postal, "Underlying and Superficial Linguistic Structure," in *Harvard Educational Review*, Vol. 34, No. 2 (1964), pp. 246–66. Note especially pages 249–58. We consider this article to be one of the finest examples of TGG methodology.

Transformations change sentences without changing their meaning. Question, negation, and the like are found in the deep structure. The transformations discussed in this unit are listed below. Briefly describe what each does.

Passive ______________________________

______________________________

Yes-no question ______________________________

______________________________

Cleft ______________________________

______________________________

Relative clause ______________________________

______________________________

Relative ***BE*** deletion ______________________________

______________________________

Adjective ______________________________

______________________________

Infinitive complementizer ______________________________

______________________________

Extraposition ______________________________

______________________________

# 12

# Meaning

## EXERCISE 1: Semantic Distinctive Features

The business of distinguishing one word from another is made much easier by dividing the meanings of words into elements, much as a chemist lists the elements present in his chemical compounds. These elements are called *semantic distinctive features.* To see how this works, look at the grid below. A plus sign for a particular word at a particular feature means that that feature is present in the word's meaning, and a minus means that that feature is not present. For example, the grid defines ***piano*** as 'a keyboard instrument that produces sound when its strings are hit.' The chart makes clear that the harpsichord differs from the piano in that its strings are plucked, not hit.

**Figure 12-1** Musical Instruments

| | String | Percussion | Plucked | Keyboard | | |
|---|---|---|---|---|---|---|
| 1. piano | + | + | − | + | | |
| 2. harpsichord | + | − | + | + | | |
| 3. ______ | | | | | | |
| 4. ______ | | | | | | |
| 5. ______ | | | | | | |

How could the harp be fit in here so that it would be neatly distinguished from the piano and the harpsichord? Enter ***harp*** on line 3 and fill in the grid. Note that the features already present can do the job of defining the harp. Now put ***harmonium*** on line 4. You will need a new feature, for the harmonium is a reed instrument. Fill in the new feature and the plus and minus symbols in the grid. Note that when a new feature is added, the previous words, as well as the new word, have to be marked plus or minus for that feature. Now put the word ***accordion*** on line 5, and fill in the grid. The harmonium and the accordion are not distinguished on the grid; there are not enough features. Both instruments, being reed instruments, are operated by blowing air past the reeds. They could be differentiated by the type of power driving the bellows; the harmonium is a foot-bellows instrument, and the accordion is a hand-bellows instrument. Fill in the grid so that these words are differentiated by these two features.

In Figure 12–2 fill in the names of musical instruments that fit the feature descriptions, or invent new instruments.

**Figure 12–2** Stringed Instruments

| | Percussion | Plucked | Keyboard |
|---|---|---|---|
| None such exists. Perhaps a combination piano and harpsichord, with a foot pedal giving the player his choice, or two keyboards. | + | + | + |
| | + | + | − |
| | + | − | + |
| | + | − | − |
| | − | + | + |
| | − | + | − |
| | − | − | + |
| | − | − | − |

Below is a list of eight wind instruments with an incomplete grid. Your task is to find the features that will discriminate them, with the aid of the instructions that follow the grid.

First separate the trombone from the other instruments by making a feature out of its unique method of control. Then separate the bassoon and oboe from the rest on the basis of the method of sound production. Do this by entering a second feature in the grid and filling in the plus and minus symbols. Now separate the trumpet, French horn, and tuba from the rest by concentrating on how these three are controlled or on how the other instruments (except the trombone) are controlled. Make a feature of the difference, and fill in the

**Figure 12-3** Wind Instruments

| | | | | Range |
|---|---|---|---|---|
| 1. trumpet | | | | |
| 2. French horn | | | | |
| 3. tuba | | | | |
| 4. flute | | | | *low* |
| 5. piccolo | | | | *high* |
| 6. bassoon | | | | |
| 7. oboe | | | | |
| 8. trombone | | | | |

grid. Note that you now have four groups: instruments 1, 2, 3; 4, 5; 6, 7; and 8. Each instrument in the first three groups is distinguished from the others in its group by musical range; for example, the piccolo is a higher-pitched instrument than the flute. Use the words ***high, middle,*** and ***low*** in the fourth column to discriminate among the instruments of the first and third groups. The second group has been done for you.

It is interesting that we are able to distinguish the three brasses from the two woodwinds without mentioning this traditional method of classification. This is partly because we are working with only eight instruments, and it is easy to distinguish them with few features. The purpose of the grid is to discriminate the words in a group, not to give each word in the group its full meaning. The most important meaning of each of these words might be considered the quality of sound of each of the instruments. This is impossible to define in an ordinary dictionary or in a grid of this sort. Another important kind of meaning for these words, or for any words, is the way they are used by speakers to build sentences. This also is ignored in semantic grids.

Grid-makers are sometimes foolish. A story is told that some early Greek sophists were wondering how 'featherless biped' would work as a definition of ***human being*** until a cynic threw a live plucked chicken into their midst.

## EXERCISE 2: Antonyms

Grids sometimes give unexpected results. For example, examine the simplified grid below, in which ***man*** and ***woman*** are antonyms.

**Figure 12-4**

| | Adult human being | Male | |
|---|---|---|---|
| 1. man | + | + | |
| 2. woman | + | − | |

As it stands here, the grid defines ***woman*** as 'an adult human being without maleness,' but it says nothing, for instance, about the fact that a woman has female reproductive organs and not simply an absence of male reproductive organs. We could define '− male' as '+ female,' but this would be an ad hoc definition. It would not simplify the grids of such groups as ***child, pup, kitten,*** and ***fawn.*** To avoid the ad hoc definition, one must make ***female*** a feature here, as well as ***male.*** Please do so above, and fill in the grid. What does the grid say now about ***woman?*** ____________________

____________________

Now compare Figure 12–5 to Figure 12–4.

**Figure 12-5**

| | Male human being | Adult | Pre-pubescent |
|---|---|---|---|
| 1. man | + | + | − |
| 2. boy | + | − | + |
| 3. ________ | | | |

Figure 12–5 looks like the completed Figure 12–4. Yet ***man*** and ***boy*** are not antonyms in the same way as ***man*** and ***woman.*** If an adult human being is not biologically a man, then she must necessarily be a woman. The third possibility is rare. ***Man*** and ***woman*** form a pair that covers the field. ***Man*** and ***boy*** have meanings in opposition, like the first pair, but do not cover all the possibilities. The words ***man*** and ***boy,*** with the meanings assigned to them by the grid above, have ranges that are neatly complementary with ***youth*** in its not uncommon meaning of 'pubescent male.' Complete the grid above, and note how the three words form an antonymous group (given the choice of possible meanings assigned to them in this exercise).

There is a pair of words that are fully antonymous and express something of the idea of ***man*** and ***boy,*** though with more precision: ***adult*** and ***minor,*** as used in a legal context. Construct a grid for these words.

**Figure 12-6**

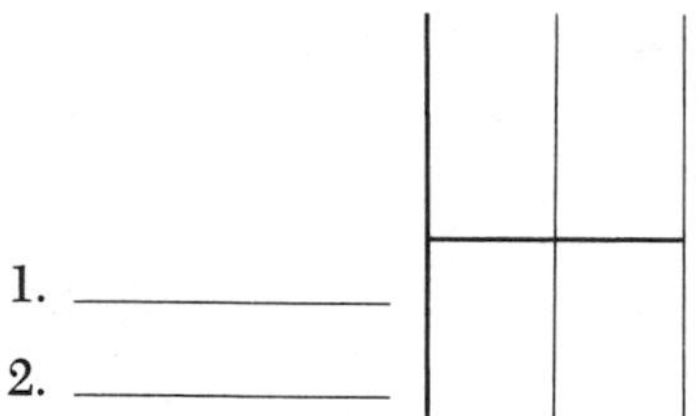

Notice that ***man, boy,*** and ***youth*** together form a relatively well-defined group: a male human being must be either man, boy, or adolescent, as we have defined the terms here.

There are many such groups, and some are of indefinite size. One group that is limited but difficult to enumerate is the words for young mammals: ***child, pup, kitten, fawn,*** and so on. Construct a grid for these four.

**Figure 12–7**

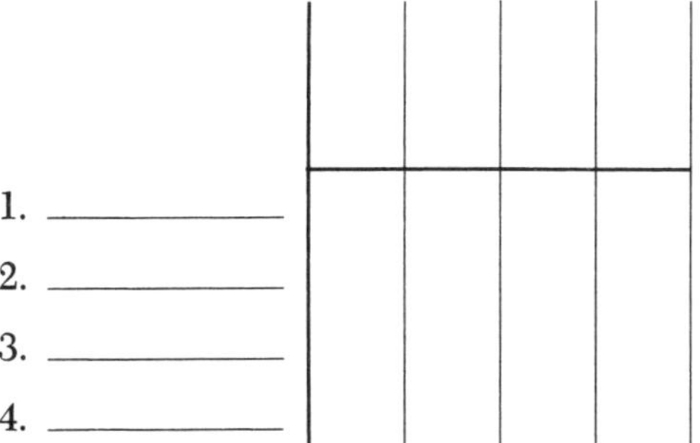

Many words that are usually considered antonyms are not complete antonyms. For example, ***decry*** and ***praise*** come close, but ***decry*** has an element of appeal to public opinion that is not necessarily present in ***praise.*** Fill in the chart below for ***decry, praise,*** and ***extol,*** after looking the words up in a good desk-size dictionary, such as the *Standard College Dictionary* or *Webster's Seventh New Collegiate Dictionary.*[1] (Not all desk dictionaries mention the element of appeal to public opinion in ***decry.*** Dictionaries do not usually give all the important elements of words.)

In order to fill in this grid, you will need a new symbol, ±, which signifies that for the relevant word the feature thus marked can be either present or absent.

**Figure 12–8**

| | To present strong polarized opinion about | | | Public statement |
|---|---|---|---|---|
| decry | | | | |
| praise | | | | |
| extol | | | | |

***Wet*** and ***dry*** might be considered complete antonyms until one thinks of a word such as ***moist*** or ***damp.*** A noise can be ***loud, soft,*** or ***moderate,*** and even with these three words the field is not covered. There are many such pairs of words in English. Write some of them below, and add the third word or phrase that, like ***moist,*** breaks the antonymy.

1. *wet–dry* ________ *moist* ________
2. ________ ________

[1] *Standard College Dictionary* (New York: Harcourt, Brace & World, 1966). *Webster's Seventh New Collegiate Dictionary* (Chicago: G. and C. Merriam Company, 1963).

3. ______________________ ______________________

4. ______________________ ______________________

Construct grids for the following pairs of words that will show in what ways they are antonyms and what extra features they might have that make them incomplete antonyms, like ***decry*** and ***praise.***

sophisticated–immature  weak–courageous
imminent–distant  ignorant–smart

Notice how much more difficult these words are to control than are words for manmade objects, such as musical instruments.

## EXERCISE 3: Synonyms

Synonyms are words that have their most important features in common. ***Puppy, child,*** and ***kitten*** are not synonyms, because they do not have in common the feature that tells the species of each, though they have 'young mammal' in common. But ***urchin*** and ***brat*** are synonyms. They have their most important feature in common.

**Figure 12-9**

| | Human child | Ragged | Ill-behaved |
|---|---|---|---|
| urchin | + | + | ± |
| brat | + | ± | + |

Fill out the grid for the words ***callow*** and ***immature.***

**Figure 12-10**

| | Not mature | |
|---|---|---|
| callow | + | + |
| immature | + | ± |

Can you say with assurance that these words are synonyms? Not synonyms? They might be in one circumstance, and not in another.

The following grid has four verbs that are not close synonyms, but still can be studied together. Most words have several meanings. The words used here are to be considered as used in a sentence such as ***John exiled Jim.*** This will limit us to one or a group of closely related meanings for each word.

**Figure 12-11**

| | Official | Membership or personal relationship lost | Wish or hope that the object will change | | | |
|---|---|---|---|---|---|---|
| 1. excommunicate | + | + | + | | | |
| 2. exile | + | + | ± | | | |
| 3. reprimand | + | ± | + | | | |
| 4. censure | + | ± | ± | | | |
| 5. ____________ | | | | | | |
| 6. ____________ | | | | | | |
| 7. ____________ | | | | | | |
| 8. ____________ | | | | | | |
| 9. ____________ | | | | | | |
| 10. ____________ | | | | | | |

Notice that the three features, with three possible values on each one, are capable of discriminating a fairly large number of words—twenty-seven, to be exact. Enter the following words in the grid, and give the values of the three features for each word: ***dun, condemn, admonish, dislike, reproach, blame.*** You will need to make extensive use of a dictionary to do this.

What word is ***reproach*** similar to? ____________ You will need another feature to distinguish ***reproach*** from ***admonish.*** To find out what this is, look in a dictionary for a synonym list with these words in it. Words considered to be synonyms are often carefully discriminated from one another in a list of synonyms that follows the entry of one of the words in the synonymy. The *Standard College Dictionary* discusses the noun forms of ***reproach*** and ***admonish*** after the entry for ***reproof***: "***Reproach*** expresses personal hurt or displeasure, as at thoughtlessness or selfishness. ***Admonition*** is warning or counsel, looking to future conduct rather than to past misdeeds." *Webster's Seventh New Collegiate Dictionary* says this: "***Admonish*** suggests earnest or friendly warning and counsel; ***Reproach*** and ***chide*** suggest displeasure or disappointment expressed in mild reproof or scolding." What feature do both dictionaries attribute to ***reproach*** that they do not attribute to ***admonish?*** ______________________________

______________________________

Write this new feature at the top of the fourth column, and fill in the +, −, or ± for each word.

The grid says little about the meanings of ***dislike*** and ***blame*** except that they belong with a group of words expressing disapproval. What feature can you find that will distinguish these two words? ______________________________
Enter that feature in the fifth column, and fill in the grid.

These five features adequately discriminate these words, but by no means do they give an adequate difinition of the words. As an example, consider the feature 'superiority.' It is not needed to distinguish between any two of these words, but it is an essential feature of ***excommunicate, exile, reprimand, censure,*** and ***dun,*** and a possible but not necessary feature of the others.

Besides being inadequate as a description of the full meanings of these words, the semantic grid does not give other kinds of information necessary to a user of the language in building sentences with these words. For example, some of the ten words can occur with a following infinitive (although none require it): ***The judge condemned him to die.*** A native speaker of English would not use a following infinitive with ***reproach*** in a parallel structure: ****John reproached him to leave.*** In the sixth column in Figure 12–11, give a ± to each word that occurs with or without a following infinitive in a sentence parallel in structure to that above. Give a minus to each word that cannot occur with a following infinitive.

## EXERCISE 4: Selection Information

An ordinary dictionary gives at least three kinds of information in describing a word; it gives pronunciation, grammatical classification, and meanings. For example, the *Standard College Dictionary* entry for ***extensile*** is "(ik·sten′sil) *adj.* 1. Capable of being extended, as the tongue. 2. Extensible." The second part, the grammatical classification, is devoted to helping a user of the language build sentences. The sixth column in Figure 12–11 gives such information.

The third part of an entry in a dictionary of the future, the meaning, might give semantic features. It might also give means of determining what kinds of words the word being defined can occur with. This would help explain how English speakers use the word in building sentences. For example, the verb ***gallop*** has as its core meaning a certain gait of a quadruped. The selection information in a dictionary of the future would specify that this word cannot be used unless there is some reference in the sentence to a quadruped capable of this gait. The sentence ****The boy galloped up the drive,*** in a context that makes it clear that he has no horse, is deviant although possibly quite effective. Its deviance and possible effectiveness depend upon the speaker's not following the selection information of ***gallop.*** The selection information would look like this: <+ quadruped>. It would follow the other parts of the dictionary entry. A phrase that lacked a word with a meaning including this semantic feature could not include the word ***gallop.*** A dictionary could thus tell us in what way the sentence above is deviant.[2]

Consider the sentence ****The dog laid an egg.*** This is clearly deviant. For the meaning of ***lay*** as it pertains to birds, the selection information is < + bird or + lizard, or . . . >. ***Lay*** with this meaning must occur in a phrase in which some other word has one or another of these features present. The sentence ****The dog laid an egg*** would not follow the selection information of its verb. Using an encyclopedia if you need to, work out the selection information of the verbs listed below enough to avoid any nonsensical sentences with animal names as subjects. You can check your correctness by making a sentence for each of the verbs with ***turtle, dog, robin, lizard, mayfly,*** and ***bass.*** If your selection restrictors keep you from making nonsense sentences, then they are correct.

engender ____________________ suckle ____________________

brood ____________________ gestate ____________________

lay ____________________ spawn ____________________

Write out the selection restrictors for the following words that will keep them from combining with the wrong kind of living creatures. For simplicity's sake, think of the *habitual* action characteristic of a particular kind of creature.

move ____________________ crawl ____________________

rack ____________________ slither ____________________

hike ____________________ fly ____________________

The selection information indicates which meaning of a word can be properly used in a particular sentence, as well as which words can be properly used. For example, the noun ***needle*** has several different meanings. The selection information automatically assigns the meaning that is relevant to each particular use of the word.

| | | |
|---|---|---|
| ***needle*** (noun) | 1. 'hypodermic syringe' | <+ medicine> |
| | 2. 'a steel instrument with an eye at one end used in sewing' | <+sewing> |
| | 3. 'a narrow pointed crystal' | <+ crystallography> |

[2]For some of the ideas of this exercise, see Jerrold J. Katz, *The Philosophy of Language* (New York: Harper & Row, 1966), Chapters 4 and 5.

When the word ***needle*** is used in a sentence, the presence of one of these three semantic features attached to one of the words in the sentence or in the immediate context will automatically assign the relevant meaning to ***needle.*** The sentence ***That is a nice tourmaline needle*** automatically assigns meaning 3, 'a narrow pointed crystal,' to ***needle*** because the semantic features of ***tourmaline*** include 'crystal.'

With the aid of your dictionary, write out three other meanings with selection information for ***needle*** (noun).

4. ______________________________

______________________________

5. ______________________________

______________________________

6. ______________________________

______________________________

Do the same for two or three meanings of each of the following words.

flat (adjective) 1. ______________________________

2. ______________________________

3. ______________________________

negative (noun) 1. ______________________________

2. ______________________________

3. ______________________________

referee 1. ______________________________

2. ______________________________

# 13

## Mind in the Grip of Language

### EXERCISE 1: More Meanings of Musical Instruments

In the last chapter, we discussed the possibility that a meaning of a word can be described with semantic features. The features were chosen by analysis: you inferred the existence of a feature by the existence of a difference in meaning between two words. The difference between ***harpsichord*** and ***harp*** led you to the feature 'keyboard.'

Besides this analytical meaning, other kinds of meaning are important. The meaning of ***lion*** is not simply the list of objective characteristics a zoologist would come up with. We must include subjective associations such as 'king of beasts' and 'Tarzan's enemy.' The meaning of ***flute*** includes our reactions to its tonal qualities, and our memories of flute music we have heard and flute players we have known. Often the majority of people in a community agree on a group of associations that cluster around a concept. Such is the case with many of the associations around ***lion.***

The semantic-feature chart can be extended to present such information. This exercise shows how it might be done.[1] The immediate subject of the exercise is the various clusters of associations that inhere in the words for some musical instruments.

On each section of the chart below you will find the name of a musical instrument followed by a number of scales. The first musical instrument is the bagpipe. The authors rated this instrument themselves. The first instrument you will rate is the harp. If you feel that ***harp*** is "very closely related" to a word at one end of the scale, place a check mark on the line next to that word.

good _X_ : ____ : ____ : ____ : ____ : ____ : ____ bad

or

good ____ : ____ : ____ : ____ : ____ : ____ : _X_ bad

If it is "quite closely related," place a check on the line one step farther in.

good ____ : _X_ : ____ : ____ : ____ : ____ : ____ bad

or

good ____ : ____ : ____ : ____ : ____ : _X_ : ____ bad

[1] This exercise is based on the work of Charles Osgood, George Suci, and Percy Tannenbaum in *The Measurement of Meaning* (Urbana, Ill.: University of Illinois Press, 1957).

If it is "only slightly related," place the mark like this:

good ____ : ____ : __X__ : ____ : ____ : ____ : ____ bad

or

good ____ : ____ : ____ : ____ : __X__ : ____ : ____ bad

If you associate the instruments with each word equally, or if you have no associations, check the center space. Please do not omit any decisions. Your word associations are important, not your sense of logic. Fill in the charts before you go on to read the instructions telling you how to handle the data.

1. Bagpipe

| | | | | | | | | | |
|---|---|---|---|---|---|---|---|---|---|
| a. | good | | | X | | | | | bad |
| b. | hard | | X | | | | | | soft |
| c. | passive | | | | | | | X | active |
| d. | stable | | | | X | | | | changeable |
| e. | defensive | X | | | | | | | aggressive |
| f. | optimistic | | X | | | | | | pessimistic |
| g. | calm | | | | | | | X | excitable |
| h. | colorful | X | | | | | | | colorless |
| i. | negative | | | | | | | X | positive |
| j. | masculine | | X | | | | | | feminine |
| k. | cold | | | | | | X | | hot |
| m. | sane | | | | X | | | | insane |
| n. | competitive | | | | | | | X | cooperative |
| p. | insensitive | | | | | | X | | sensitive |
| q. | severe | | | | | X | | | lenient |
| r. | rash | | | | X | | | | prudent |
| s. | humble | | X | | | | | | proud |
| t. | interesting | | | X | | | | | boring |

2. Harp

| | | | | | | | | | |
|---|---|---|---|---|---|---|---|---|---|
| a. | good | | | | | | | | bad |
| b. | hard | | | | | | | | soft |
| c. | passive | | | | | | | | active |
| d. | stable | | | | | | | | changeable |
| e. | defensive | | | | | | | | aggressive |
| f. | optimistic | | | | | | | | pessimistic |
| g. | calm | | | | | | | | excitable |
| h. | colorful | | | | | | | | colorless |

i. negative ____:____:____:____:____:____:____ positive
j. masculine ____:____:____:____:____:____:____ feminine
k. cold ____:____:____:____:____:____:____ hot
m. sane ____:____:____:____:____:____:____ insane
n. competitive ____:____:____:____:____:____:____ cooperative
p. insensitive ____:____:____:____:____:____:____ sensitive
q. severe ____:____:____:____:____:____:____ lenient
r. rash ____:____:____:____:____:____:____ prudent
s. humble ____:____:____:____:____:____:____ proud
t. interesting ____:____:____:____:____:____:____ boring

3. Banjo

a. good ____:____:____:____:____:____:____ bad
b. hard ____:____:____:____:____:____:____ soft
c. passive ____:____:____:____:____:____:____ active
d. stable ____:____:____:____:____:____:____ changeable
e. defensive ____:____:____:____:____:____:____ aggressive
f. optimistic ____:____:____:____:____:____:____ pessimistic
g. calm ____:____:____:____:____:____:____ excitable
h. colorful ____:____:____:____:____:____:____ colorless
i. negative ____:____:____:____:____:____:____ positive
j. masculine ____:____:____:____:____:____:____ feminine
k. cold ____:____:____:____:____:____:____ hot
m. sane ____:____:____:____:____:____:____ insane
n. competitive ____:____:____:____:____:____:____ cooperative
p. insensitive ____:____:____:____:____:____:____ sensitive
q. severe ____:____:____:____:____:____:____ lenient
r. rash ____:____:____:____:____:____:____ prudent
s. humble ____:____:____:____:____:____:____ proud
t. interesting ____:____:____:____:____:____:____ boring

4. Guitar

a. good ____:____:____:____:____:____:____ bad
b. hard ____:____:____:____:____:____:____ soft
c. passive ____:____:____:____:____:____:____ active
d. stable ____:____:____:____:____:____:____ changeable
e. defensive ____:____:____:____:____:____:____ aggressive
f. optimistic ____:____:____:____:____:____:____ pessimistic

g. calm ___:___:___:___:___:___:___ excitable
h. colorful ___:___:___:___:___:___:___ colorless
i. negative ___:___:___:___:___:___:___ positive
j. masculine ___:___:___:___:___:___:___ feminine
k. cold ___:___:___:___:___:___:___ hot
m. sane ___:___:___:___:___:___:___ insane
n. competitive ___:___:___:___:___:___:___ cooperative
p. insensitive ___:___:___:___:___:___:___ sensitive
q. severe ___:___:___:___:___:___:___ lenient
r. rash ___:___:___:___:___:___:___ prudent
s. humble ___:___:___:___:___:___:___ proud
t. interesting ___:___:___:___:___:___:___ boring

5. Violin

a. good ___:___:___:___:___:___:___ bad
b. hard ___:___:___:___:___:___:___ soft
c. passive ___:___:___:___:___:___:___ active
d. stable ___:___:___:___:___:___:___ changeable
e. defensive ___:___:___:___:___:___:___ aggressive
f. optimistic ___:___:___:___:___:___:___ pessimistic
g. calm ___:___:___:___:___:___:___ excitable
h. colorful ___:___:___:___:___:___:___ colorless
i. negative ___:___:___:___:___:___:___ positive
j. masculine ___:___:___:___:___:___:___ feminine
k. cold ___:___:___:___:___:___:___ hot
m. sane ___:___:___:___:___:___:___ insane
n. competitive ___:___:___:___:___:___:___ cooperative
p. insensitive ___:___:___:___:___:___:___ sensitive
q. severe ___:___:___:___:___:___:___ lenient
r. rash ___:___:___:___:___:___:___ prudent
s. humble ___:___:___:___:___:___:___ proud
t. interesting ___:___:___:___:___:___:___ boring

6. Piano

a. good ___:___:___:___:___:___:___ bad
b. hard ___:___:___:___:___:___:___ soft
c. passive ___:___:___:___:___:___:___ active
d. stable ___:___:___:___:___:___:___ changeable

e. defensive ____:____:____:____:____:____:____ aggressive
f. optimistic ____:____:____:____:____:____:____ pessimistic
g. calm ____:____:____:____:____:____:____ excitable
h. colorful ____:____:____:____:____:____:____ colorless
i. negative ____:____:____:____:____:____:____ positive
j. masculine ____:____:____:____:____:____:____ feminine
k. cold ____:____:____:____:____:____:____ hot
m. sane ____:____:____:____:____:____:____ insane
n. competitive ____:____:____:____:____:____:____ cooperative
p. insensitive ____:____:____:____:____:____:____ sensitive
q. severe ____:____:____:____:____:____:____ lenient
r. rash ____:____:____:____:____:____:____ prudent
s. humble ____:____:____:____:____:____:____ proud
t. interesting ____:____:____:____:____:____:____ boring

7. Harpsichord

a. good ____:____:____:____:____:____:____ bad
b. hard ____:____:____:____:____:____:____ soft
c. passive ____:____:____:____:____:____:____ active
d. stable ____:____:____:____:____:____:____ changeable
e. defensive ____:____:____:____:____:____:____ aggressive
f. optimistic ____:____:____:____:____:____:____ pessimistic
g. calm ____:____:____:____:____:____:____ excitable
h. colorful ____:____:____:____:____:____:____ colorless
i. negative ____:____:____:____:____:____:____ positive
j. masculine ____:____:____:____:____:____:____ feminine
k. cold ____:____:____:____:____:____:____ hot
m. sane ____:____:____:____:____:____:____ insane
n. competitive ____:____:____:____:____:____:____ cooperative
p. insensitive ____:____:____:____:____:____:____ sensitive
q. severe ____:____:____:____:____:____:____ lenient
r. rash ____:____:____:____:____:____:____ prudent
s. humble ____:____:____:____:____:____:____ proud
t. interesting ____:____:____:____:____:____:____ boring

Osgood, Suci, and Tannenbaum, the authors of *The Measurement of Meaning*, have worked extensively with the pairs of words in this exercise and have found that college undergraduates tend to group some of the pairs together as if they had much the same associations. Such a group is ***good-bad, optimistic-pessimistic,*** and ***positive-negative.*** The students rated a concept such as 'foreigner' about the same on each of these three pairs. The investigators studied many pairs and tried to discover how the students grouped them. On the basis of this information, the eighteen pairs of this exercise appear to fall into six groups with three pairs each. The names for the groups are strictly intuitive.

I. Evaluation

a. ***good-bad;*** f. ***optimistic-pessimistic;*** i. ***positive-negative***

II. Potency

b. ***hard-soft;*** j. ***masculine-feminine;*** q. ***severe-lenient***

III. Activity

c. ***active-passive;*** g. ***excitable-calm***; k. ***hot-cold***

IV. Collectedness

d. ***stable-changeable;*** m. ***sane-insane;*** r. ***prudent-rash***

V. Tautness

e. ***aggressive-defensive;*** n. ***competitive-cooperative;*** s. ***proud-humble***

VI. Receptivity

h. ***colorful-colorless;*** p. ***sensitive-insensitive;*** t. ***interesting-boring***

We will investigate how you rate each musical instrument according to each group. In order to do this, you will need to make some computations.

I. Evaluation

Fill out the chart below for the three pairs of the first group: a. ***good-bad;*** f. ***optimistic-pessimistic;*** i. ***positive-negative.*** You can do this by assigning numbers to the spaces on each scale:

good $\underline{+3}$ : $\underline{+2}$ : $\underline{+1}$ : $\underline{0}$ : $\underline{-1}$ : $\underline{-2}$ : $\underline{-3}$ bad

Instrument 1, the bagpipe, is filled in as a model. Notice that on the large chart you have already filled in, i is given as ***negative-positive.*** The order was reversed on that chart to keep the more dynamic or positive word from consistently being associated with the plus (+3, +2 . . .) side of the chart. For this reason, many of the pairs are reversed. Consequently, you must reverse the score of such pairs as ***negative-positive.*** If it was +3 it will become a −3. The pairs of words to be reversed are marked on the charts below for you.

| Pairs | 1 | 2 | 3 | 4 | 5 | 6 | 7 |
|---|---|---|---|---|---|---|---|
| a | +1 | | | | | | |
| f | +2 | | | | | | |
| Reverse i | +3 | | | | | | |
| Sums of the columns | +6 | | | | | | |

**Figure 13-1**

Now add up the scores in each column. Addition of plus and minus scores is just like moving on a ruler. To add +3, −2, and −2, start on the ruler at zero. Then move three places to the *right* for *plus* 3. Add *minus* 2: move two places to the *left*. You are now at +1. Add *minus* 2 again: move two more places to the *left*. The final sum of +3, −2, and −2 is −1.

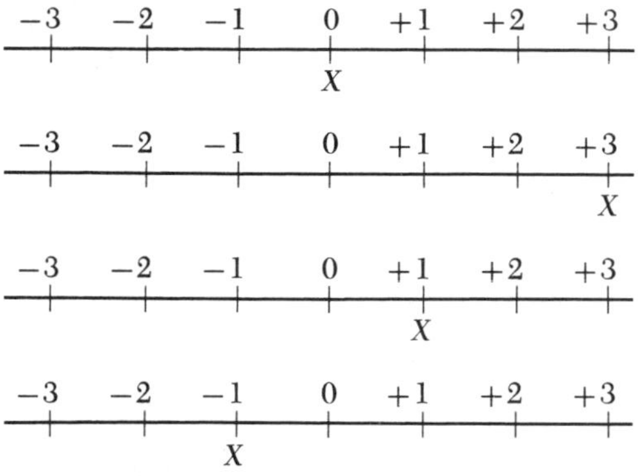

−3 −2 −1 0 +1 +2 +3
X (at 0)

−3 −2 −1 0 +1 +2 +3
X (at +3)

−3 −2 −1 0 +1 +2 +3
X (at +1)

−3 −2 −1 0 +1 +2 +3
X (at −1)

**Figure 13-2**

II. Potency

Fill in this chart the same way you filled in the last one. The relevant pairs are b, j, and q. None are reversed.

Instruments

| Pairs | 1 | 2 | 3 | 4 | 5 | 6 | 7 |
|---|---|---|---|---|---|---|---|
| b | +2 | | | | | | |
| j | +2 | | | | | | |
| q | −1 | | | | | | |
| Sums | +3 | | | | | | |

**Figure 13-3**

III. Activity

Pairs: c, g, and k. Reverse the scores of all three. It might be easier for you to add them all first and then reverse the sums.

Instruments

| Pairs | 1 | 2 | 3 | 4 | 5 | 6 | 7 |
|---|---|---|---|---|---|---|---|
| c | −3 | | | | | | |
| g | −3 | | | | | | |
| k | −2 | | | | | | |
| Reverse sums | +8 | | | | | | |

**Figure 13-4**

IV. Collectedness

Pairs: d, m, and r. Reverse the scores of r.

Instruments

| Pairs | 1 | 2 | 3 | 4 | 5 | 6 | 7 |
|---|---|---|---|---|---|---|---|
| d | 0 | | | | | | |
| m | 0 | | | | | | |
| Reverse r | 0 | | | | | | |
| Sums | 0 | | | | | | |

**Figure 13-5**

V. Tautness

Pairs: e, m, and s. Reverse the scores of e and s.

Instruments

| Pairs | 1 | 2 | 3 | 4 | 5 | 6 | 7 |
|---|---|---|---|---|---|---|---|
| Reverse e | −3 | | | | | | |
| n | −3 | | | | | | |
| Reverse s | −2 | | | | | | |
| Sums | −8 | | | | | | |

**Figure 13-6**

VI. Receptivity

Pairs: h, p, and t. Reverse the scores of p.

Instruments

| Pairs | 1 | 2 | 3 | 4 | 5 | 6 | 7 |
|---|---|---|---|---|---|---|---|
| h | +3 | | | | | | |
| Reverse p | +2 | | | | | | |
| t | +1 | | | | | | |
| Sums | +6 | | | | | | |

**Figure 13-7**

Now combine your sums into one chart.

|  | Bagpipe | Harp | Banjo | Guitar | Violin | Piano | Harpsi-chord | Totals |
|---|---|---|---|---|---|---|---|---|
| Evaluation | +6 |  |  |  |  |  |  |  |
| Potency | +3 |  |  |  |  |  |  |  |
| Activity | +8 |  |  |  |  |  |  |  |
| Collectedness | 0 |  |  |  |  |  |  |  |
| Tautness | −8 |  |  |  |  |  |  |  |
| Receptivity | +6 |  |  |  |  |  |  |  |

**Figure 13-8**

After filling in this chart, add up each row and place the totals in the last column. These totals give your overall reactions to this set of musical instruments. Inspect the last column: did you rate the instruments low on the potency and activity groups? Can you guess how the authors' choice of musical instruments affected the totals of the last column? For example, what might have happened if the list had left off the ***violin, harp,*** and ***harpsichord,*** and had included the ***sitar, electric guitar,*** and ***drums?***

________________________________________

________________________________________

Inspect your totals for each musical instrument. How did you differ on the ***banjo*** and the ***harp?*** Which is the most potent instrument? Which is the least potent? ____________

________________________________________

________________________________________

## EXERCISE 2: Political and Social Terms

Follow the instructions for Exercise 1 on page 191.

1. A member of the John Birch Society
   - a. good ___:___:___:___:___:___:___ bad
   - b. hard ___:___:___:___:___:___:___ soft
   - c. passive ___:___:___:___:___:___:___ active
   - d. stable ___:___:___:___:___:___:___ changeable
   - e. defensive ___:___:___:___:___:___:___ aggressive
   - f. optimistic ___:___:___:___:___:___:___ pessimistic
   - g. calm ___:___:___:___:___:___:___ excitable
   - h. colorful ___:___:___:___:___:___:___ colorless

i. negative ____:____:____:____:____:____:____ positive

j. masculine ____:____:____:____:____:____:____ feminine

k. cold ____:____:____:____:____:____:____ hot

m. sane ____:____:____:____:____:____:____ insane

n. competitive ____:____:____:____:____:____:____ cooperative

p. insensitive ____:____:____:____:____:____:____ sensitive

q. severe ____:____:____:____:____:____:____ lenient

r. rash ____:____:____:____:____:____:____ prudent

s. humble ____:____:____:____:____:____:____ proud

t. interesting ____:____:____:____:____:____:____ boring

2. A liberal

a. good ____:____:____:____:____:____:____ bad

b. hard ____:____:____:____:____:____:____ soft

c. passive ____:____:____:____:____:____:____ active

d. stable ____:____:____:____:____:____:____ changeable

e. defensive ____:____:____:____:____:____:____ aggressive

f. optimistic ____:____:____:____:____:____:____ pessimistic

g. calm ____:____:____:____:____:____:____ excitable

h. colorful ____:____:____:____:____:____:____ colorless

i. negative ____:____:____:____:____:____:____ positive

j. masculine ____:____:____:____:____:____:____ feminine

k. cold ____:____:____:____:____:____:____ hot

m. sane ____:____:____:____:____:____:____ insane

n. competitive ____:____:____:____:____:____:____ cooperative

p. insensitive ____:____:____:____:____:____:____ sensitive

q. severe ____:____:____:____:____:____:____ lenient

r. rash ____:____:____:____:____:____:____ prudent

s. humble ____:____:____:____:____:____:____ proud

t. interesting ____:____:____:____:____:____:____ boring

3. A conservative

a. good ____:____:____:____:____:____:____ bad

b. hard ____:____:____:____:____:____:____ soft

c. passive ____:____:____:____:____:____:____ active

d. stable ____:____:____:____:____:____:____ changeable

e. defensive ____:____:____:____:____:____:____ aggressive

f. optimistic ___:___:___:___:___:___:___ pessimistic
g. calm ___:___:___:___:___:___:___ excitable
h. colorful ___:___:___:___:___:___:___ colorless
i. negative ___:___:___:___:___:___:___ positive
j. masculine ___:___:___:___:___:___:___ feminine
k. cold ___:___:___:___:___:___:___ hot
m. sane ___:___:___:___:___:___:___ insane
n. competitive ___:___:___:___:___:___:___ cooperative
p. insensitive ___:___:___:___:___:___:___ sensitive
q. severe ___:___:___:___:___:___:___ lenient
r. rash ___:___:___:___:___:___:___ prudent
s. humble ___:___:___:___:___:___:___ proud
t. interesting ___:___:___:___:___:___:___ boring

4. A radical
a. good ___:___:___:___:___:___:___ bad
b. hard ___:___:___:___:___:___:___ soft
c. passive ___:___:___:___:___:___:___ active
d. stable ___:___:___:___:___:___:___ changeable
e. defensive ___:___:___:___:___:___:___ aggressive
f. optimistic ___:___:___:___:___:___:___ pessimistic
g. calm ___:___:___:___:___:___:___ excitable
h. colorful ___:___:___:___:___:___:___ colorless
i. negative ___:___:___:___:___:___:___ positive
j. masculine ___:___:___:___:___:___:___ feminine
k. cold ___:___:___:___:___:___:___ hot
m. sane ___:___:___:___:___:___:___ insane
n. competitive ___:___:___:___:___:___:___ cooperative
p. insensitive ___:___:___:___:___:___:___ sensitive
q. severe ___:___:___:___:___:___:___ lenient
r. rash ___:___:___:___:___:___:___ prudent
s. humble ___:___:___:___:___:___:___ proud
t. interesting ___:___:___:___:___:___:___ boring

5. A hippie
a. good ___:___:___:___:___:___:___ bad
b. hard ___:___:___:___:___:___:___ soft
c. passive ___:___:___:___:___:___:___ active

| | | | |
|---|---|---|---|
| d. | stable | ____:____:____:____:____:____:____ | changeable |
| e. | defensive | ____:____:____:____:____:____:____ | aggressive |
| f. | optimistic | ____:____:____:____:____:____:____ | pessimistic |
| g. | calm | ____:____:____:____:____:____:____ | excitable |
| h. | colorful | ____:____:____:____:____:____:____ | colorless |
| i. | negative | ____:____:____:____:____:____:____ | positive |
| j. | masculine | ____:____:____:____:____:____:____ | feminine |
| k. | cold | ____:____:____:____:____:____:____ | hot |
| m. | sane | ____:____:____:____:____:____:____ | insane |
| n. | competitive | ____:____:____:____:____:____:____ | cooperative |
| p. | insensitive | ____:____:____:____:____:____:____ | sensitive |
| q. | severe | ____:____:____:____:____:____:____ | lenient |
| r. | rash | ____:____:____:____:____:____:____ | prudent |
| s. | humble | ____:____:____:____:____:____:____ | proud |
| t. | interesting | ____:____:____:____:____:____:____ | boring |

6. A politician

| | | | |
|---|---|---|---|
| a. | good | ____:____:____:____:____:____:____ | bad |
| b. | hard | ____:____:____:____:____:____:____ | soft |
| c. | passive | ____:____:____:____:____:____:____ | active |
| d. | stable | ____:____:____:____:____:____:____ | changeable |
| e. | defensive | ____:____:____:____:____:____:____ | aggressive |
| f. | optimistic | ____:____:____:____:____:____:____ | pessimistic |
| g. | calm | ____:____:____:____:____:____:____ | excitable |
| h. | colorful | ____:____:____:____:____:____:____ | colorless |
| i. | negative | ____:____:____:____:____:____:____ | positive |
| j. | masculine | ____:____:____:____:____:____:____ | feminine |
| k. | cold | ____:____:____:____:____:____:____ | hot |
| m. | sane | ____:____:____:____:____:____:____ | insane |
| n. | competitive | ____:____:____:____:____:____:____ | cooperative |
| p. | insensitive | ____:____:____:____:____:____:____ | sensitive |
| q. | severe | ____:____:____:____:____:____:____ | lenient |
| r. | rash | ____:____:____:____:____:____:____ | prudent |
| s. | humble | ____:____:____:____:____:____:____ | proud |
| t. | interesting | ____:____:____:____:____:____:____ | boring |

7. A protester

| | | | |
|---|---|---|---|
| a. | good | ____:____:____:____:____:____:____ | bad |
| b. | hard | ____:____:____:____:____:____:____ | soft |

c. passive ___:___:___:___:___:___:___ active
d. stable ___:___:___:___:___:___:___ changeable
e. defensive ___:___:___:___:___:___:___ aggressive
f. optimistic ___:___:___:___:___:___:___ pessimistic
g. calm ___:___:___:___:___:___:___ excitable
h. colorful ___:___:___:___:___:___:___ colorless
i. negative ___:___:___:___:___:___:___ positive
j. masculine ___:___:___:___:___:___:___ feminine
k. cold ___:___:___:___:___:___:___ hot
m. sane ___:___:___:___:___:___:___ insane
n. competitive ___:___:___:___:___:___:___ cooperative
p. insensitive ___:___:___:___:___:___:___ sensitive
q. severe ___:___:___:___:___:___:___ lenient
r. rash ___:___:___:___:___:___:___ prudent
s. humble ___:___:___:___:___:___:___ proud
t. interesting ___:___:___:___:___:___:___ boring

I. Evaluation

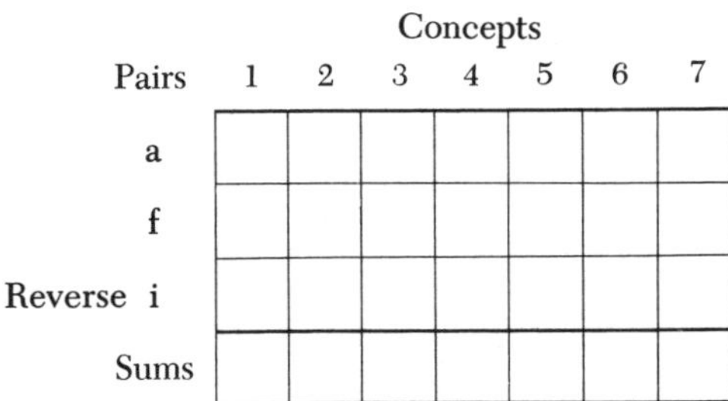

| | Concepts | | | | | | |
|---|---|---|---|---|---|---|---|
| Pairs | 1 | 2 | 3 | 4 | 5 | 6 | 7 |
| a | | | | | | | |
| f | | | | | | | |
| Reverse i | | | | | | | |
| Sums | | | | | | | |

**Figure 13–10**

II. Potency

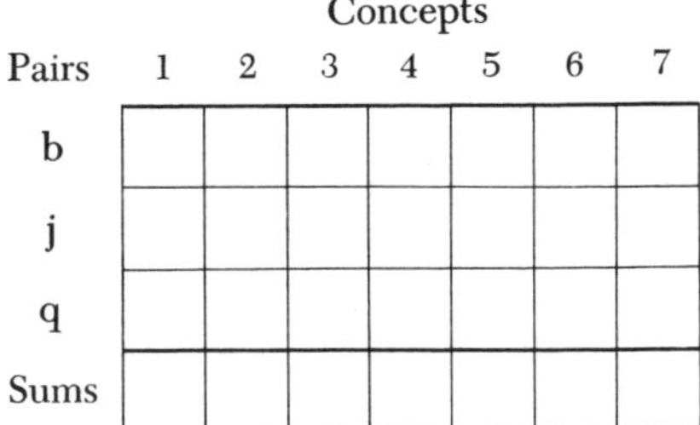

| | Concepts | | | | | | |
|---|---|---|---|---|---|---|---|
| Pairs | 1 | 2 | 3 | 4 | 5 | 6 | 7 |
| b | | | | | | | |
| j | | | | | | | |
| q | | | | | | | |
| Sums | | | | | | | |

**Figure 13–11**

## III. Activity

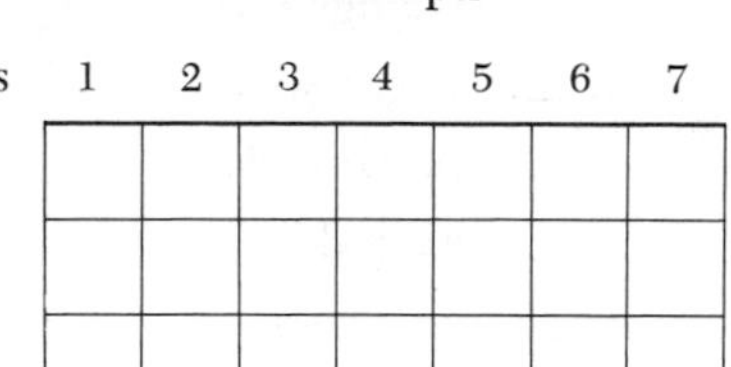


**Figure 13-12**

## IV. Collectedness

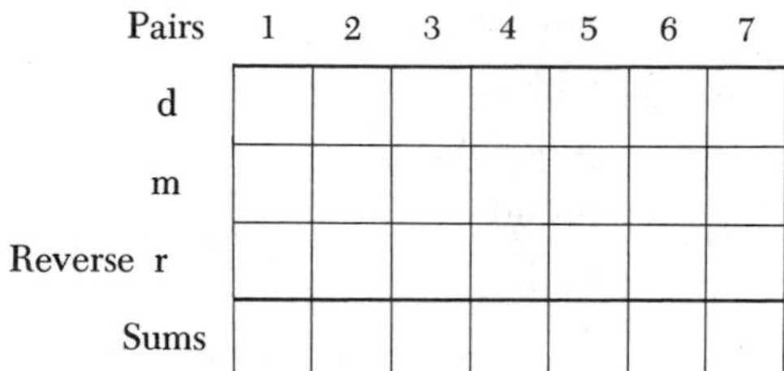


**Figure 13-13**

## V. Tautness

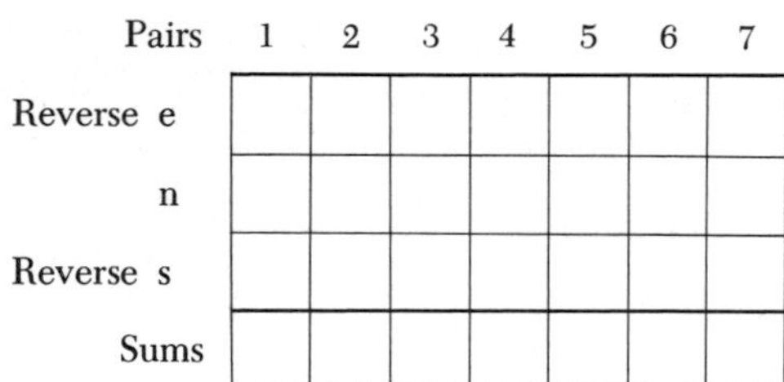


**Figure 13-14**

## VI. Receptivity

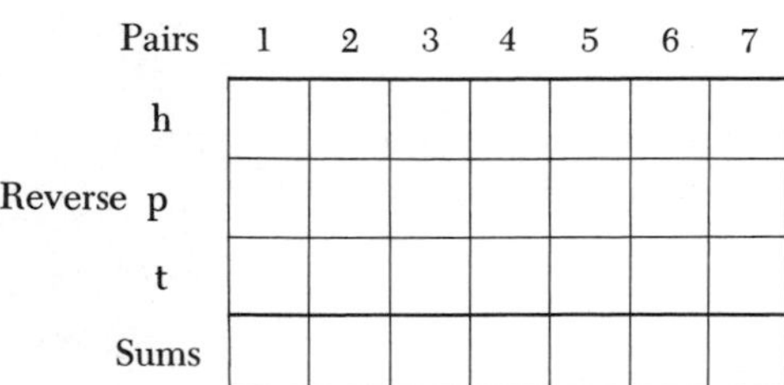


**Figure 13-15**

| | A member of the John Birch Society | A liberal | A conservative | A radical | A hippie | A protester | A politician | Totals |
|---|---|---|---|---|---|---|---|---|
| | A | B | C | D | E | F | G | |
| Evaluation | | | | | | | | |
| Potency | | | | | | | | |
| Activity | | | | | | | | |
| Collectedness | | | | | | | | |
| Tautness | | | | | | | | |
| Receptivity | | | | | | | | |

**Figure 13-16**

One interesting result of the comparatively tense current domestic political scene is that several words that one would ordinarily consider neutral have come to carry strong negative or positive judgments when used by some speakers. For example, look at the noun ***protester.*** If you had a chance to study the final charts of your classmates, you might find that some people would evaluate the word high, and others low. The middle ground might not be as well populated as one might predict, basing the prediction on the list of dictionary meanings of the word. Study your reactions to the word ***hippie.*** Do you find some possible contradictions? For example, do you find the word high on the receptive scale and low on the potency and activity scales? How do your reactions here compare to your reactions for the musical instruments? Do they match any of them approximately? __________ Do they match the ratings for any other of the political terms? __________ Have you tended to put the political terms into two groups? If so, what are they? ____________________ Which of the six scales gives the greatest differences for these two groups? __________ __________________ Can you account for this? ______________________________

## EXERCISE 3: Entertainment Terms

Follow the instructions for Exercise 1 on page 191.

1. Fun
   a. good ___:___:___:___:___:___:___ bad
   b. hard ___:___:___:___:___:___:___ soft
   c. passive ___:___:___:___:___:___:___ active
   d. stable ___:___:___:___:___:___:___ changeable

e. defensive ___:___:___:___:___:___:___ aggressive
f. optimistic ___:___:___:___:___:___:___ pessimistic
g. calm ___:___:___:___:___:___:___ excitable
h. colorful ___:___:___:___:___:___:___ colorless
i. negative ___:___:___:___:___:___:___ positive
j. masculine ___:___:___:___:___:___:___ feminine
k. cold ___:___:___:___:___:___:___ hot
m. sane ___:___:___:___:___:___:___ insane
n. competitive ___:___:___:___:___:___:___ cooperative
p. insensitive ___:___:___:___:___:___:___ sensitive
q. severe ___:___:___:___:___:___:___ lenient
r. rash ___:___:___:___:___:___:___ prudent
s. humble ___:___:___:___:___:___:___ proud
t. interesting ___:___:___:___:___:___:___ boring

2. Sport

a. good ___:___:___:___:___:___:___ bad
b. hard ___:___:___:___:___:___:___ soft
c. passive ___:___:___:___:___:___:___ active
d. stable ___:___:___:___:___:___:___ changeable
e. defensive ___:___:___:___:___:___:___ aggressive
f. optimistic ___:___:___:___:___:___:___ pessimistic
g. calm ___:___:___:___:___:___:___ excitable
h. colorful ___:___:___:___:___:___:___ colorless
i. negative ___:___:___:___:___:___:___ positive
j. masculine ___:___:___:___:___:___:___ feminine
k. cold ___:___:___:___:___:___:___ hot
m. sane ___:___:___:___:___:___:___ insane
n. competitive ___:___:___:___:___:___:___ cooperative
p. insensitive ___:___:___:___:___:___:___ sensitive
q. severe ___:___:___:___:___:___:___ lenient
r. rash ___:___:___:___:___:___:___ prudent
s. humble ___:___:___:___:___:___:___ proud
t. interesting ___:___:___:___:___:___:___ boring

3. Party

a. good ___:___:___:___:___:___:___ bad
b. hard ___:___:___:___:___:___:___ soft

| | | | |
|---|---|---|---|
| c. | passive | ____:____:____:____:____:____:____ | active |
| d. | stable | ____:____:____:____:____:____:____ | changeable |
| e. | defensive | ____:____:____:____:____:____:____ | aggressive |
| f. | optimistic | ____:____:____:____:____:____:____ | pessimistic |
| g. | calm | ____:____:____:____:____:____:____ | excitable |
| h. | colorful | ____:____:____:____:____:____:____ | colorless |
| i. | negative | ____:____:____:____:____:____:____ | positive |
| j. | masculine | ____:____:____:____:____:____:____ | feminine |
| k. | cold | ____:____:____:____:____:____:____ | hot |
| m. | sane | ____:____:____:____:____:____:____ | insane |
| n. | competitive | ____:____:____:____:____:____:____ | cooperative |
| p. | insensitive | ____:____:____:____:____:____:____ | sensitive |
| q. | severe | ____:____:____:____:____:____:____ | lenient |
| r. | rash | ____:____:____:____:____:____:____ | prudent |
| s. | humble | ____:____:____:____:____:____:____ | proud |
| t. | interesting | ____:____:____:____:____:____:____ | boring |

4. Orgy

| | | | |
|---|---|---|---|
| a. | good | ____:____:____:____:____:____:____ | bad |
| b. | hard | ____:____:____:____:____:____:____ | soft |
| c. | passive | ____:____:____:____:____:____:____ | active |
| d. | stable | ____:____:____:____:____:____:____ | changeable |
| e. | defensive | ____:____:____:____:____:____:____ | aggressive |
| f. | optimistic | ____:____:____:____:____:____:____ | pessimistic |
| g. | calm | ____:____:____:____:____:____:____ | excitable |
| h. | colorful | ____:____:____:____:____:____:____ | colorless |
| i. | negative | ____:____:____:____:____:____:____ | positive |
| j. | masculine | ____:____:____:____:____:____:____ | feminine |
| k. | cold | ____:____:____:____:____:____:____ | hot |
| m. | sane | ____:____:____:____:____:____:____ | insane |
| n. | competitive | ____:____:____:____:____:____:____ | cooperative |
| p. | insensitive | ____:____:____:____:____:____:____ | sensitive |
| q. | severe | ____:____:____:____:____:____:____ | lenient |
| r. | rash | ____:____:____:____:____:____:____ | prudent |
| s. | humble | ____:____:____:____:____:____:____ | proud |
| t. | interesting | ____:____:____:____:____:____:____ | boring |

5. Recreation

a. good ____:____:____:____:____:____:____ bad
b. hard ____:____:____:____:____:____:____ soft
c. passive ____:____:____:____:____:____:____ active
d. stable ____:____:____:____:____:____:____ changeable
e. defensive ____:____:____:____:____:____:____ aggressive
f. optimistic ____:____:____:____:____:____:____ pessimistic
g. calm ____:____:____:____:____:____:____ excitable
h. colorful ____:____:____:____:____:____:____ colorless
i. negative ____:____:____:____:____:____:____ positive
j. masculine ____:____:____:____:____:____:____ feminine
k. cold ____:____:____:____:____:____:____ hot
m. sane ____:____:____:____:____:____:____ insane
n. competitive ____:____:____:____:____:____:____ cooperative
p. insensitive ____:____:____:____:____:____:____ sensitive
q. severe ____:____:____:____:____:____:____ lenient
r. rash ____:____:____:____:____:____:____ prudent
s. humble ____:____:____:____:____:____:____ proud
t. interesting ____:____:____:____:____:____:____ boring

6. Amusement

a. good ____:____:____:____:____:____:____ bad
b. hard ____:____:____:____:____:____:____ soft
c. passive ____:____:____:____:____:____:____ active
d. stable ____:____:____:____:____:____:____ changeable
e. defensive ____:____:____:____:____:____:____ aggressive
f. optimistic ____:____:____:____:____:____:____ pessimistic
g. calm ____:____:____:____:____:____:____ excitable
h. colorful ____:____:____:____:____:____:____ colorless
i. negative ____:____:____:____:____:____:____ positive
j. masculine ____:____:____:____:____:____:____ feminine
k. cold ____:____:____:____:____:____:____ hot
m. sane ____:____:____:____:____:____:____ insane
n. competitive ____:____:____:____:____:____:____ cooperative
p. insensitive ____:____:____:____:____:____:____ sensitive
q. severe ____:____:____:____:____:____:____ lenient
r. rash ____:____:____:____:____:____:____ prudent

s. humble ____:____:____:____:____:____:____ proud
t. interesting ____:____:____:____:____:____:____ boring

7. Binge
a. good ____:____:____:____:____:____:____ bad
b. hard ____:____:____:____:____:____:____ soft
c. passive ____:____:____:____:____:____:____ active
d. stable ____:____:____:____:____:____:____ changeable
e. defensive ____:____:____:____:____:____:____ aggressive
f. optimistic ____:____:____:____:____:____:____ pessimistic
g. calm ____:____:____:____:____:____:____ excitable
h. colorful ____:____:____:____:____:____:____ colorless
i. negative ____:____:____:____:____:____:____ positive
j. masculine ____:____:____:____:____:____:____ feminine
k. cold ____:____:____:____:____:____:____ hot
m. sane ____:____:____:____:____:____:____ insane
n. competitive ____:____:____:____:____:____:____ cooperative
p. insensitive ____:____:____:____:____:____:____ sensitive
q. severe ____:____:____:____:____:____:____ lenient
r. rash ____:____:____:____:____:____:____ prudent
s. humble ____:____:____:____:____:____:____ proud
t. interesting ____:____:____:____:____:____:____ boring

I. Evaluation

| | Concepts | | | | | | |
|---|---|---|---|---|---|---|---|
| Pairs | A | B | C | D | E | F | G |
| a | | | | | | | |
| f | | | | | | | |
| Reverse i | | | | | | | |
| Sums | | | | | | | |

**Figure 13-17**

## II. Potency

Concepts

| Pairs | A | B | C | D | E | F | G |
|---|---|---|---|---|---|---|---|
| b | | | | | | | |
| j | | | | | | | |
| q | | | | | | | |
| Sums | | | | | | | |

**Figure 13-18**

## III. Activity

Concepts

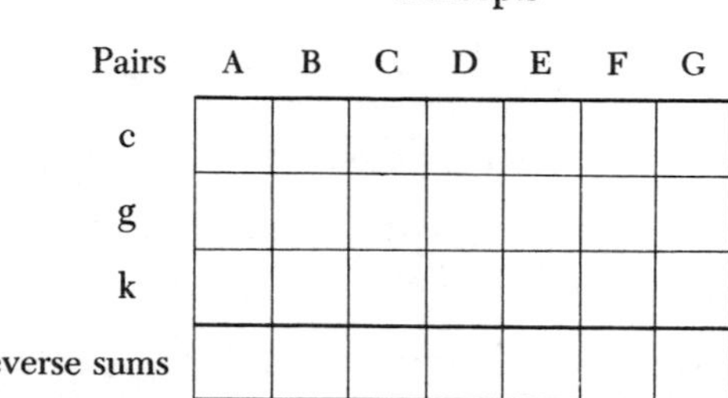

| Pairs | A | B | C | D | E | F | G |
|---|---|---|---|---|---|---|---|
| c | | | | | | | |
| g | | | | | | | |
| k | | | | | | | |
| Reverse sums | | | | | | | |

**Figure 13-19**

## IV. Collectedness

Concepts

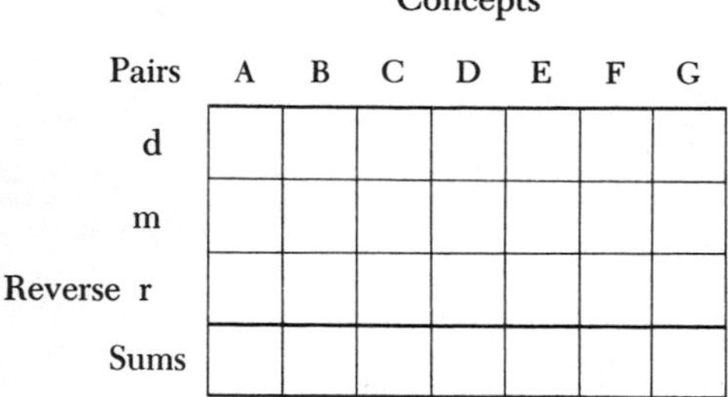

| Pairs | A | B | C | D | E | F | G |
|---|---|---|---|---|---|---|---|
| d | | | | | | | |
| m | | | | | | | |
| Reverse r | | | | | | | |
| Sums | | | | | | | |

**Figure 13-20**

## V. Tautness

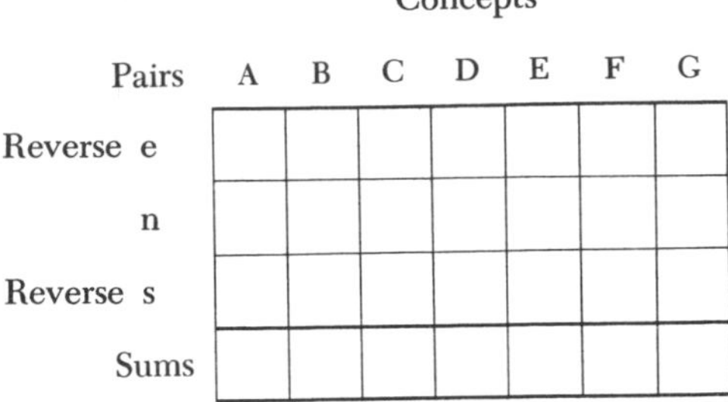

| Pairs | A | B | C | D | E | F | G |
|---|---|---|---|---|---|---|---|
| Reverse e | | | | | | | |
| n | | | | | | | |
| Reverse s | | | | | | | |
| Sums | | | | | | | |

(Column heading over A–G: Concepts)

**Figure 13-21**

## VI. Receptivity

| Pairs | A | B | C | D | E | F | G |
|---|---|---|---|---|---|---|---|
| h | | | | | | | |
| Reverse p | | | | | | | |
| t | | | | | | | |
| Sums | | | | | | | |

(Column heading over A–G: Concepts)

**Figure 13-22**

| | Fun | Sport | Revel | Orgy | Recreation | Amusement | Totals |
|---|---|---|---|---|---|---|---|
| Evaluation | | | | | | | |
| Potency | | | | | | | |
| Activity | | | | | | | |
| Collectedness | | | | | | | |
| Tautness | | | | | | | |
| Receptivity | | | | | | | |

**Figure 13-23**

What are your overall reactions to the whole class of words? Find this out by adding up each row and entering the result in the last column. Does any result stand out? How do your reactions in this column differ from those of the person sitting next to you in class?

Were they closer than you would have expected? ______

Which word did you list as least taut? ______ Least collected? ______ Most active? ______

Is one of the words more potent than the others? ______
Did you notice a contradiction between your evaluation (moral reaction to) of any of these words and their receptivity, potency, and activity? ______

______

## EXERCISE 4: Favorable and Unfavorable Naming

Words embody attitudes. The charts in this chapter are one way of investigating these attitudes. Dr. S. I. Hayakawa, in *Language in Thought and Action,*[2] made use of an idea of Lord Bertrand Russell's to show clearly how words embody attitudes. Consider the following "conjugations":

I may not know much about art, but I know what I like.
You could profit by a course in art history.
He is an uncultured ignoramus.

Or: My son is rambunctious and high-spirited.
Your son is maladjusted and deprived.
His son is a little hoodlum.

"Conjugate" the following statements in a similar way.

1. I am slender. ______

______

______

2. I am a trifle overweight. ______

______

______

3. I am a statesman. ______

______

______

4. I collect rare, old objects of art. ______

______

______

[2] 2nd ed. (New York: Harcourt, Brace & World, 1964), pp. 95–96. Items 1, 2, 4, and 5 in this exercise are from page 96.

5. I believe in old-fashioned, laissez-faire capitalism. ______________________________

________________________________________________________________

________________________________________________________________

________________________________________________________________

6. I am a police officer. ________________________________________________

________________________________________________________________

________________________________________________________________

7. I am a semanticist. __________________________________________________

________________________________________________________________

________________________________________________________________

8. I am a peace marcher. ________________________________________________

________________________________________________________________

________________________________________________________________

# 14

## Some Practical Matters

### EXERCISE 1: The *Third New International Dictionary:* On Pronunciation

Merriam-Webster's *Third New International Dictionary* of 1961 is based scrupulously on the actual practice of English speakers and on the statements of the grammarians who suggest how men ought to speak. The dictionary records both. If someone wanted to find out how a word, say ***wharf,*** is pronounced by cultured people across the country, he would do well to look in this dictionary. It lists eight pronunciations, in abbreviated form. Write them out in full here. ______________________________________________

______________________________________________________________

______________________________________________. What does the dictionary say about the status of these pronunciations? Are any of them necessarily forbidden to an educated person? Would any of them necessarily cause an adverse reaction in an educated audience in his own part of the country? The dictionary gives such information. Study the section on pronunciation in the "Explanatory Notes," which starts on page 16a. Does the lack of a usage label or mark perhaps signify that a pronunciation is heard in all parts of the country? __________ What exactly does the fact that a pronunciation is unmarked signify?

______________________________________________________________

______________________________________________________________

What are the acceptable pronunciations of the following words? (Underline the pronunciation that you use.)

foreign ______________________________________________________

barn ________________________________________________________

with ________________________________________________________

aunt ________________________________________________________

fog _________________________________________________________

new _________________________________________________________

______________________________________________________________

The pronunciation of words is necessarily affected by the sounds in surrounding words. Webster's *Third* gives these variations in pronunciations for some words. Supply the variations for these two words and the environments that cause the variation.

creel ______________________________

root ______________________________

The dictionary sometimes marks a pronunciation as coming from a particular region. Write down the regional pronunciation and name the region for the following words. (The small number at the beginning of the word will help lead you to the right entry.)

greasy ______________________________

[1]creek ______________________________

[1]Negro ______________________________

[1]the ______________________________

[1]-ing (verbal suffix) ______________________________

Some of the words have pronunciations that are labeled "substandard" or "chiefly substandard." Look in the "Explanatory Notes" for the label "substandard" and summarize what is meant by the term. ______________________________

______________________________

______________________________

Look up the following words and write down the substandard pronunciations and their full labels.

because ______________________________

ask ______________________________

athlete ______________________________

didn't ______________________________

[1]extra ______________________________

The editors had difficult decisions to make in applying the labels "substandard" and "chiefly substandard." The first two of the three words discussed below have pronunciations marked "chiefly substandard" or "chiefly in substandard speech," and the third is bluntly marked "substandard." There are not many words with this blunt label in the dictionary. In the light of the information given below about these words, discuss on what basis Webster's *Third* applied these different labels. ______________________________

______________________________

______________________________

______________________________

______________________________

***wash*** \ˈwo(ə)rsh, ˈwärsh\ Webster's *Third* labels these "chiefly substandard." Hans Kurath and Raven I. McDavid, Jr., basing their statement on the evidence gathered for the *Linguistic Atlas of the United States and Canada*, say that "In Pennsylvania west of the Susquehanna River and in West Virginia, an /r/ rather generally makes its appearance between the low back vowel and the /š/ of ***wash*** and ***Washington.*** This usage survives also in the Valley of Virginia and the Pennsylvania settlements farther south. In other areas that preserve postvocalic /r/, this intrusive /r/ is rare."[1]

***borrow*** \ˈbärē, ˈbäri\ Webster's *Third* labels this "chiefly in substandard speech." Kurath and McDavid write, "The variant ending in /i/ is characteristic of Southern and South Midland folk speech; it occurs here also, with varying frequency, in the speech of the middle class, but is rare in cultivated speech. Outside the South and the South Midland only scattered instances of /i/ have been observed, except in southeastern Maine and adjoining parts of New Hampshire."[2] The incidence of /i/ in cultivated speech is about 4 per cent.

***Once, twice*** \ˈwənzt, -n(s)t\, \ˈtwīst\ Webster's *Third* spells these ***oncet*** and ***twicet,*** and labels these "substandard." Kurath and McDavid write, "An added /t/ occurs in ***once*** and ***twice*** throughout the Midland and the South, excepting only the Piedmont of Virginia. It is more frequent in ***once*** than in ***twice.*** Though most common in folk speech, it is widely used by middle-class speakers, especially in the South Midland."[3]

It is a curious fact that some words have common pronunciations that many people dislike. These pronunciations are marked with ÷, which is called an *obelus*. Summarize what this symbol means.

____________________________________________________________

____________________________________________________________

Write down first what your own pronunciations of the following words are, and then the pronunciations that the dictionary has marked with the obelus as disapproved of by many people.

eczema __________________________________________________

baptist __________________________________________________

February ________________________________________________

licorice __________________________________________________

rodeo ___________________________________________________

pumpkin ________________________________________________

Is there a pronunciation of ***licorice*** acceptable everywhere? __________________

Can a pronunciation marked with an obelus still be an accepted pronunciation? __________

[1] Hans Kurath and Raven I. McDavid, Jr., *The Pronunciation of English in the Atlantic States* (Ann Arbor, Michigan: University of Michigan Press, 1961), pp. 169–70. The status labels of ***once, twice, borrow,*** and ***wash*** were first studied by Jean Malmstrom, "Webster's Third on Nonstandard Usage," *Publication of the American Dialect Society,* 41 (April, 1964), pp. 1–6.

[2] *Ibid.,* p. 173.

[3] *Ibid.,* p. 179.

## EXERCISE 2: The *Third New International Dictionary:* On Word Usage

Look up the phrase ***greasy grind.*** How does the dictionary label it? ____________

______________________________

Summarize the definition of this label that is given in the "Explanatory Notes." ____________

______________________________

Can a word that has the label "slang" ever be used in contexts that are not marked by extreme informality? ____________ Give the meanings of the words and phrases below that are labeled "slang."

mary ______________________________

up for grabs ______________________________

cornball ______________________________

Look up the word [5]***like*** as used in ***he talked stuttering-like.*** How is it labeled? ____________

____________ What does this label mean? (For information, go to the "Explanatory Notes.") ______________________________

______________________________

What are the differences between the meanings of this label and "slang"? ____________

______________________________

Look up the following words and give the meanings that are labeled "substandard" and the exact full wording of the label.

learn (meaning 'teach') ______________________________

wore out ______________________________

[2]suspicion ______________________________

Some of the words in the dictionary are proper only to certain areas of the country or to certain countries. Look up the words below and pick out the restricted meaning and the region to which it is restricted.

mary ______________________________

lay by ______________________________

leave out ______________________________

leave over ______________________________

mutton corn ______________________________

screw ______________________________

The information in the dictionary that is at once the most plentiful and the most difficult to use as a source of information about usage is the citation. This is the quotation, often ascribed to a particular person or publication, that illustrates the word in use. Consider the word [1]*eve.* One citation is clearly poetical: <from morn to noon he fell, from noon to dewy *eve*—John Milton>. No label is needed to show that the word is part of the language of poetry. Look up the word *morn* and write the names and occupations of the people quoted. (You may not be able to find the occupations of all of them.) In what contexts would you expect to find it used? ____________________

Look up the citations for the following words and describe the contexts in which they would appear to be especially appropriate.

pearly (meanings 4, 5, and 6) ____________________

pearl (meaning teeth) ____________________

lay off (as in *lay off me*—note the style of the citation) ____________________

[3]even (meaning 1b) ____________________

sputnik ____________________

husband (meaning 'hoarder') ____________________

mark (meaning 'one to be swindled') ____________________

neck (meaning 'fondle and kiss') ____________________

## EXERCISE 3: The *Third New International Dictionary:* On Inflections

The dictionary gives information about the appropriateness of various inflected forms. Write down the labels for the following italicized words in the use illustrated.

*brung* (preterite) ____________________

have *wore* ____________________

you *was* (plural) ____________________

you *is* (plural) ____________________

*ain't* (meaning 'have not') ____________________

John and *her* are here ____________________

between you and *he* ____________________

Often the labels are not definite; usage is somewhat divided. Summarize the information contained in the entries for the following underlined words.

He talked to my sister and *I.* ____________________

Our people and ***us*** are here. ________________________________

________________________________

The dictionary often makes distinctions between speech and writing in its discussions of usage, especially usage of inflections. Your summaries of some of the usage information just above should carefully discriminate between what is proper to speech and what is proper to writing. Write summaries of what Webster's *Third* has to say about the following forms in both speech and writing. Note also the differences between the facts of actual usage and the positions taken by some grammarians.

ain't (meaning 1c) ________________________________

________________________________

me (as in ***it's me***) ________________________________

________________________________

me (as in ***me and John went yesterday***) ________________________________

________________________________

us (as in ***it was us***) ________________________________

________________________________

which (as in ***it was raining there yesterday, which kept us from going***) ________________

________________________________

________________________________

whom (as in ***the man whom you took to dinner***) ________________________________

________________________________

## EXERCISE 4: The Desk Dictionary

There is much more in a good desk dictionary than is apparent in casual, everyday use. You have already been introduced to its etymological information in Chapter 7. This exercise is designed to introduce you to some of the principles and practices of your own dictionary. If the desk dictionary you use does not have the information requested, indicate this in the space provided for the answer.

A. The Main Entry

1. What is the name of your dictionary? ________________________________

   Does your dictionary carry not just words, but also phrases, as main entries? ________

   If so, give one. ________________________________

   Does it carry phrases within the main entries? ____________ If so, give an example.

   ________________________________

2. Where does your dictionary carry names of places? ______________________

3. Where does it carry abbreviations and their meanings? ______________________

______________________________________________________________

4. Where does it carry biographical names? ______________________

5. Does your dictionary have separate main entries for ***junior*** used as noun and as adjective? ______________________

   If not, how are these two words separated? ______________________

6. Does your dictionary give any principles of order that determine whether the noun or the adjective form of ***junior*** should come first? (Look in the front matter, the introductory material of the dictionary.) In some dictionaries the older forms come first. ______________________

______________________________________________________________

7. How does your dictionary indicate word division for purposes of hyphenation?

______________________________________________________________

8. Where are variant spellings of the word ***pajamas*** listed? Does ***pyjamas*** have its own main entry? ______________________

9. What are the variants of ***dexterous?*** ______________________

   Of ***caddy?*** ______________________

   Which of the two spellings of each word is preferred by the dictionary? ____________

   ______________________ Give the page of the front matter on which the principle is stated by which you decided which, if either, is preferred.

   ______________________________________________________________

10. Write the American spelling of the following words.

    gaol ______________________

    kerb ______________________

    tyre ______________________

    cyder ______________________

    cheque ______________________

    colour ______________________

    behaviour ______________________

11. Does your dictionary set apart in some way words and phrases it considers foreign?

    ____________ How? ______________________

B. Pronunciation

1. Copy the vowel and diphthong symbols that your dictionary uses for English sounds. For each sound you use in your own speech write two words in which the sound is used. Do not use the same examples as the dictionary.

2. How does your dictionary mark the varying degrees of stress within a word? Give one example.

3. Earlier in this chapter you investigated the pronunciations of ***wharf*** and what the *Third New International Dictionary* says about the status of these pronunciations.

Compare your own dictionary with Webster's *Third.* Below, give the variant pronunciations of the word ***wharf.*** Indicate which one is yours by underlining it. Spell each pronunciation out completely: do not use abbreviations. ______

______

What does your dictionary say about the status of these pronunciations? Are they all used by educated speakers? ______

______

What determines which pronunciation comes first? ______

______

______

Does your dictionary state that the first pronunciation is preferred? ______

On what page? ______

4. What labels does your dictionary use to indicate that the acceptability of a pronunciation is restricted in some way? (Be sure you include regional as well as usage labels.) ______
5. If your dictionary does not list a particular pronunciation of a word, does this mean that pronunciation is in some way proscribed or necessarily characteristic only of uneducated speakers? (Look in the front matter for this information.) ______

______

______

C. Parts of Speech

What are the functional labels or parts of speech given in the dictionary for the following italicized words in the given contexts?

1. Do you ***like*** working there? ______
2. ***Like*** father, ***like*** son. ______
3. He bought a suit of ***like*** cut. ______
4. Is the iron hot enough to melt ***solder?*** ______
5. Please ***solder*** this joint. ______

D. Inflected Forms

Write all the forms the dictionary gives for the following. Indicate the usage level of each form.

1. plural of ***brother-in-law*** ______
2. plural of ***cupful*** ______
3. plural of ***index*** ______

4. plural of ***datum*** ______________________________

5. plural of ***alumnus*** ______________________________

6. preterite of ***dive*** ______________________________

7. past participle of ***dive*** ______________________________

8. past participle of ***drank*** ______________________________

9. preterite of ***work*** ______________________________

E. Capitalization

Underline the letters that should be capitalized.

1. schick test
2. ouija board
3. caustic soda
4. garand rifle
5. artesian well
6. verner's law
7. irish setter
8. marcel wave
9. peking man
10. crepe de chine

F. Definitions

1. Read the explanatory notes of your dictionary to see what meaning of a word is listed first. Is the oldest meaning given first, the most common, or what? __________

______________________________

Is the order of the meanings always the same? ______________________________

2. The word ***float*** can mean one thing to a zoologist and another to the pilot of a seaplane. Sometimes these specialized meanings are marked by special lables, such as *Aeron.* or *Zool.* Give a specialized meaning of each of the following words.

1. set ______________________________
2. rest ______________________________
3. fundamental ______________________________
4. highball ______________________________
5. free ______________________________

3. Compose six short sentences using six of the different senses of ***needle.*** A reader should be able to guess your meaning from the sentence. (Remember your exercise with this word in Chapter 12.)

1. ______________________________
2. ______________________________
3. ______________________________
4. ______________________________
5. ______________________________
6. ______________________________

4. Often, instead of giving a full definition of a word, a dictionary will give a synonym. Or, in addition to a definition, the dictionary will refer the reader to another word or words, where more information is given. Look through your dictionary and write two words for which synonyms rather than definitions are given. Write the synonyms also.

   *dispend* ______ *Obs. to pay out, expend, spend* ______

   ______ ______

   ______ ______

   Write below two words for which meanings are supplemented by cross-references to other words. Give the words that supplement the definition.

   *hobble* ______ *fetter, hamper, impede* ______

   ______ ______

   ______ ______

G. Miscellaneous Sections

Most dictionaries give a variety of information in other parts of the book besides the main vocabulary. Different dictionaries give different information. Does your dictionary discuss punctuation? ______ Manuscript preparation? ______ Does it give proofreading symbols? ______ A history of the English language? ______ An essay on dialect and usage? ______ Detailed information on pronunciation? ______ A section on English given names? ______ Italicization? ______ Capitalization? ______ Rimes? ______ Does it have an index? ______

H. Sources of Information

The dictionary maker does not compose his own definitions arbitrarily but bases his definitions and usage statements on how words are actually used and sometimes on how some grammarians say they ought to be used. Read the preface to your dictionary, and anything else of relevance, to find what the sources of information were for your dictionary. Be as detailed as possible.

______

______

______

______

______

______

______

## EXERCISE 5: Readings in Doctrines of Usage

**Seventeenth- and Eighteenth-Century England:**

Browsing through grammars of English from the last three centuries turns up interesting ideas about "good English" and the task of the grammarian.

This passage is from the dedicatory poem in *The English Grammar* by Joseph Aickin (London, 1693) and is addressed to Aickin.

> Great *Chaucer* did at first the Tongue refine
> But you from all its dregs have clear'd the wine.
> *Wallis*, and *Cooper* did with *Wharton* try,
> And by degrees the Tongue did Rectifie.
> But still there wanted a more perfect Rule,
> An *English Grammar* for the English School.

The dedication gives to the grammarian the task of perfecting the language by giving it rules, something the four named poets could not do completely. The following passage from Aickin's *Grammar* opens his preface.

> The Daily obstructions and difficulties, that occur in teaching and Learning our Mother Tongue, proceed from the want of an English Grammar, by Law establish'd, the Standard of education, as in other Tongues; For no Tongue can be acquired without Grammatical rules; since then all other Tongues, and Languages are taught by Grammar, why ought not the English Tongue to be taught so too. Imitation will never do it, under twenty years; I have known some Foreigners who have been longer in learning to speak English and yet are far from it: the not learning by Grammar, is the true cause. Hence it cometh, that Children go ten or eleven years or more to School, and yet do not attain the Perfection of the English Tongue: Nay some scarce learn to read and write well in that time: but are forced at length to go to Latin Schools to attain its perfection: and sooner become masters of the Latine, than their own Tongue. The want of such a Grammar, which ought to be the standard of the English Tongue, is the cause of all this. . . .

Aickin assumes that everyone should learn English like a foreign language from a grammar book, even native speakers. What does Aickin consider the task of the grammarian?

________________________________________

________________________________________

________________________________________

Aickin's statement betrays a basic distrust of the normal English of his time, even that of the children of well-educated parents.

Bishop Robert Lowth, publishing about seventy years later, also distrusted the language. The passage below is from the preface of his *A Short Introduction to English Grammar* (London, 1762).

> The English Language hath been much cultivated during the last two hundred years. It hath been considerably polished and refined; it hath been greatly enlarged in extent and compass; its force and energy, its variety, richness, and elegance, have been tried with good success, in verse and in prose,

upon all subjects, and in every kind of stile: but whatever other improvements it may have received, it hath made no advances in Grammatical accuracy.

It is now about fifty years since Doctor *Swift* made a public remonstrance, addressed to the Earl of Oxford, then Lord Treasurer, of the imperfect State of our Language; alledging in particular, that in many instances it "offended against every part of Grammar." *Swift* must be allowed to have been a good judge of this matter. He was himself very attentive to this part, both in his own writings, and in his remarks upon those of his friends: he is one of our very best prose writers. Indeed the justness of this complaint, as far as I can find, hath never been questioned; and yet no effectual method hath hiterto been taken to redress the grievance of which he complains.

But let us consider how, and in what extent, we are to understand this charge brought against the *English* Language. Does it mean, that the *English* Language as it is spoken by the politest part of the nation, and as it stands in the writings of our most approved authors, oftentimes offends against every part of Grammar? Thus far, I am afraid, the charge is true.

Can you conjecture what Bishop Lowth means by *Grammar* in the next to last sentence?

________________________________________

________________________________________

Later in the preface he laments the trust people have in the way they speak.

It is not owing then to any peculiar irregularity or difficulty of our Language, that the general practice both of speaking and writing it is chargeable with inaccuracy. It is not the Language, but the practice, that is in fault. The truth is, Grammar is very much neglected among us: and it is not the difficulty of the Language, but on the contrary the simplicity and facility of it, that occasions this neglect. Were the Language less easy and simple, we should find ourselves under a necessity of studying it with more care and attention. But as it is, we take for granted, that we have a competent knowledge and skill, and are able to acquit ourselves properly, in our own native tongue: a faculty solely acquired by use, conducted by habit, and tried by the ear, carries us on without reflection; we meet with no rubs or difficulties in our way, or we do not perceive them; we find ourselves able to go on without rules, and we do not so much as suspect that we stand in need of them.

By asserting the simplicity of English, Bishop Lowth is saying that it has fewer inflections than Latin. He is apparently under the impression that children learning a highly inflected language from their parents, such as Russian children, have great difficulty with the task. Bishop Lowth wrote that "It is not the Language, but the practice, that is in fault." What source of information about the English *language* can you imagine that would give data significantly at odds with the actual *practice* of English speakers? ________________

________________________________________

________________________________________

Bishop Lowth himself limits his sources of information. He would not, of course, study the common speech. On the other hand, he writes:

Our best Authors for want of some rudiments of this kind have sometimes fallen into mistakes, and been guilty of palpable errors in point of Grammar. The examples there given [in Notes which give common errors of usage by these best authors] are such as occurred in reading, without any very curious or methodical examination: and they might easily have been much increased in number by any one, who had leisure or phlegm enough to have gone through a regular course of reading with this particular view.

He rejects both the common speech and the writings of the best authors. What is the source of his data? ______________________________

______________________________

One of Bishop Lowth's Notes on errors of usage appears on page 99 in the first edition of his book.

"Tell who *loves who:* what favours some partake, And who is jilted for another's sake." Dryden, Juvenal, Sat.vi. "Those, *who* he *thought* true to his party." Clarendon, Hist. Vol. I. p. 667.8vo. "*Who* should I *meet* the other night, but my old friend?" Spect. No 32. "*Who* should I *see* in the lid of it, but the Doctor?" Addison, Spect. No 57. "He knows, *who* it is proper to *expose* foremost." Swift, Tale of a Tub, Conclusion. It ought in all these places to be *whom.*

**Nineteenth-Century America:**

Samuel Kirkham in *English Grammar in Familiar Lectures* (Rochester, New York, 1823) followed Bishop Lowth and the traditions of the eighteenth-century English grammarians. Let us start with several of his key definitions. "English Grammar is the art of speaking and writing the English language with propriety." The standard is "the established practice of the best speakers and writers by whom it is used."

By the phrase, *established practice,* is implied reputable, national, and present usage. A usage becomes *good* and *legal,* when it has been long and generally adopted. *The best speakers and writers,* or such as may be considered good authority in the use of language, are those who are deservedly in high estimation; speakers, distinguished for their elocution and other literary attainments, and writers, eminent for correct taste, solid matter, and refined manner. (1835, 41st edition, pp. 17–18)

How do you think Kirkham would distinguish those writers deservedly in high estimation from those undeservedly in high estimation? What down-to-earth method of choosing would he have? ______________________________

______________________________

______________________________

______________________________

The eighteenth-century English pronouncements on usage were generally *ipse dixit* in base, even though the grammarians said they only followed good usage. Kirkham does the same: in a note later in his text (page 35) he betrays his attitude toward the "best writers."

To demonstrate the utility, and enforce the necessity, of exercising the learner in correcting *false Syntax,* I need no other argument than the interesting and undeniable fact, that Mr. Murray's labours, in this department, have effected a complete revolution in the English language, in point of verbal accuracy. Who does not know, that the best writers of this day, are not guilty of *one* grammatical inaccuracy, where those authors who wrote before Mr. Murray flourished, are guilty

> of *five*? And what has produced this important change for the better? Ask the hundreds of thousands who have studied "Mr. Murray's exercises in *False Syntax*."

Kirkham refers to "the best writers" both here and in his definitions reprinted above. Does he actually use their practice as his standard? ________ On what standard did Mr. Murray base his principles? ____________________ Could he have based it on the standard of the best writers of his day? Why? ______________________________

______________________________

______________________________

______________________________

We have seen what Kirkham's attitude toward the best speakers and writers was; let us look at his attitude toward the English language. He expresses it in an apology for his book near the end of his preface.

> That the work is defective, the author is fully sensible: and he is free to acknowledge, that its defects arise, in part, from his own want of judgment and skill. But there is another and a more serious cause of them, namely the anomalies and imperfections with which the language abounds. This latter circumstance is also the cause of the existence of so widely different opinions on many important points; and, moreover, the reason that the grammatical principles of our language can never be indisputably settled. But principles ought not to be rejected because they admit of exceptions. He who is thoroughly acquainted with the genius and structure of our language, can duly appreciate the truth of these remarks.

The word *genius* here is of uncertain meaning, but the attitude toward English is clear. What is the task of the grammarian, according to Kirkham?

______________________________

______________________________

______________________________

Kirkham expresses the old idea that language improves with age.

> In the early and rude state of society, mankind are quite limited in their knowledge, and having but few ideas to communicate, a small number of words answers their purpose in the transmission of thought. This leads them to express their ideas in short, detached sentences, requiring few or none of those *connectives*, or words of transition, which are afterwards introduced into language by refinement, and which contribute so largely to its perspicuity and elegance. The argument appears to be conclusive, then, that every language must necessarily have more parts of speech in its refined, than in its barbarous state. (p. 28)

Where else in these readings has the idea of the progress of English been expressed?

______________________________

______________________________

One of the most interesting passages in Kirkham's little book is the exhortation "to the young learner," much of which is reprinted on the following pages.

You are about to enter upon one of the most useful, and, when rightly pursued, one of the most interesting studies in the whole circle of science. If, however, you, like many a misguided youth, are under the impression that the study of grammar is dry and irksome, and a matter of little consequence, I trust I shall succeed in removing from your mind, all such false notions and ungrounded prejudices; for I will endeavour to convince you, before I close these lectures, that this is not only a pleasing study, but one of real and substantial utility; a study that directly tends to adorn and dignify human nature, and meliorate the condition of man. Grammar is a leading branch of that learning which alone is capable of unfolding and maturing the mental powers, and of elevating man to his proper rank in the scale of intellectual existence;—of that learning which lifts the soul from earth, and enables it to hold converse with a thousand worlds.

The similarity to a passage from the 1693 *English Grammar* of Joseph Aickin is striking:

Learning is an inestimable Jewel, exceeding the worth of all the Riches of the Earth; for it makes men fit for any Employment either in Church or State. It restores that Knowledge of good, which *Adam* lost by his fall, and thereby entailed Ignorance upon his Posterity. It distinguisheth Man from Beasts, and all Terrestrial Creatures. It teacheth us the Knowledge of God and the true way to Heaven.

Kirkham resumes:

In pursuing any and every other path of science, you will discover the truth of these remarks, and feel its force; for you will find, that, as grammar opens the door to every department of learning, a knowledge of it is indispensable: and should you not aspire at a distinction in the republick of letters, this knowledge cannot fail of being serviceable to you, even if you are destined to pass through the humblest walks of life. I think it is clear, that, in one point of view, grammatical knowledge possesses a decided advantage over every other branch of learning. Penmanship, arithmetick, geography, astronomy, botany, chymistry, and so on, are highly useful in their respective places; but not one of them is so universally applicable to practical purposes, as this. In every situation, under all circumstances, on all occasions;—when you speak, read, write, or think, a knowledge of grammar is of essential utility.

Note the appeal to usefulness; this is a distinctively American passage. Kirkham continues:

You are aware, my young friend, that you live in an age of light and knowledge;—an age in which science and the arts are marching onward with gigantick strides. You live, too, in a land of liberty;—a land on which the smiles of Heaven beam with uncommon refulgence. The trump of the warriour and the clangour of arms no longer echo on our mountains, or in our valleys; "the garments died in blood have passed away;" the mighty struggle for independence is over; and you live to enjoy the rich boon of freedom and prosperity which was purchased with the blood of our fathers. These considerations forbid that you should ever be so unmindful of your duty to your country, to your Creator, to yourself, and to succeeding generations, as to be content to grovel in ignorance. Remember that "knowledge is power;" that an enlightened and virtuous people can never be enslaved; and that, on the intelligence of our youth, rest the future liberty, the prosperity, the happiness, the grandeur, and the glory of our beloved country. Go on, then, with a laudable ambition, and an unyielding perseverance, in the path which leads to honour and renown. Press forward. Go, and gather laurels on the hill of science; linger among her unfading beauties; "drink

> deep" of her crystal fountain; and then join in "the march of fame." Become learned and virtuous, and you will be great. Love God and serve him, and you will be happy.

(Place in parentheses the phrases of the above passages by Kirkham relating grammar to patriotism.) [Place in brackets the phrases which relate grammar to other virtues.] Underline phrases which relate success in reputation, power, or money, to grammar. The mix of values presented in this passage is typically American.

A 0
B 1
C 2
D 3
E 4
F 5
G 6
H 7
I 8
J 9